THE OAKWOOD PRESS

# The Essential Guide to Austrian Railways and Tramways

*by*
*Mervyn Jones*

## THE OAKWOOD PRESS

© Oakwood Press & Mervyn Jones 2008

British Library Cataloguing in Publication Data
A Record for this book is available from the British Library
ISBN 978 0 85361 674 0

Typeset by Oakwood Graphics.
Repro by pkmediaworks, Cranborne, Dorset.
Printed by Cambrian Printers Ltd, Aberystwyth, Ceredigeon.

*All rights reserved. No part of this book may be reproduced or transmitted in any form or by any means, electronic or mechanical, including photocopying, recording or by any information storage and retrieval system, without permission from the Publisher in writing.*

# About the Author

Mervyn Jones began his interest in UK railways in the early 1950s. He joined the British Police Service in 1962 and over the following 35 years he served in a number of forces before retiring towards the end of 1997. Since then he has travelled the world extensively on behalf of the United Kingdom's Foreign and Commonwealth Office teaching senior members of developing governments how to cope with natural and man-made disasters. On one occasion he taught in (Outer) Mongolia travelling there and back with his wife on the Trans-Siberian and Trans-Mongolian railways.

He is the holder of a Master of Science degree in Social Policy from Cranfield University and prior to writing books on European Railways he published numerous articles on academic subjects as well as a book on organizational behaviour. He lives with his wife, Caroline, half of the year at their home on the North Wales, Shropshire and Cheshire borders and the other half in the south of France close to Avignon and Nîmes.

His previous railway publications were *The Essential Guide to French Heritage and Tourist Railways* (2006) and *The Essential Guide to Swiss Heritage and Tourist Railways* (2007) also published by Oakwood Press. He and his wife are currently researching, photographing and writing for the next guide on the Alpine Railways of France, Switzerland, Italy, Austria, Germany and Slovenia.

*Front Cover:* Taurus class '1016' No. 022-4 hauling a car-carrying train from Böckstein via the Tauern tunnel arrives at Mallnitz on 17th October, 2007. *Author*

*Title page:* Club U44's 1949-built 0-8-2 No. 83.180 ex-FTB (Bosnia) crossing the Grub viaduct north of Weiz on 14th October, 2007. *Caroline Jones*

*Rear cover:* Trams travel the Landstraße in Linz towards the Haupplatz on 29th June, 2007. The elaborate building with the twin spires left of centre is the *Ursulinenkirche* located at 31 Landstraße. It was built between 1736 and 1772. *Author*

Published by The Oakwood Press (Usk), P.O. Box 13, Usk, Mon., NP15 1YS.
E-mail: sales@oakwoodpress.co.uk
Website: www.oakwoodpress.co.uk

# Contents

| | Introduction | 4 |
|---|---|---|
| | Acknowledgements | 5 |
| Chapter One | Austria - the country, its people and administration | 7 |
| | History | 7 |
| | Geography | 10 |
| | Climate | 10 |
| | Government | 10 |
| | Population | 10 |
| | Religion | 11 |
| | Economy | 11 |
| | Currency | 11 |
| | Transportation | 12 |
| Chapter Two | A Brief History of Austrian Railways | 13 |
| Chapter Three | Getting the best out of this guide | 18 |
| Chapter Four | Austria's National Railway (ÖBB) | 21 |
| Chapter Five | Austria's Railways and Tramways by State | 43 |
| | Burgenland | 43 |
| | Carinthia (Kärnten) | 45 |
| | Lower Austria (Niederösterreich) | 57 |
| | Salzburg | 87 |
| | Styria (Steiremark) | 98 |
| | Tyrol (Tirol) | 122 |
| | Upper Austria (Oberösterreich) | 140 |
| | Vienna (Wien) | 164 |
| | Vorarlberg | 172 |
| Chapter Six | Austria's Rail Freight Companies | 176 |
| Chapter Seven | Funicular operations in Austria | 179 |
| Chapter Eight | Austria's International Railway Relationships | 191 |
| Appendix | UK's Austrian Railway Group | 203 |
| | Glossary | 204 |
| | Bibliography | 205 |
| | Interesting Websites | 206 |
| | Index | 207 |

# Introduction

This guide, third in the series, has been written to appeal to railway enthusiasts, holiday-makers and travellers who are interested in visiting the beautiful countryside of Austria. This guide lists a total of 172 entries throughout Austria where heritage, tourist and general railways as well as related activities can be found. Of these, the author has identified 47 specific routes operated by Austrian Federal Railways [Österreichische Bundesbahnen (ÖBB)] including the world famous Semmeringbahn in Lower Austria (*see entry 50*). Also listed are 12 museums including the National Transport Museum at Strasshof in Lower Austria and ÖGEG's superb collection at Ampflwang in Upper Austria (*see entry 118*). Five companies providing freight services have been included as have 15 funicular/cable car operations. To conclude there is a description of the railway links with Austria's eight neighbouring countries. The situation towards the end of 2007 was that all but one was fully active although some had restricted operations due to recent flood damage, the Pinzgauerbahn in Salzburgland, for example (*see entry 65*). Many of the organizations shown have preserved much traction and rolling stock some of which is stored and often on display or accessible to view on prior application. Moreover, much material has been kept in or restored to full working order and is used from time to time for excursions on ÖBB tracks. ÖBB must be applauded in this regard for it is particularly active in maintaining a *Nostalgie* fleet of railway material which is deployed regularly and frequently in an annual comprehensive programme of excursions throughout Austria.

An important question in writing a book such as this is what to and what not to include. 'Heritage' railways are relatively speaking easy to identify but where do regular routes qualify as being of 'tourist' interest? Given the outstanding natural beauty of most of Austria, it is difficult to determine which routes do and do not qualify. All the railways identified in the book travel on a variety of routes, both long and short, invariably through beautiful countryside and therefore have been included even though they could be defined by some as 'commuter' routes. However, it is the contention of the author and his wife that they merit inclusion. It is hoped that the reader and perhaps the traveller to Austria agrees.

Innsbruck tram No. 52 descending the Mittelgebirgbahn to Innsbruck on 26th June, 2007.
*Author*

# Acknowledgements

The author wishes to acknowledge the help, support, advice and, indeed, friendship, he has received from many quarters during the research for and the writing of this guide. The author is particularly indebted to many enthusiasts, including those professionally employed as well as the legion of volunteers, for the assistance and advice provided and the supply of up-to-date information about current activities and future plans.

Important sources of information in writing this guide have been by making visits to many of the railways and museums and learning at first hand about their history and current operations. Discussions enjoyed with organizers, enthusiasts and travellers, who were always found to be willing to share their valuable knowledge, proved most fruitful.

Other sources of information found to be important in compiling this guide were the many websites on the Internet which have been written and published on all aspects of railways in Austria. The author, therefore, is indebted to the webmasters of the many sites visited. Whilst all copyright has been respected, it is acknowledged and appreciated by the author how useful these sites have been in compiling information for this guide.

The author also wishes to express his appreciation to the UK's Austrian Railway Group (ARG) of which he is a member. The officers and members of the Group have been particularly helpful as has been much of the content of ARG's excellent quarterly Journal. More information about ARG and its activities in the UK can be found in the Appendix. Special thanks must go to Howard Lawrence, the secretary and treasurer of the ARG, who spent much of his free time reading the first draft of the manuscript and making helpful suggestions and corrections. However, any errors and omissions found in this the final publication are the sole responsibility of the author. It would be remiss not to mention and express appreciation for the encouragement, help and advice that was forthcoming from Oakwood Press and in particular their Ian Kennedy.

Finally, the author wishes to give special thanks to his wife, Caroline, who supported him throughout the project in many, many ways including the taking of numerous photographs, some of which are featured in this book. This book is dedicated to Dr Stefan Popper, sometime Her Majesty's Coroner for South Yorkshire - West District.

Zillertalbahn's 1902-built Krauss (Linz) No. 3 *Tirol* heads down the valley towards Mayrhofen on 27th June, 2007. *Author*

The Hohen Tauern is just one of the many magnificent mountain ranges of Austria. This photograph is taken from Mallnitz station on 17th October, 2007. *Author*

The *Michaelertor* entrance to the palace of Emperor Franz-Josef I is just one of the many beautiful buildings of Vienna. *Author*

# Chapter One

# Austria
# The country, its people and administration

Austria is a landlocked country in Central Europe. In the German language the country is known as *Österreich* which in English translates as 'eastern empire'. The name is derived from the old German word *Ostarrîchi*. It has borders with eight countries - Germany and the Czech Republic to the north, Slovakia and Hungary to the east, Slovenia and Italy to the south, and Switzerland and Liechtenstein to the west. The capital of Austria is the beautiful city of Vienna which is located on the eastern side of the country close to its international frontier with Slovakia. The national flag is rectangular and consists of two red horizontal bars separated by a white horizontal bar. The country's national anthem is *Land der Berge, Land am Strome* which in German aptly describes Austria - Land of Mountains, Land on the River.

## History

The origins of modern Austria date back to the ninth century, when the countryside of upper and lower Austria became increasingly populated. The name *Ostarrîchi* is first documented in an official document dated 996. Since then the word has evolved into the German word 'Österreich'.

Austria has experienced frequent, dramatic and sometimes violent changes throughout its long history. From 996 to about 1500, Austria was smaller in geographical size than it is today. After 1500, it grew in size and became 'imperial' and remained so for over 400 years. Since the end of World War I Austria has been a republic.

The first event that perhaps marks the creation of modern-day Austria goes back to 976 when the German king installed a Babenburg margrave with land in the Danube valley. The word 'margrave', used in both English and French, comes from the German word *markgraf* which was used in medieval times as a term for a military governor of a *Carolingian mark*. A mark was a border province and the word *Carolingian* referred to a particular dynasty known variously as the *Carlovingians* or *Karlings* with its members being drawn from a Frankish noble family.

In 1156, Austria became an independent unit within the German Empire and almost 40 years later the country began to expand with the annexation of Styria. An important, if not the most important, milestone in Austria's history followed in the middle to late 13th century when the Babenburgs as a ruling family became extinct with the last survivor, Frederick II, being killed in battle in 1246. There followed a 36 year interregnum when powerful families fought for control but eventually, in 1282, the Habsburgs became dominant and took power adopting at the time the title 'House of Austria'. The country again expanded with Carinthia and Carniola, a region in what is now Slovenia, coming under Habsburg rule in 1335 followed by Tyrol in 1363.

Another key event was in 1493 when Maximilian I became the Holy Roman Emperor. This saw the beginning of Austria's expansionism internationally much being achieved by way of inter-dynastic marriages. For example, Maximilian himself married the heiress of Burgundy, thus acquiring most of the territory in the Low Countries. Maximilian's son, Philip the Handsome, married well in the form of the heiress of Castile and Aragon and as a consequence Spain and its Italian, African, and New World territories came to the Habsburg family. In the early 16th century Archduke Ferdinand I was elected as King of Bohemia and King of Hungary. During the 17th and early 18th centuries the Habsburgs were involved in a number of wars, for example, the Thirty Years' War (1618-1648); conflicts with the Turks during the reign of Leopold I (1657-1705); the Third Dutch War (1672-1679); the War of the League of Augsburg sometimes referred to as the 'Nine Years' War' (1688-1697); a series of campaigns which returned Hungary to Austrian control by the Treaty of Carlowitz in 1699; and, finally, the War of the Spanish Succession (1701-1713). Most of these conflicts extended the Habsburgs' territory and enhanced their power base.

However, these achievements were not long-lasting. Towards the end of the reign of Charles VI (1711-1740) Austria relinquished many of these gains principally because Charles, who, without a male heir, anticipated the demise of the House of Austria (Habsburg). As a consequence he exchanged land for what turned out to be worthless assurances from other powers to ensure that his daughter Maria Theresa would be allowed to succeed. Charles died in 1740 heralding the War of the Austrian Succession (1740-1748). Eventually, Maria Theresa's husband Francis of Lorraine, Grand Duke of Tuscany, was elected Emperor, restoring control to the Habsburgs or, rather, to the House of Habsburg-Lorraine. Maria Theresa with her husband consolidated the 'House of Austria' into a 'modern', for the time, state and *Monarchia Austriaca* (Austrian Monarchy) became the norm.

In 1804, Francis I, on seeing Napoleon declare himself Emperor of France, proclaimed himself Emperor (Kaiser) of Austria and thus the creation of *Kaisertum Österreich* (Austrian Empire). The Napoleonic Wars, however, took their toll on Austrian possessions. By the Treaty of Pressburg in 1805, Austria was obliged to give up Dalmatia to France, Venetia to Napoleon's Kingdom of Italy, Tyrol to Bavaria, and various Swabian territories to Baden and Württemberg. However, as some compensation, Salzburg was allowed to be annexed to Austria.

The Napoleonic Wars ended with the Treaty of Vienna in 1815 and it was Prince Klemens Wenzel von Metternich, a German-Austrian politician, who played an important role in the advantageous diplomatic solution that that treaty brought to Austria. Metternich continued to dominate Austrian political life for over 40 years and, because of his distrust of people power, ran it largely as a police state. Austria also experienced, as did many other countries in Europe, the 1848 Revolutions. The conclusion for Austria was the departure of Metternich and the abdication of the mentally handicapped Emperor Ferdinand I in favour of his nephew, Franz Josef I.

Conflict was far from over after Franz Josef's succession. The defeat of Austrian forces in the 1866 Austro-Prussian War led to Austria's exclusion from Germany when the German Confederation was dissolved. Franz Josef's weak position internationally led him to concede internal reforms, one of which was to appease Hungarian nationalism by agreeing a deal with Hungarian nobles. This led to the creation in 1867 of the Dual Monarchy of Austria-Hungary. Austria was declared the western part of the empire.

Over the next 40 years Austria experienced much in the way of construction, expansion of the cities and, in particular, the railway lines, as well as a rapid growth in industrialisation throughout the country, the only exception being in the Tyrol which retained its largely agricultural base.

The Austro-Hungarian Empire, however, did not give up its policy of imperial expansion. In 1878, Bosnia and Herzegovina, were occupied followed by other new Balkan states in 1907. All were subsequently subjected to the joint rule of the governments of Austria and Hungary. Nationalistic strife in the Balkans was an inevitable consequence culminating in Franz Josef's presumed heir, Archduke Franz Ferdinand, being assassinated in Sarajevo in 1914. World War I followed.

With the defeat in 1918 of the 'Central Powers' - Germany, Austria-Hungary, the Ottoman Empire and Bulgaria - the break up of the Austro-Hungarian Empire followed. Emperor Karl of Austria, who had succeeded Franz Josef after his death in 1916, went into exile and the First Austrian Republic was later proclaimed. The next two decades were not easy for the new Austria as it searched for an identity. In the early 1930s with the strong influences of the Christian Social Party, Austrian government moved increasingly towards the centralization of power based on a fascist model. In 1932, the Dollfuß became Chancellor and the following year a procedural voting error allowed him to dissolve the National Council and vest legislative power in his executive by using an emergency provision enacted during World War I. Attempts by the Socialist opposition party failed to resolve the crisis peacefully and in 1934 the new Austro-fascist regime provoked the Austrian Civil War. The socialist party was weak and the uprising by its supporters was quickly put down. A ban followed on the socialist party and related organizations. The Dollfuß executive approved a new constitution abolishing the freedom of the press and establishing a one party system, 'The Patriotic Front', which remained in force until Austria became part of the Third Reich in 1938. The Patriotic Front government however frustrated the pro-Hitler sympathizers in Austria who wished to have both greater political influence and unification with Germany. Dollfuß held out but was seen by pro-German factions as too much of an obstruction; he was assassinated in July 1934. His successor, Schuschnigg, maintained Dollfuß's restrictive policies but he was forced to resign in March 1938 following Hitler's demand to allow power-sharing with the pro-German groups. Following Schuschnigg's resignation, German troops, in what is known as the *Anschluss*, occupied Austria without resistance. There followed the Nazi occupation of Austria which was annexed into Germany's Third Reich. Interestingly during that time and even though Adolf Hitler was Austrian (born at Braunau am Inn in Upper Austria) the Nazis denied Austrian nationals the use of the word 'Austria'.

World War II followed in 1939.

In 1945, after the defeat of the Axis powers the Second Austrian Republic was formed. The helpful outcome for Austria can be credited to a politically adept Austrian statesman, Karl Renner. Even before the war in Europe had come to an end, in the April of 1945, he had declared Austria a separate state from Germany and set up a government which deliberately included a broad political mix. There is no doubt that this clever action impressed the Allies who went on to treat Austria more as a liberated country from Nazi oppression, rather than a defeated warmonger. Under the Allied Commission for Austria the country was occupied from May 1945 with four zones created in the country and occupied respectively by the British, French, American and the Soviets. Vienna was also divided into four occupied sections together with a fifth being an international zone at its centre for which responsibility revolved between the individual four occupying powers.

Austria remained occupied by the Allied forces under these arrangements for 10 years until and when the Austrian State Treaty was signed and Austria regained its full sovereignty. The country declared at the same time its neutrality which was enshrined in its new constitution.

Austria has continued to develop since that time. In 1995, it joined the European Union and has since adopted the Euro (€). (*Sources: Wikipedia, Insight-Austria and Insight-Great Railway Journeys.*)

## Geography

Austria is a largely mountainous country located in the Alps. The Central Eastern Alps, Northern Limestone Alps and Southern Limestone Alps are all partly in Austria. Of the total area of Austria only about a quarter can be considered low lying, and only 32 per cent of the country is below 500 metres (1,640 feet). The high mountainous Alps in the west of Austria become the low lands and plains in the east.

Austria can be divided into five different areas. The biggest area of the country, at 60 per cent of the land mass, is that containing the Austrian Alps. The Austrian foothills at the base of the Alps and the Carpathians account for a further 12 per cent. The foothills in the east amount to about another 12 per cent. The second greatest mountainous area, but much lower than the Alps, is located to the north and is known as the Austrian granite plateau and accounts for about 10 per cent. The Austrian portion of the Viennese basin makes up about four per cent. Austria is about 580 km across its width and has a total area of 83,858 sq. km (32,378 sq. miles). Vienna is the country's capital and is also its largest city.

## Climate

The greater part of Austria lies in the cool/temperate climate zone in which humid westerly winds dominate. With over half of the country in the Alps the alpine climate predominates. In the east, in the Pannonian Plain and along the Danube valley, the climate reflects continental characteristics with less rain than in the alpine region.

## Government

Austria is a parliamentary democracy consisting of nine federal states and is one of six European countries that have declared permanent neutrality. Austria has been a member of the United Nations since 1955, joined the European Union in 1995 and adopted the euro currency in 2002. The prime political parties are the Austrian People's Party (ÖVP) and the Social Democratic Party (SPÖ) who have been in coalition since the beginning of 2007. The opposition parties are the Green Party of Austria and the Freedom Party of Austria (FPÖ). Alfred Gusenbauer has been the leader of the SPÖ since 2000 and became Austria's Chancellor in January 2007.

## Population

The population in 2006 was 8,292,322 having risen by an estimated 259,000 since the last official census which took place in 2001. Vienna's population is about 1.6 million or 2.2 million when one includes those living in the suburbs. The second largest city, Graz, is home to 250,099 people, followed by Linz with 188,968, Salzburg with about 150,000, and Innsbruck with 117,346. All other centres of population total less than 100,000. The official language is German with 88.6 per cent of the population speaking it followed by Turkish (2.3 per cent), Serbian (2.2 per cent), Croatian (1.6 per cent), Hungarian (0.5 per cent) and Bosnian (0.4 per cent). Slovenian, Croatian, Hungarian are all officially recognised as regional languages.

Austria's Parliament buildings on the Ringstrasse in Vienna. It is almost impossible in photographing any of the beautiful buildings of Vienna not to include the ubiquitous tram!　　　　　　　　　　　　　　　　　　　　　　　　　　　　　　　　　　*Author*

## Religion

By the year 2000, 73 per cent of Austria's population was registered as Roman Catholics. About five per cent identified themselves as Protestants. About 12 per cent of the population say that they do not belong to any church or religious community. Of the remainder, about 180,000 are members of the Eastern Orthodox Church, about 7,300 are Jewish, 300,000 are registered as members of various Muslim communities and 20,000 are committed Buddhists.

## Economy

Austria has a well-advanced social market economy and enjoys a high standard of living. In keeping with some other European Countries until the 1980s many of Austria's largest industries were in state ownership; however, in recent years, privatisation has reduced the number of state run companies.

Historically, Germany has been the main trading partner of Austria bringing a dependent relationship on Germany's economy. When there was growth in Germany, Austria invariably benefitted and conversely any slow down was extended across the frontier as was the case in 2001 when growth amounted to less than one per cent. Austria, on becoming a member state of the European Union, however, has reduced its dependency on Germany. The country now experiences increasingly stronger relationships with other European member states. Improved foreign investment brought about by Austria's convenient geographical location close to other EU aspiring economies to the east has no doubt also helped.

## Currency

The official currency is the euro, prior to that it was the Austrian schilling. At the time of writing (January 2008) the euro was worth 75 pence sterling.

Given the extensive electrified network in Austria, routine maintenance is critical. Here No. X 534.063 is being deployed on line inspection on the Brennerbahn on 26th June, 2007. *Author*

## Transportation

Railway track in Austria (not just that managed by ÖBB) totals 6,123 km of which 3,523 km has been electrified. Standard gauge (1.435 m) accounts for 5,639 km of which 3,429 km has been electrified. Narrow gauge amounts for another 481 km made up of 468 km of 760 mm gauge of which 94 km has been electrified and 13 km of 600 mm gauge of which only 3 km has been electrified.

The length of made-up roads totals 200,000 km which includes more than 2,000 km of toll motorways. Incidentally, toll fees are not collected on the route as in some other European countries, France and Spain, for example; rather, it is essential for the vehicle driver to buy a vignette on arrival at an Austrian border or beforehand by post or personal visit or to a local country-based Austrian Tourist Office. A vignette for visitors can be issued for 10 days or two months. There are strict penalties for not displaying a current motorway vignette.

Having much of the River Danube within Austria's boundary, the River Rhine and the Rhine-Main-Danube Canal close to it in Germany, water-borne transportation is also important. The Danube enters Austria at Passau on the German border and continues south-eastwards through Linz and Vienna, to Bratislava just over the border in Slovakia. Tributaries of the Danube in Austria include the Inn (forming part of Austria's German border), Traun, Enns, and Ybbs rivers. In the south, other important rivers are the Mur and the Mürz. In addition to the rivers, there are numerous lakes, notably Lake Constance (Bodensee), forming the western border with Liechtenstein and Switzerland, and Neusiedler Lake in Burgenland, near to the Hungarian border.

Serfaus, in the district of Landeck in the Tyrol, is the only municipality in Austria which does not allow automobile traffic at certain times of the year. The village (about 1,200 inhabitants) is well known for its tiny subway system - the Dorfbahn Serfaus. With four stations and a length of 1,280 m it allows for a complete ban of cars within the town, while at the same time maintaining the village's attraction to tourists, especially winter skiers (*see entry 104*).

# Chapter Two

# A Brief History of Austrian Railways

The first railways introduced to Austria were those developed at the beginning of the 19th century and were not powered by steam at all but literally by horsepower. In 1810, a horse-drawn railway was opened at the Styrian Erzberg - the Ore Mountain - for the transportation of ore. This railway, incidentally, was the forerunner of the Erzbergbahn (*see entry 74*). Much later, in August 1832, a horse-drawn railway was opened between Budweis and Linz which eventually operated over a length of almost 129 km and is claimed to be the first inter-urban railway in Europe. However, things did not move on so quickly in Austria compared to other leading countries in Europe and tended to lag behind.

Such lack of development frustrated many. Professor Franz Riepl of the University of Vienna was one such critic. He decided to design a railway network for Austria which, had it been built, would have been about 2,200 km long. His proposed network was to link the major cities of Austria (including Trieste with its access to the Mediterranean) for the transportation of important commodities of the time, i.e. cereals, wood and salt. He also believed that in the developing Industrial Age aided especially by the steam engine, coal would become the necessary, indeed vital, fuel to achieve economic success.

Riepl's proposals interested the banker Salomon von Rothschild who was willing to commit finance for the construction of a railway line, expecting, as did many other entrepreneurs of the time, significant profits from the investment. Rothschild wished for a railway linking Vienna with the coal mines of Moravia-Silesia, so he applied in 1830 for a concession to construct a line from Vienna to Krakow in Poland. However, it was not until a change of monarch in 1835 when Emperor Ferdinand I succeeded Franz I, that approval was forthcoming. Construction began in 1836 of what became named as 'Kaiser Ferdinand's Nordbahn'. The following November the first train travelled the initial section - Floridsdorf to Wagram. This was the turning point in the development of railways for Austria.

Other entrepreneurs saw the opportunities in developing their own railways but it was quickly realised that profits for investors were taking precedence over the State's desire to have a coherent railway system for the whole of the country. As a consequence, in the early 1840s, the State stepped in, the driving force at the time being the Finance Minister, a man named Kübeck who presented his own plan for a railway network. In Austria in 1840 there was only 144 km of railway lines but, following State intervention, by 1854 there was a total of 994 km State Railways accounting for almost 70 per cent of the country's total. Incidentally, the Semmeringbahn (*see entry 50*) was one of those built during this period as was construction begun of Riepl's dream, the line from Vienna to Trieste which eventually opened in 1857.

However, it was in the mid-1850s that State involvement in railways came to an end with Emperor Franz Josef I's foreign policy bringing Austria to the brink of war. As a consequence there were difficult economic times and the continuing construction and development of the State railways became a casualty. Private investors were encouraged to get involved and concessions were extended from 50 to 90 years with the State guaranteeing rewarding levels of interest. Furthermore, all of the existing State railways were sold off at knock-down prices, in some instances to foreign investors, the French for example, thus diminishing some of Austria's national wealth.

The memorial to Dr Carl Ritter von Ghega the founding father of the Semmeringbahn.
*Author*

From 1854 onwards, there followed the construction of numerous private railways; however, by 1859 this came to a sudden halt as a result of international conflict. When the war with Prussia came to an end in 1866, railway construction recommenced in earnest aided by a strong economic boom. However, this again came to an abrupt halt in 1873 when the Stock Exchange crashed. A number of private railways became insolvent and it was necessary for the State to take them over. The economic crisis also slowed the construction of private railways so it was necessary for State to invest once again in order to develop the country's transport system as well as provide much needed jobs.

In July 1884 the *k.k. Generaldirektion der Staatsbahnen* (Imperial General Directorate of State Railways) was founded and entrusted with the management of the total of 5,103 km of railway track. Thereafter, *kaiserlich-königliche Staatsbahnen* (*k.k. StB*) became the monopoly for all railways in Austria by taking over the existing private railways (the KJB, KFNB, ÖNWB, StEG, etc.). Up until the end of the monarchy in 1918, the only major private railway which was not nationalized was the Südbahn. This meant that by the beginning of World War I, out of a total of 22,981 km of railway track in Austria, 18,859 or just over 82 per cent was either State-owned or were private railways being run by the State.

The next phase in the history of Austrian railways began at the end of World War I and at the time after the Monarchy had ended. The day after Armistice Day in 1918 the Republic of Austria assumed power. The consequence for the railways was that those parts of the *k.k. StB* remaining in the new republic became part of the *Deutsch-Österreichische Staatsbahnen (DÖStB)* (German-Austrian State Railways) and in October 1919 the Austrian part was re-named the *Österreichische Staatseisenbahnen (ÖStB)* (Austrian State Railways) and from the following April became known as *Österreichische Bundesbahnen* (Austrian Federal Railways) adopting BBÖ as its abbreviation.

An early priority was to move to electrification especially as coal supplies to maintain steam working were difficult to obtain. The situation was not helped when Czechoslovakia, a new State and formerly part of the Austro-Hungarian Empire and an important source of coal supplies, chose to boycott the Austrian economy. The new government of the republic decided to build hydro-power stations and put them under the control of railway management. The government also set about re-organizing the State railways to run on commercial principles in order to improve profitability and efficiency. This led directly to BBÖ becoming an independent economic unit. Unfortunately by the early 1930s, because of the absence of injections of cash to meet outstanding debts with which the railways had become saddled, they became bankrupt. This in turn became very political and contributed directly to the fall of the First Republic.

Matters improved however when the global economy began to recover. This was helped in 1936 by a political rapprochement between Germany and Italy bringing about a much-needed boost in coal transit traffic. However, this improvement in the fortunes of the railways was short-lived and although loans were granted to the financially stricken company it was only the annexation of Austria by the German Reich in March 1938 that saved the BBÖ from what was fast becoming the inevitable - total collapse.

The annexation of Austria by Germany ushered in the *Reichsbahn* period in the history of Austria's railways. Six days after the German Wehrmacht troops entered Austria the *Österreichische Bundesbahnen* was dissolved and the management of the railways passed to the *Deutsche Reichsbahn* (DRB). Given Germany by then was developing its war machine a great number of locomotives which had been previously mothballed by BBÖ for many years were reactivated by the DRB. Following the outbreak of World War II, freight traffic increased significantly with the emphasis on military movement and war-related freight.

During the war Austria, like Germany, did not fare well with much of the country being hit by Allied Bombing. By 1945 the war was over leaving the country in a pitiful state especially the railway infrastructure much of which had been deliberately destroyed by the German *Wehrmacht* in order to thwart the rapidly advancing Red Army.

In April 1945, the German Reichsbahn in Austria came to an end and with the agreement of the Soviet occupying forces the Austrian railway employees established the Railway Directorate of Vienna. Three other Directorates were formed a short time later at Linz, Villach and Innsbruck. The railways were critical to the reconstruction of Austria in its newly created form as the Second Republic. Railway operations had to be re-started as quickly as possible not least of all to supply the population with the food.

However, the situation was not helped by the existence of the four Railway Directorates in the Allied occupation zones. It made for the development of an Austria-wide railway network a difficult if not an impossible task. Different Allied forces exerting major influences parochially in their regions meant that an overall coherent plan could not be pursued. Something had to be done. In August 1945, following a decision of the Allied Council, the Railway Directorate of Vienna was established as the General Directorate of the Austrian State Railways (*Österreichische Staatseisenbahnen* - ÖStB) and subsequently its responsibility expanded to the entire area of the new Austrian Federal State with the individual State railways being placed under combined management. At the same time a new and separate Railway Directorate was introduced for Vienna.

By August 1947, *Österreichische Staatseisenbahnen* had become *Österreichische Bundesbahnen* (Austrian Federal Railways) but it did not adopt its abbreviation ÖBB until 1953. The first priorities after the end of the war were the repair of the damage cause by the hostilities. Thereafter the priorities were electrification and in turn the abandonment of steam traction, the renewal of the rolling stock and the building of several new stations. The creation of Vienna's S-Bahn was also one of the benefits of this period.

*Right:* A view of the cogwheel on Achenseebahn's locomotive No. 2 *Jenbach* on 27th June, 2007. *Author*

*Below:* This photograph shows one of the Schneebergbahn's *Salamander* sets which benefits from the Abt system. *Author*

The Schafbergbahn's steam locomotive No. Z14 utilizing the Abt rack system brings down the midday train from the summit on 30th June, 2007. *Author*

# A BRIEF HISTORY OF AUSTRIAN RAILWAYS

*Österreichische Bundesbahnen* logo.

In the March 1966 elections, the Austrian People's Party won an absolute majority. The subsequent newly-formed government declared as one of its objectives the 'commercialisation' of the State railways thus sounding the death knell of direct involvement in their running. A Federal Railway Act of 1969 created a new *Österreichische Bundesbahnen*. A number of re-organizations followed, as they did again in 1989 when the 'New Railway' programme was adopted focusing ÖBB on delivering a modern transportation system. In 1992, another major re-structuring followed the Federal Railways Act 1992, which allowed for ÖBB to become a company in its own right and then in 2003 the Federal Railway Structure Act permitted ÖBB to re-structure to its present legal structure - the ÖBB Holding Group AG.

Since then, ÖBB Holding Group AG, and its sub-groups, by adopting strong commercial principles has continued to reflect upon their core business which, in some instances is or has led to the selling off of aspects into private hands, the Schneebergbahn (*see entry 49*) for example. (*Sources: Horn, A (ÖBB), Insight-Great Railway Journeys, Platform 5, Schweers + Wall and Geramond-Österreich.*)

## Rack/cogwheel systems utilised in Austria

There are two rack/cogwheel systems operated in Austria. The first is that which was invented by Niklaus Riggenbach and is reputed to be the oldest form of rack railway/cogwheel system in the world. It is formed by steel plates or channels connected by round or square rods at regular intervals. The Riggenbach system being the first designed suffers from the fact that its fixed rack is much more complex and expensive to build than the other, later designs. Incidentally, this system is sometimes also referred to as the Marsh system, because of its invention about the same time by an American inventor of that name who was the builder of the Mount Washington Cog Railway in the United States of America. The Riggenbach system is used on just one railway in Austria, the Achenseebahn (*see entry 95*) although it is also used on the Zugspitzbahn on the Austro-Germany border (*see entry 162*).

The second system is that devised by Roman Abt, a Swiss locomotive engineer. Abt at the time was working for a rack/cogwheel railway utilising the Riggenbach design which he thought could be much improved. The Abt rack features steel plates mounted vertically and in parallel to the rails, with rack teeth machined to a precise profile within them. These engage with the locomotive's pinion teeth much more smoothly than the Riggenbach system. Two or three parallel sets of Abt rack plates are used, with a corresponding number of driving pinions on the locomotive which ensures that at least one pinion tooth is always securely engaged. The Abt system is used on the Schneebergbahn (*see entry 49*) and the Schafbergbahn (*see entry 122*).

# Chapter Three

## Getting the best out of this Guide

To assist the reader in orientating him or herself relative to what is on offer and perhaps for planning a visit or visits to Austria, the railways and other locations identified in this guide have been organized as follows. Firstly, on a national basis the biggest provider, the Austrian Federal Railways (ÖBB) can be found in Chapter Four (*entry 1 on page 21*). Within this chapter Austrian Federal Railways Nostalgia Fleet Operations are described (*entries begin at page 27*). The second grouping in Chapter Five identifies those railways distributed on a state basis, i.e. Burgenland (*entries begin at page 43*), Carinthia (Kärnten) (*page 45*), Lower Austria (Niederösterreich) (*page 57*), Salzburg (*page 87*), Styria (Steiermark) (*page 98*), Tyrol (*page 122*), Upper Austria (Oberösterreich) (*page 140*), Vienna (Wien) (*page 164*) and Vorarlberg (*page 172*). (NB: The states or 'bunds' are arranged in alphabetical order according to their spelling in English. On this point, the author has also tended, but not always, to use English spellings, where they exist, for the names of the cities, towns and villages. Alternative spellings in Austro-German, as much as possible, have been included, not least of all to aid map reading.)

Chapter Six describes very briefly some of Austria's freight operations (*page 176*). In Chapter Seven some 15 funicular operations are described (*entries begin at page 179*). Finally, in Chapter Eight, Austria's relationships with its eight neighbouring countries are briefly explored (*page 191*).

All nine states in Austria have something to offer the railway enthusiast, the traveller and the family holiday-maker. The book describes railways of all gauges and types, museums, and, finally, items of related railway or general transport interest. It also gives some information about some funiculars but not cable cars, of which there are a great number in Austria. The guide, hopefully, has avoided becoming over detailed about the material which is held, in favour of listing, where known, of what may be seen and indicating where more information may be found. Having said that, some comprehensive lists have been provided for some of the larger operations where the information has fallen easily to hand. Those who want more detail invariably will find that a good starting point is the organization's website. There are many of these for Austrian Railways, which, experience has shown, contain a wealth of information. To assist in this respect, websites and e-mail addresses, where they exist, are provided. Websites are a very helpful means of obtaining current information but it is worth noting that some are not always regularly maintained or have been moved to a new address (URL) leaving the web browser or search engine at a loss. Similarly, some e-mail addresses are not always effective. At the time of going to print (early 2008) all the websites and e-mail addresses have been checked, found to be active and to be what they purported to be. Incidentally, where a website is listed, shown in brackets immediately after is the language or languages in which the information is written i.e. German (de), French (fr), Italian (it), English (en), Dutch (nl), Japanese (jp), Spanish (es), Portuguese (pt), Russian (ru), Slovenian (sv), Chinese (zh) and Korean (kr).

Each entry also identifies the location by town or city, its canton and proximity to a major centre of population as well as the state's capital. Route directions are not provided but a grid reference drawn from the *Michelin Map Number 730 – Austria* is given. Consideration was given to including GPS references but from the author's experience it is just as easy to enter the destination rather than provide data which have a huge potential for error. Contact details such as addresses, telephone and fax number where

# GETTING THE BEST OUT OF THIS GUIDE

known are listed. It will be noted that the numbers given are shown in a format as if one is dialling from within Austria. If dialling from abroad start the call with the international dialling code – in the UK it is 00 – followed by the code for Austria which is 43; then drop the first digit – the 0 – then follow it with the number. For example, the number in Austria for the Zillertalbahn (*entry 107*) is 0 52 44 60 60 but if calling from the UK dial the following: 00 43 52 44 60 60. Other information provided includes dates of opening, hours of operation, examples of the charges levied and train journey times which normally are for a single direction unless otherwise indicated. The year in brackets after the entry indicates when the information was obtained.

Every attempt has been made to ensure that all the information in this guide is correct and up-to-date, but it is important to render a health warning. Before travelling any distance in Austria to any of the locations listed herein, it is wise, in order to avoid disappointment, to check the state of current operations. There are many factors in heritage and tourist railway operations, short of closure or suspension, which can alter the availability of a service, not least the changing condition of many of the ageing locomotives and other rolling stock. Also, much of the Austrian preserved railway material can and does move around the country so if one wishes to see something particular, it is wise to check beforehand that it is where it is supposed to be!

Foreign languages can sometimes present a barrier to some in gaining more information. Therefore, to assist those who may have some understanding of German a glossary of 60 of the more common railway or railway related terms has been included.

Finally, for planning all journeys within Austria, it is worth noting that all tickets, timetables, fares and special offers are available at manned railway stations, travel agencies, or via the ÖBB Call Centre on +43 (0)5-1717 (code as if calling internationally) or by way of ÖBB's excellent website which is helpfully presented in both German and English languages.

The author is always keen to keep the information correct and up-to-date. By the nature of things, this guide has limitations in that it can only provide a 'snapshot' of what the state of affairs was at a particular time. The source material for this book was gathered towards the end of 2007 and the beginning of 2008. Much of the information contained herein will not change, well at least, not significantly. Other detail, however, will alter; for example, operating dates of the heritage railways, timetables, tariffs, rolling stock, company names and so on. Having said that, if this publication is used as is its intention, as a guide, then it is hoped that the contents will have relevance for some time to come. Operating dates for the preserved railways are a good example; whilst precise dates have been given for 2007, this year and beyond they will obviously change. However, it is the author's experience in Austria and elsewhere that whilst that may be true, the pattern of activity often remains more or less the same.

Writing a guide such as this presents special challenges. The author estimates that this guide holds in excess of 20,000 separate items of factual information. Getting it right first time has always been the author's goal but inevitably, given the enormity of the task, errors can and, regrettably, do creep in but it is hoped that any of these do not mar the reader's enjoyment of the guide. The author, therefore, calls for help from the readership. Contributions are invited if any inaccuracies are identified in this book, changes have been found to the operating circumstances or new facilities have become available. Such information can be sent to the author who can be contacted by e-mail at info@rail-guides.eu or c/o Oakwood Press. Secondly the author has developed a website - www.rail-guides.eu - which has been written for the sole purpose to support not only this book but the previous publications - *The Essential Guide to French Heritage and Tourist Railways* and *The Essential Guide to Swiss Heritage and Tourist Railways*.

Dual-voltage *Taurus* No. 1116 113-0 arriving at Linz Hbf on 29th June, 2007. *Author*

A 'Postbus' sporting the 100th anniversary livery standing at Selzthal station on 10th July, 2007. *Author*

# Chapter Four

# Austria's National Railway (ÖBB)

## 1 Austrian Federal Railways (Österreichische Bundesbahnen - ÖBB)

ÖBB-Holding AG is the parent company of the ÖBB Group and was established on 20th April, 2004 with the authority of *Bundesbahnstrukturgesetz 2003* (Federal Railways Structure Act, 2003). The Republic of Austria through the Austrian Federal Ministry of Transport, Innovation and Technology owns 100 per cent of the shares. ÖBB-Holding AG oversees the subsidiary companies referred as sub-groups of the ÖBB Group which all began operations on 1st January, 2005. The sub-groups are: ÖBB-Personenverkehr, Rail Cargo Austria (*see also entry 145*), ÖBB-Infrastruktur Betrieb and ÖBB-Infrastruktur Bau.

ÖBB-Personenverkehr carrying annually a grand total of 443 million passengers and with a market share of *circa* 90 per cent is the largest provider of public rail and bus transport services in the whole of Austria. In 2006 about 196 million passengers, of whom 29 million were long distance, were carried by rail. The ÖBB-Postbus service, with a fleet of about 2,100 buses, provides Austria-wide bus routes. In 2006, about 247 million passengers were carried by bus.

ÖBB-Traktion GmbH is the largest provider of traction in Austria delivering annually something in the order of 131 million train-kilometres and 7.4 million man-hours in traction vehicle services. Annually, ÖBB-Traktion performs about one million man-hours in car and carriage inspection and servicing through 500,000 repair and maintenance operations and 100,000 vehicle checks.

The fleet comprises 1,096 locomotives, 392 railcars, 3,016 passenger carriages and 108 luggage vans or mail cars. Classes '1016,' '1116' and '1216' *Taurus Eurosprinter* locomotives (*see pictures above and at entries 5, 25, 101, 121, and 143*) built by Siemens-Krauss-Maffei are the current mainstay of the fleet with 332 on the books and a further 50 of the class '1216' ordered in 2006 of which 18 had been delivered by the end of 2006. These new '1216s' are capable of speeds of up to 230 kmh for long-distance passenger transport and for hauling considerably greater weights of freight.

Rail Cargo Austria (*see entry 145*) operated with 17,635 freight cars in 2006 and transported 92.7 million tons. ÖBB operates on a network distance of 5,683 km with 11,000 km of track. ÖBB is a big employer with over 42,200 employees including 1,242 apprentices.

*Timetables and fare structures*

Timetable services for trains running throughout Austria can be found on-line at www. oebb. at/en ; for travelling further afield the on-line timetable for most European services, including all Austrian can be found at reiseauskunft.bahn.de/bin/query.exe/en

The cost of almost all train standard fares for journeys within Austria but not across international frontiers can also be found on-line at ÖBB's website. There also exists a discount card called the 'VORTEILScard'. This is a customer card which currently is held by over 1,000,000 passengers and offer up to 45 per cent discounts when purchasing tickets at a station ticket office - *Reisebüro am Bahnhof* - and up to 50 per cent if booking on-line or at an unmanned ticket machine. The VORTEILScard holder can also obtain even greater discounts (up to 60 per cent) for travelling to certain special events. The card holder can also obtain particularly good value tickets through many

ÖBB's Siemens class '5022' *Desiro* No. 014-4 awaiting later departure from Linz Urfahr station on 29th June, 2007. *Author*

ÖBB's Railcargo carries all manner of freight. Here a consignment of BMW Z5s and Z3s valued at over £4 million passes through Selzthal station. *Author*

## AUSTRIA'S NATIONAL RAILWAY (ÖBB)

European countries and with 'RAILPLUS' save 25 per cent on cross-border rail services. ÖBB also offer the '1-PLUS-Freizeitticket' which allows small groups to travel by rail at low cost with discounts for second and subsequent passengers.

*Fahrgäst Osterrreich* is the body representing passengers using Austrian public transport and can be found at www.fahrgast.at/~english.htm ; visitors to Austria may also find helpful the official site for Austrian Tourist Information at www.austria.info/english/

### Austria's Principal Routes operated by Austrian Federal Railways (ÖBB)

### 2 Nordbahn

*Locations*: Vienna and Breclav in the Czech Republic.
*Michelin map references*: V4 and W2 respectively.
*Operated by*: ÖBB.
*Official line number*: 214.
*Timetable number*: 930.
*Route*: North from Vienna Floridsdorf or Vienna Floridsdorf to Breclav in the Czech Republic via Gänserndorf and Hohenau, a total distance of 83 km.
*Journey time*: 1 hour 11 minutes to Breclav and between 46 and 56 minutes to Hohenau.
*Gauge*: Standard by adhesion only.
*Electrified*: Yes, 15 kV AC 16.7 Hz.
*Places to see*: The Austrian National Railway Museum is at Strasshof on this route (*see entry 51*).
*Website*: www.oebb.at/en
*Operating*: Daily all the year round every hour.
*Tariff*: A 2nd class adult single to Hohenau from Vienna (Floridsdorf) is €10.90 (2007).
*Comments*: Is one of the four routes from Austria into the Czech Republic eventually reaching Brno.

*Taurus* No. 1116 149-4 on the Nordbahn passing the Strasshof Museum and heading for Breclav on 3rd July, 2007.         *Author*

Hungarian MAV *Taurus* No. 1047 010-2, a regular traveller on the Ostbahn, stands at Vienna's Westbahnhof on 6th July, 2007. *Author*

ÖBB's 'Talent' class '4024' No. 104-4 at Mürzzuschlag about to leave for Vienna via the Semmeringbahn on 11th October, 2007. *Author*

## 3 Ostbahn

*Location*: Vienna and Györ in Hungary.
*Michelin map references*: V4 and off the map but east of X6 respectively.
*Operated by*: ÖBB.
*Official line number*: 218.
*Timetable numbers*: 700 & 701.
*Route*: East from Vienna Südbahnhof (and sometimes the Westbahnhof) to Györ in Hungary via Bruck a.d. Leitha, a total distance of about 140 km.
*Journey time*: 1 hour 28 minutes.
*Gauge*: Standard gauge by adhesion only.
*Electrified*: Yes, 15 kV AC 16.7 Hz.
*Websites*: www.oebb.at/en and www.mav.hu and www.gysev.hu
*Operating*: Daily all year round every hour.
*Tariff*: A 2nd class adult single from Vienna Südbahnhof to Bruck a.d. Leitha costs €9.30 (2007).
*Comments*: Is one of the seven routes from Austria into Hungary (*see entry 166*).

## 4 Südbahn

*Location*: Vienna and Graz.
*Michelin map references*: V4 and S7.
*Operated by*: ÖBB.
*Official line numbers*: 205 to Mürzzuschlag, 805 from Mürzzuschlag to Werndorf south of Graz and then 705 (to Spielfeld-Straß).
*Timetable numbers*: 500, 501, 600, 250, 501 (to Spielfeld-Straß).
*Route*: From Vienna Südbahnhof to Graz and on to Spielfeld-Straß on the Slovenian border, a total distance of 261 km.
*Journey time*: 3 hours 12 minutes without changes.
*Gauge*: Standard by adhesion only.
*Electrified*: Yes, 15 kV AC 16.7 Hz and voltage supply changes to 3000 V DC down to Maribor in Slovenia.
*Website*: www.oebb.at/en and www.slo-zelcznice.si/en/
*Operating*: Daily all the year round every hour.
*Tariff*: An adult 2nd class single ticket from Vienna to Graz is €30.20 (2007).
*Comments*: The Südbahn has as on its route the World Heritage site the Semmeringbahn (*see entry 50*). The Südbahn offers one of the four routes into Slovenia with this one to the town of Maribor (SLO) (*see entry 170*).

## 5 Westbahn

*Location*: Vienna and Bregenz.
*Michelin map references*: V4 and B6 respectively.
*Operated by*: ÖBB.
*Official line numbers*: 103, 201, 230, 401, 501, 601 and 602.
*Timetable numbers*: 100, 101, 110, 201, 300, 400 and 401.
*Route*: From Vienna Westbahnhof to Bregenz in Austria's Vorarlberg, a total distance of 770 km (including the section through Germany (D). The line continues from

*Taurus* No. 1116 112-2 approaches Timelkam station on the Westbahn at speed on 1st July, 2007.
*Author*

*Nostalgie* fleet electric locomotive No. 1010.10 leaves Payerbach station on the Semmeringbahn on 14th October, 2007.
*Author*

# AUSTRIA'S NATIONAL RAILWAY (ÖBB)

Bregenz to Lindau on the Bodensee (Lake Constance) in Germany. From Salzburg the Westbahn travels through Germany to Kufstein (A) via Rosenheim (D).
*Journey time*: 7 hours 36 minutes without changes.
*Gauge*: Standard by adhesion only.
*Electrified*: Yes, 15 kV AC 16.7 Hz.
*Website*: www.oebb.at/en (de en) and www.slo-zeleznice.si/en/ (de en).
*Operating date*s: Daily all year round with services every one to two hours.
*Tariff*: An adult 2nd class single is €61.70 (2007).
*Comments*: Given the geographical shape of Austria it is hardly surprising that the east to west route is the longest in the country. The Westbahn passes through the 10.25 km Arlberg tunnel.

## Austrian Federal Railways Nostalgia Fleet Operations

### 6  E1 - Erlebniszug Zauberberge

*Locations*: Vienna and Mürzzuschlag.
*Michelin map references*: V4 and S6 respectively.
*Operated by*: ÖBB Erlebnisbahn.
*Route*: From Vienna Südbahnhof to Mürzzuschlag in Styria, a distance of 119 km.
*Journey time*: 2 hours 2 minutes.
*Gauge*: Standard gauge by adhesion only.
*Traction utilised*: Electric-powered (15 kV AC 16.7 Hz).
*Rolling stock*: *Nostalgie E-loks* either from class '1010', '1041' or '1046'.
*Places to see*: Visit the Südbahn Kulturbahnhof at Mürzzuschlag (*see entry 92*) and the Semmeringbahn exhibition at Semmering station (*see entry 50*).
*Contact details*: Verein Erlebnis Bahn und Schiff, Bahngasse 2, Bad Fischau-Brunn, A-2721. Telephone: 0664 200 1500. E-mail: bestellung@erlebnis-bahn.at
*Website*: www.erlebnis-bahn-schiff.at
*Operating dates*: Saturdays, Sundays and public holidays all year round. Trains leave Vienna at 0814 hours arriving at Mürzzuschlag at 1016 hours and leave Mürzzuschlag at 1605 hours for the return journey and arrive back at Vienna at 1808 hours. The train also operates another service on the same day from Mürzzuschlag (leaving at 1203 hours) to Wiener Neustadt arriving at 1325 hours and leaving there at 1400 hours arriving back at Mürzzuschlag at 1514 hours (2007).
*Comments*:   Probably one of the most enjoyable ways of experiencing the Semmeringbahn (*see entry 50*). There are no fewer than seven versions of this service offered throughout the operating year.

### 7  E2 - Erlebniszug Wiener Alpen

*Location*: Bratislava in Slovakia to Mürzzuschlag via Wiener Neustadt in Lower Austria.
*Michelin map references*: X4 and S6 respectively.
*Operated by*: ÖBB Erlebnisbahn.
*Route*: From Bratislava Petr. to Mürzzuschlag, distance of approximately 175 km.
*Journey time*: 3 hours 5 minutes.

Electric locomotive No. 1046 016-0 on the 'Erlebniszug Wiener Alpen' excursion crosses the Wagnergraben viaduct (142 m) of the Semmeringbahn on 13th October, 2007. *Author*

The track nearest to camera is the ÖBB's standard gauge at Puchberg am Schneeberg station. The train set in the background is sporting the *Salamander* livery of the Schneebergbahn.
*Author*

# AUSTRIA'S NATIONAL RAILWAY (ÖBB)

*Gauge*: Standard by adhesion only.
*Traction utilised*: Electric- and diesel-powered.
*Rolling stock*: *Nostalgie E-Lok* class '1046' or a diesel-powered locomotive of class *Hercules* '2016' or diesel locomotive No. 2143.040
*Places to see*: As with E1 above, visit the Südbahn Kulturbahnhof at Mürzzuschlag (*see entry 92*) and the Semmeringbahn exhibition at Semmering station (*see entry 50*).
*Contact details*: Verein Erlebnis Bahn und Schiff, Bahngasse 2, Bad Fischau-Brunn, A-2721. Telephone: 0664 200 1500. E-mail: bestellung@erlebnis-bahn.at
*Website*: www.erlebnis-bahn-schiff.at
*Operating dates*: Saturdays, Sundays and Public Holidays all year round. Trains leave Bratislava at 0651 hours arriving at Mürzzuschlag at 0956 hours and leave Mürzzuschlag at 1649 hours for the return journey and arrive back at Bratislava at 1953 hours. Another service is also operated on these days between Wiener Neustadt (leaving at 0905 hours) and Gutenstein (arriving at 1007 hours). The return journey leaves Gutenstein at 1653 hours and arrives back at Wiener Neustadt an hour later. (2007).
*Comments*: Again perhaps one of the most enjoyable ways of experiencing the Semmeringbahn (*see entry 50*). There are no fewer than six versions of this service offered throughout the operating year.

## 8  E3 - Erlebniszug Schneebergland

*Locations*: Vienna Südbahnhof (one service), Puchberg am Schneeberg and from Wiener Neustadt (an additional three services).
*Michelin map references*: V4, T5 and U5 respectively.
*Operated by*: ÖBB Erlebnisbahn.
*Routes*: From Vienna Südbahnhof to Puchberg am Schneeberg, a total distance of about 84 km. From Wiener Neustadt to Puchberg am Schneeberg, a total distance of 27 km.
*Journey time*: From Vienna Südbahnhof to Puchberg am Schneeberg, 2 hours and from Wiener Neustadt to Puchberg am Schneeberg, 47 minutes.
*Gauge*: Standard by adhesion only.
*Traction utilised*: Electric- and diesel-powered.
*Rolling stock*: From Vienna to Wiener Neustadt an *E-Lok* and from Wiener Neustadt to Puchberg am Schneeberg a class '2016' diesel locomotive.
*Places to see*: The Schneebergbahn (*see entry 49*).
*Contact details*: Verein Erlebnis Bahn und Schiff, Bahngasse 2, Bad Fischau-Brunn, A-2721. Telephone: 0664 200 1500. E-mail: bestellung@erlebnis-bahn.at
*Website*: www.erlebnis-bahn-schiff.at
*Operating dates*: Saturdays, Sundays and Public Holidays all year round. The first train of the day leaves Vienna Südbahnhof at 0823 hours and arrives at Puchberg am Schneeberg at 1023 hours. The only return of the day to Vienna Südbahnhof leaves Puchberg am Schneeberg at 1635 hours arriving back in Vienna at 1845 hours. Three other services operate from Wiener Neustadt leaving at 1136, 1336 and 1536 hours. Return services leave Puchberg am Schneeberg at 1035, 1235 and 1435 hours (2007).
*Comments:* A useful and enjoyable way of reaching Puchberg to travel the rack railway up the Schneeberg. There are six versions of this service offered throughout the operating year.

The 'Wachau Express' crosses a viaduct near to St Nikola-Struden on 8th October, 2007. 'A class '2043' leads the way. *Author*

Diesel locomotive No. 2043 012-0 heads the Strudengau service on 8th October, 2007. Here it is emerging from the river mist and running alongside the Danube towards Grein. *Author*

## 9  E4 - Erlebniszug Wachau

*Locations*: Vienna Südbahnhof and St Valentin in Lower Austria.
*Michelin map references*: V4 and P4 respectively.
*Operated by*: ÖBB Erlebnisbahn.
*Route*: From Vienna Südbahnhof to St Valentin in Lower Austria via Tulln, Krems a.d. Donau, Spitz a.d. Donau and Grein, a total distance of about 210 km.
*Journey time*: 6 hours 12 minutes.
*Gauge*: Standard by adhesion only.
*Traction utilised*: Electric- and diesel-powered.
*Rolling stock*: A *Nostalgie E-Lok* is used from Vienna to Krems a.d. Donau and from there to St Valentin a class '2143' or a class '2043' diesel locomotive.
*Places to see*: The impressive Melk Abbey (*de Stift Melk*) which can be seen clearly from the train was built in 1683 after the previous construction was burnt down by the Turks. Originally a castle stood on this site and was the Babenburg family's first residence in Austria in the year 976. The ceiling frescoes are particularly outstanding.
*Contact details*: Verein Erlebnis Bahn und Schiff, Bahngasse 2, Bad Fischau-Brunn, A-2721. Telephone: 0664 200 1500. E-mail: bestellung@erlebnis-bahn.at
*Website*: www.erlebnis-bahn-schiff.at
*Operating dates*: Daily from the end of March to almost the end of October with one service in each direction. The service leaves Vienna Südbahnhof at 0711 hours and arrives at Spitz a.d. Donau at 1002 hours and St Valentin at 1323 hours. Thirty minutes later it leaves St Valentin and arrives at Aggsbach Markt at 1607 hours and back at Vienna Südbahnhof at 1859 hours (2007).
*Comments*: This route runs alongside the River Danube ('Donau') for almost the entire journey passing through the outstandingly beautiful Wachau Valley with its hectares and hectares of vineyards. This is an excursion not to be missed. There are eight versions of this service offered throughout the operating year.

## 10  E5 - Erlebniszug Strudengau

*Location*: Linz in Upper Austria and Krems a.d. Donau in Lower Austria.
*Michelin map references*: O4 and S3 respectively.
*Operated by*: ÖBB Erlebnisbahn.
*Route*: From Linz to Krems a.d. Donau, a total distance of about 140 km.
*Journey time*: 3 hours 17 minutes.
*Gauge*: Standard by adhesion only.
*Traction utilised*: Diesel-powered.
*Rolling stock*: Class '2043' or class '2143' diesels.
*Places to see*: The beautiful city of Linz and, of course, the River Danube for a pleasure cruise. Krems is a mecca for art lovers with its 'Karikaturmuseum' and 'Kunsthalle Krems'.
*Contact details*: Verein Erlebnis Bahn und Schiff, Bahngasse 2, Bad Fischau-Brunn, A-2721. Telephone: 0664 200 1500. E-mail: bestellung@erlebnis-bahn.at
*Website*: www.erlebnis-bahn-schiff.at
*Operating dates*: Daily from the end of March to almost the end of October with one service in each direction from Linz (leaves at 0824) to Krems a.d. Donau (arrives 1141 hours) and return (leaves Krems at 1558 and arrives back at Linz at 2025 hours). An

The 'Danube Express' service was being performed by class '1044' No. 055-0 on 8th October, 2007. This class is slowly being replaced by *Taurus* class '1116s'. *Author*

An Ennstal service from Stainach-Irdning hauled by No. 1044 122-8 approaches a level crossing near Liezen heading for Selzthal on 9th October, 2007. *Author*

additional service leaves Spitz a.d. Donau at 1455 and arrives at Krems a.d. Donau at 1523 hours. A service leaves Spitz a.d. Donau at 1334 hours and arrives at Spitz a.d. Donau at 1403 hours (2007).
*Comments*: This journey is a shorter version of the Wachau Express (*entry 9 above*) enjoying as it does the magnificent scenery of the Strudengau and the Wachau valley as it hugs the River Danube along its route. There are no fewer than five versions of this service offered throughout its operating year.

## 11  E6 - Erlebniszug Donau

*Locations*: Vienna Südbahnhof and Passau in Germany.
*Michelin map references*: V4 and M3 respectively.
*Operated by*: ÖBB Erlebnisbahn.
*Route*: From Vienna Südbahnhof to Passau in Bavaria, Germany, a total distance of about 285 km.
*Journey time*: 5 hours 13 minutes.
*Gauge*: Standard by adhesion only.
*Traction utilised*: Electric-powered.
*Rolling stock*: Usually hauled by an *E-Lok* class '1044' a class which is steadily being replaced on ÖBB's regular fleet by *Taurus* class '1116s'.
*Places to see*: This service can offer visitors staying in Vienna a 7½ hour visit to the beautiful city of Linz; however, it does make for a long day!
*Contact details*: Verein Erlebnis Bahn und Schiff, Bahngasse 2, Bad Fischau-Brunn, A-2721. Telephone: 0664 200 1500. E-mail: bestellung@erlebnis-bahn.at
*Website*: www.erlebnis-bahn-schiff.at
*Operating dates*: Daily all the year round with one service in each direction from Vienna Südbahnhof leaving at 0740 hours to Passau arriving at 1253 hours and returning from Passau at 1714 hours and arriving back at Vienna Südbahnhof at 2233 hours. An additional service leaves Passau at 1315 hours and arrives at Linz at 1443 hours. A service also leaves Linz at 1517 hours and arrives at Passau at 1653 hours (2007).
*Comments*: This service travels on ÖBB's Westbahn. There are no fewer than 11 versions of this service offered throughout the operating year.

## 12  E7 - Erlebniszug Ennstal

*Locations*: Vienna and Bischofshofen in the state of Salzburg.
*Michelin map references*: V4 and L6 respectively.
*Operated by*: ÖBB Erlebnisbahn.
*Route*: From Vienna Südbahnhof to Bischofshofen via Selzthal, a total distance of about 350 km.
*Journey time*: 5 hours 56 minutes.
*Gauge*: Standard by adhesion only.
*Traction utilised*: Electric-powered.
*Rolling stock*: An *E-Lok* from the *Nostalgie* fleet.
*Places to see*: The Ennstal route passes through the awe-inspiring Gesäuse valley (*see entry 76*).
*Contact details*: Verein Erlebnis Bahn und Schiff, Bahngasse 2, Bad Fischau-Brunn, A-2721. Telephone: 0664 200 1500. E-mail: bestellung@erlebnis-bahn.at

Class '1144' locomotives are class '1044s' fitted for push-pull working. Here No. 1144.277 stands at Neusiedl am See station on 5th July, 2007. *Author*

Diesel No. 2143.35, a locomotive of a class being phased out of regular operations (note the old logo), here heads the 'Reblaus Express' on 6th October, 2007 having left Hofern and heading down to Retz. *Author*

*Website*: www.erlebnis-bahn-schiff.at
*Operating dates*: Saturdays, Sundays and Public Holidays throughout the year. The service leaves Vienna Südbahnhof at 0740 hours and arrives at Bischofshofen at 1334 hours. A return service leaves at 1426 hours and arrives back in Vienna at 2038 hours.
*Comments*: There are no fewer than 13 versions of this service offered throughout the operating year.

### 13  E8 - Erlebniszug Neusiedlersee

*Locations*: Vienna Südbahnhof and Neusiedlersee in Burgenland.
*Michelin map references*: V4 and W5 respectively.
*Operated by*: ÖBB Erlebnisbahn.
*Route*: From Vienna Südbahnhof (Ost) to Neusiedlersee, a total distance of 60 km.
*Journey time*: 41 minutes.
*Gauge*: Standard by adhesion only.
*Traction utilised*: Electric-powered.
*Rolling stock*: At weekends and on public holidays a *Nostalgie E-Lok* class '2050' is operated with another *E-Lok* class being deployed on weekdays.
*Contact details*: Verein Erlebnis Bahn und Schiff, Bahngasse 2, Bad Fischau-Brunn, A-2721. Telephone: 0664 200 1500. E-mail: bestellung@erlebnis-bahn.at
*Website*: www.erlebnis-bahn-schiff.at
*Operating dates*: Daily from end of March to almost the end of October. Services leave Vienna Südbahnhof (Ost) at 0902 hours and arrive at Neusiedlersee at 0943 hours and return at 1826 hours arriving back at the Südbahnhof at 1908 hours
*Comments*: An enjoyable day out can be had by walkers, cyclists and bird-watchers at the lake.

### 14  E9 - Reblaus Express

*Locations*: Retz and Drosendorf (on the Czech Republic's South Moravia border) both in Lower Austria.
*Michelin map references*: T2 and S2 respectively.
*Operated by*: ÖBB Erlebnisbahn.
*Route*: From Retz to Drosendorf, a total distance of 34 km.
*Journey time*: 1 hour 35 minutes.
*Gauge*: Standard by adhesion only on a maximum gradient of 2.7 per cent.
*Traction utilised*: Diesel-powered.
*Rolling stock*: Diesel locomotives Nos. 2045.20 or 2143.35.
*Places to see*: On the first Sunday of each month there is a bus connection from Drosendorf leaving at 1100 hours and from Geras leaving at 1045 hours to Vranov in the Czech Republic (NB: passports are essential to enter and leave) and returning to Drosendorf by 1545 hours and Geras by 1605 hours both in time for the return train journey to Retz. Retz also has an underground life all of its own. An extensive subterranean network, including the largest historic wine cellar in Austria, covers a large area under the town's streets. The tunnels sometimes go three levels deep and it is possible to take a guided tour of about five per cent of the system - about 900 metres of tunnel. (*Source: Insight Guide - Austria.*)

*Contact details*: Verein Erlebnis Bahn und Schiff, Bahngasse 2, Bad Fischau-Brunn, A-2721. Telephone: 0664 200 1500. E-mail: bestellung@erlebnis-bahn.at or Ing. Alfred Polt, ÖBB-Personenverkehr, Erlebnisbahn, Reblaus Express Österreichische Bundesbahnen, Laxenburgerstraße 2, A-1100 Vienna. Telephone: 01 93000/31 98 2 Fax: 0664/617 65 79. E-mail: alfred.polt@ts.oebb.at
*Website*: www.reblaus-express.at and www.erlebnis-bahn-schiff.at
*Operating dates*: *Nostalgie* rail services operate from 1st May to 28th October. The rest of the year it functions as a bus-operated service.
*Tariff*: A single ticket for an adult is €8.80, a child (7-15 years) €4.40 and a family (two adults and two children) €17.60. A return ticket is €12.40, €6.20 and €24.80 respectively. ÖBB also offers adult return tickets from Vienna to Drosendorf for €28, for a child €14 and for a family €56. Bus return tickets from Drosendorf to Vranov are €10, €5 and €20 respectively. Bus return tickets from Geras to Vranov are €13, €6.50 and €26 respectively. Bicycles are carried free of charge on the trains. There are a variety of group discount rates depending on the size of the group (2007).
*Comments*: The line connects the Weinviertel and Waldviertel regions of Lower Austria and passes through vineyards, fields and forests to sites of cultural interest and natural beauty as well as an opportunity to visit the Czech town of Vranov with its magnificent cliff-top château.

**15 Middle Austria Excursions**

ÖBB Erlebnisbahn operates four excursions in Middle Austria operating out of Liezen/Selzthal as follows:

*Route M1* named the Salzkammergut Express from Selzthal to Ebensee/Gmunden, a total distance of about 90 km.
*Journey time*: 2 hours 55 minutes.
*Traction utilised*: Standard gauge electric-powered *Nostalgie E-Lok* class '1245' No. 005 built 1939-40 (*picture of a sister locomotive can be seen at entry 16 tour 08c below*).
*Operating dates*: In 2007 excursions were operated on 14th July, 26th July, 9th August and 25th August. On those days the train left Selzthal station at 1035 hours and arrived at Ebensee at 1325 hours. It returned from Gmunden at 1658 hours and arrived back at Selzthal at 1922 hours.
*Tariff*: Adult ticket was €43 and for a child €31 (2007).

*Route M2* named the Nationalpark Knappentour from Liezen to Eisernz, a total distance of about 60 km.
*Journey time*: 1 hour 38 minutes.
*Traction utilised*: Standard gauge electric-powered *Nostalgie E-Lok* class '1080' No. 01.
*Operating dates*: In 2007 excursions were operated on 4th August and 1st September. The trains left Liezen at 0950 hours and arrived at Eisnerz at 1128 hours. The return trains left Eisnerz at 1610 hours and arrived back at 1758 hours.
*Tariff*: Adult ticket was €43 and for a child €31 (2007).

*Route M3* named the Dreiflussefahrt from Selzthal to Passau in Bavaria, a total distance of about 179 km.
*Journey time*: 3 hours 23 minutes.

Selzthal is an important rail centre and the focal point for Middle Austria excursions. Outside Selzthal station the 2-10-0 steam locomotive No. 52.7046 of 1943 vintage is displayed.
*Author*

*Traction utilised*: Standard gauge electric-powered *Nostalgie E-Lok* class '1041' No. 022 built 1952-4.
*Operating dates*: In 2007 excursions were operated on 21st July, 18th August and 8th September. The trains left Selzthal at 0747 hours and arrived at Passau at 1110 hours. The return trains left Passau at 1707 hours and arrived back at 2022 hours.
*Tariff*: Adult ticket was €53 and for a child €27 (2007).

*Route M4* named the Südsteirische Weinberge from Liezen to Ehrenhausen, a total distance of about 161 km.
*Journey time*: 3 hours 20 minutes.
*Traction utilised*: Standard gauge electric-powered *Nostalgie E-Lok* class '1041' No. 022 built 1952-4.
*Operating dates*: In 2007 excursions were operated on 15th, 23rd and 29th September. The trains left Liezen at 0800 hours and arrived at Ehrenhausen at 1120 hours. The return trains left Ehrenhausen at 1724 hours and arrived back at 2018 hours.
*Tariff*: Adult ticket was €44 and for a child €22 (2007).

*Contact details for all these Middle Austria excursions*: Verein Erlebnis Bahn und Schiff, Bahngasse 2, Bad Fischau-Brunn, A-2721. Telephone: 0664 200 1500. E-mail: bestellung@erlebnis-bahn.at
*Website*: www.erlebnis-bahn-schiff.at

Built at the Floridsdorf locomotive factory in 1891 '17c372' has been fully restored and is now used regularly for excursions. Here it is seen at Ernstbrunn on 6th October, 2007. *Author*

Built between 1939/40 electric locomotive No. 1245.525 is safeguarded at Knittelfeld where it was seen on 7th July, 2007. '525' regularly undertakes excursion duties. Two others of this class have survived: '04' is at Salzburg and '05' at Selzthal. *Author*

## 16 Eastern Austria Excursions

ÖBB Erlebnisbahn operates 44 excursions in Eastern Austria operating mainly out of Vienna but also from Wiener Neustadt, Mödling, Villach and Knittelfeld. The following is a sample of five of the excursions available:

*Route O4* named the 'Saisoneröffnung' from Vienna Südbahnhof to Strasshof Eisenbahnmuseum via Vienna Meidling, Oberlaa, Stadlau and Süssenbrunn, a total distance of about 40 km.
*Journey time*: 1 hour 30 minutes.
*Traction utilised*: Standard gauge steam-powered *Dampflok* No. 17c372.
*Operating dates*: In 2007 the excursion operated on 22nd April. The train left Vienna Südbahnhof at 0845 hours and arrived at Strasshof Eisenbahnmuseum at 1015 hours. The return train left Strasshof Eisenbahnmuseum at 1550 hours and arrived back at 1700 hours.
*Tariff*: Adult ticket was €20 and for a child €10 (2007).

*Route O8c* named the 'Internationales Andampfen 2007 - fur Kärnten' from Villach to Knittelfeld via Feldkirchen, St Veit, Treibach, Friesach, Neumarkt, Mariahof, Scheifling, Unzmarkt, Judenburg and Zeltweg, a total distance of about 181 km.
*Journey time*: The outward journey takes 2 hours 8 minutes and return 3 hours 20 minutes.
*Traction utilised*: Standard gauge electric-powered *E-Lok* No. 1245.525.
*Operating dates*: In 2007 the excursion operated on 20th May. The train left Villach at 0820 hours and arrived at Knittelfeld at 1028 hours. The return train left Knittelfeld at 1600 hours and arrived back at 1920 hours.
*Tariff*: Adult ticket was €24, for a child €12 and for a family €48. Reduced prices apply to passengers joining the train *en route* (2007).

*Route O18* named the 'Zu den Raimundspielen nach Gutenstein' from Vienna Südbahnhof to Gutenstein, a total distance of about 69 km.
*Journey time*: 4 hours 25 minutes.
*Traction utilised*: Standard gauge steam-powered *Dampflok* No. Tfz52.
*Operating dates*: In 2007 excursions were operated on 21st July, 28th July, 4th August, 12th August and 18th August. On those days the train left Vienna Südbahnhof station at 1427 hours (except 12th August - 1345 hours) and arrived at Gutenstein at 1610 hours (on all dates). It returned from Gutenstein by bus on all dates except 12th August when it left at 2120 hours and arrived back at Vienna Südbahnhof at 2330 hours.
*Tariff*: Adult ticket was between €49.90 and €59 and for a child between €17 and €35 (2007).

*Route O22* named the 'Erlebnisweltbahn' from Vienna Südbahnhof to Ernstbrunn, a total distance of about 50 km.
*Journey time*: 2 hours 13 minutes.
*Traction utilised*: Standard gauge steam-powered *Nostalgie Dampfloks* Nos. 52.4984 or 17c372 or standard gauge *Dieselloks* classes '2050', '2045' or locomotive No. 2143.040 and *Dieseltriebwagens* Nos. VT 5041 or VT 5145 or VT 5042 14.
*Operating dates*: In 2007 excursions were operated on 8th, 9th, 15th, 16th, 22nd, 23rd, 29th and 30th September and 6th, 7th, 13th, 14th, 20th, 21st, 26th, 27th and 28th

October. The trains left Vienna Südbahnhof at 0822 hours and arrived at Ernstbrunn at 1035 hours. The return trains left Ernstbrunn at 1625 hours and arrived back at Vienna Südbahnhof at 1833 hours.
*Tariff*: An adult ticket for a steam-hauled excursion was €24 and for a child €12. An adult ticket for a diesel-hauled excursion was €18 and for a child €9 (2007).

*Routes O29a and O29b* offer two trips, the first named 'Oktoberfest' from Vienna Südbahnhof to Wiener Neustadt and a second trip named 'Kürbisfest im Retzer Land' on the same day to Retz, total distances of 54 km and 86 km respectively.
*Journey times*: 46 minutes and 2 hours 36 minutes respectively.
*Traction utilised*: Standard gauge electric-powered *Nostalgie E-Lok* class '1010' for Oktoberfest and *Nostalgie E-Lok* No. 1189 02 'Krokodil' for 'Kürbisfest im Retzer Land'.
*Operating dates*: In 2007, the two excursions operated only on 27th October. The first train left Vienna Südbahnhof at 0814 hours and arrived at Wiener Neustadt at 0900 hours returning at 1719 hours with arrival back at Vienna Südbahnhof at 1808 hours. The train for Retz left Vienna Südbahnhof at 1224 hours and arrived at Retz at 1500 hours. The return left at 2040 hours and arrived back at Vienna Südbahnhof at 2245 hours.
*Tariff*: Adult tickets were €24 for the first excursion and €20 for the second. A ticket for a child cost €8 (NB: tariff correct - no beer!) and €10 respectively. Family tickets cost €48 and €40 respectively (2007).

*Contact details for all these Eastern Austria excursions and others*: Verein Erlebnis Bahn und Schiff, Bahngasse 2, Bad Fischau-Brunn, A-2721. Telephone: 0664 200 1500. E-mail: bestellung@erlebnis-bahn.at
*Website*: www.erlebnis-bahn-schiff.at

ÖBB's preserved steam locomotive No. 17c372 powers its way towards Naglern-Simonsfeld on 6th October, 2007. *Author*

## AUSTRIA'S NATIONAL RAILWAY (ÖBB)

### 17 Southern Austria Excursions

ÖBB Erlebnisbahn operates 10 excursions in Southern Austria. The following are two examples:

*Route S2* named the 'Karawankendampf' from Ferlach to Faak am See, a total distance of 35 km.
*Journey time*: 1 hour 50 minutes.
*Traction utilised*: Standard gauge steam-powered *Nostalgie Dampflok* Tfz No. 93 1332.
*Operating dates*: In 2007 this excursion operated on 19th July, 2nd, 15th and 30th August. On those days the train left Ferlach at 0815 hours and arrived back at Ferlach at 1230 hours after a 55 minute stop at Faak am See. It ran again the same day leaving at 1530 hours and arriving back at Ferlach at 1930 hours with a shorter stop at Faak am See of 32 minutes.
*Tariff*: Adult ticket was €18, for a child €9 and for a family €36 (2007).

*Route S7* named the 'Ritterfest in der italienischen Weinstadt Cormons' from Friesach to Cormons via Klagenfurt, Villach and Tarvisio, a total distance of about 230 km.
*Journey time*: about 3 hours 40 minutes.
*Traction utilised*: Standard gauge diesel-powered *Nostalgie* class '2043' locomotive.
*Operating dates*: In 2007 the excursion ran only on 2nd September. The train left Friesach at 0720 and arrived at Cormons at about 1100 hours. The return train left Cormons at 2100 hours and arrived back at about 0030 hours.
*Tariff*: Adult ticket was €28, for a child €14 and for a family €56 (2007).

**Contact details for all these Southern Austria excursions and others**: Verein Erlebnis Bahn und Schiff, Bahngasse 2, Bad Fischau-Brunn, A-2721. Telephone: 0664 200 1500. E-mail: bestellung@erlebnis-bahn.at
*Website*: www.erlebnis-bahn-schiff.at

### 18 Western Austria Excursions

ÖBB Erlebnisbahn operates four excursions in Western Austria. Two examples are as follows:

*Route W1* named the 'Nostalgie Gisela/Tirol' from Wörgl to Zell am See, a total distance of 86 km (NB: The return journey is to Kirchberg/Tirol).
*Journey time*: to Zell am See is 2 hours 29 minutes and back to Kirchberg/Tirol, 1 hour 54 minutes.
*Traction utilised*: Standard gauge electric-powered *Nostalgie E-Lok* Nos. 1020.47 or 1245. 004 (*picture of a sister locomotive can be seen at entry 16 tour 08c*).
*Operating dates*: In 2007 excursions were operated on Thursdays between 22nd May and 25th September. On those Thursdays trains left Wörgl at 0836 hours and arrived at Zell am See at 1105 hours. It returned from Zell am See at 1200 hours and arrived at Kirchberg at 1354 hours.
*Tariff*: Adult ticket was €18 and for a child €9 (2007).

42  THE ESSENTIAL GUIDE TO AUSTRIAN RAILWAYS AND TRAMWAYS

*Route W2* named the 'Kaiser Max' from Reutte in Tirol to Jenbach, a total distance of 139 km.
*Journey time*: 3 hours 8 minutes.
*Traction utilised*: Standard gauge electric-powered *Nostalgie E-Lok* No. 1020.44.
*Operating dates*: In 2007 excursions were operated on 17th, 24th, 31st July, 7th, 14th, 15th, 21st, 28th August, 4th and 11th September. The trains left Reutte at 0820 hours and arrived at Jenbach at 1128 hours. The return trains left Jenbach at 1635 hours and arrived back at Reutte at 2025 hours.
*Tariff*: Adult ticket was €28, for a child €14 and for a family €56 (2007).

*Contact details for these excursions and others*: Verein Erlebnis Bahn und Schiff, Bahngasse 2, Bad Fischau-Brunn, A-2721. Telephone: 0664 200 1500. E-mail: bestellung@erlebnis-bahn.at
*Website*: www.erlebnis-bahn-schiff.at

The Karwendel route above Innsbruck is travelled by 'Kaiser Max' excursion. There are no fewer than 15 tunnels on the journey between Innsbruck and Seefeld in Tirol, a distance of 22 km. Here an afternoon *die Bahn* service on 21st October, 2007 crosses a viaduct near Leithen. Meanwhile two wild deer move into the scene.   *Author*

# Chapter Five

# Austria's Railways and Tramways by State

## Burgenland

Burgenland is the most eastern and least populated state in Austria. It consists of two main *stadt* (town) - Eisenstadt the capital with a population of about 12,000 and the other main town is Rust. There are a further seven districts and 171 municipalities. It is 166 km long from north to south but much narrower from east to west, for example the state is only 5 km wide at Sieggraben. Burgenland, in geographical area, is the seventh largest (3,966 sq. km) in Austria. The highest point is at Geschriebenstein (alt. 884 m) and the lowest near Apetlon (114 m). Burgenland has borders with the Austrian states of Niederösterreich and Steiermark and international frontiers with Slovakia, Hungary and Slovenia. Burgenland and Hungary share the Neusiedler See (lake).

### 19 Neusierdler Seebahn (NSB)

*Location*: Neusiedl am See, 50 km south east of Vienna and 44 km by road east of Eisenstadt.
*Michelin map reference*: W5.
*Nearest main line railway station*: Bruck a.d. Leitha and Parndorf on ÖBB's official line number 218 and timetables 700 and 701.
*Operated by*: GySEV-ROeEE.
*Official line number*: As this is not an ÖBB-operated line, even though ÖBB rolling stock uses the line (*see picture*) an official number has not been allocated.
*Timetable number*: 731.
*Route*: From Neusiedl am See south to Fertószentmiklós in Hungary, a total distance of about 54 km.

A *Talent* class '4124' (4-car unit) No. 008-6 passes the station at Weiden am See on 5th July, 2007 heading for Fertööszentmiklos. *Author*

*Journey time*: 1 hour 4 minutes.
*Gauge*: Standard by adhesion only. Local line - single track.
*Electrified*: No.
*Places to see*: Neusiedler See is a popular holiday resort and an area of ecological and ornithological interest. About 95 per cent of the lake is in Austria. The area claims over 300 days of sunshine every year and enjoys hot summers but very cold winters. There are over 2,500 km of cycle routes and bridle paths including a cycle route circling the lake giving access to the large breeding grounds for almost 300 species of bird and habitat for over 40 mammals.
*Website*: www.oebb.at/en and www.gysev.hu
*Operating dates*: Daily all year round.
*Comments*: In the summer months only there is a short tourist line known as the Kleinebahn Neusiedl am See (KNS) running from Bad Neusiedl am See to the lake at Badeanstalt.


**20 Südburgenländische Regionalbahn [SRB]** also known as **Märchenbahn**

*Location*: Oberwart, 120 km south of Vienna and 100 km south of Eisenstadt.
*Michelin map reference*: U7.
*Nearest railway station*: Oberwart.
*Operated by*: Südbergenlandische Regionalbahn.
*Official line number*: 168.
*Timetable number*: 52.

*Routes*: a) from Oberwart almost due north to the town of Oberschützen (8 km), and b) south-easterly from Oberwart to Rechnitz via Grosspetersdorf (25 km).
*Journey times*: a) by bus, 13 minutes; and b) by bus, between 30 and 40 minutes.
*Gauge*: Standard by adhesion only.
*Electrified*: No.
*Historic rolling stock*: 1928-built 2-8-2T steam locomotive No. 93.1422, 1890-built 0-6-2T No. 97.203, *Diesellok* No. M31 and a former Pressburgerbahnwagen, all based at SRB's depot at Grosspetersdorf.
*Places to see*: There is a rare (for Austria) Calvinist church located in Oberwart.
*Contact details*: Bahnstrasse 1, A–7508 Grosspetersdorf. Telephone: 03362/25 91-25 Fax: 03362/25 91-13. E-mail: adolf.schuch@schuch-reisen.at
*Websites*: www.maerchenbahn.at/start.htm and www.schienenbahnen.at/Mitglieder/SRB.pdf
*Operating dates*: From mid-July to late August on Sundays and Public Holidays at 1430 hours.
*Tariff*: For the journey on the *Nostalgie* train an adult ticket is €10 and for a child (3-13 years) €7 (2007).
*Comments*: Connects to the ÖBB network (line number 168) at Oberwart south of Friedberg on the Aspangbahn. Regular passengers are now catered for by bus-operated services. Rail services still work the line but concentrate on the movement of freight. This was one of the routes leading to the frontier crossing into Hungary (*see entry 166*).

## Carinthia (Kärnten)

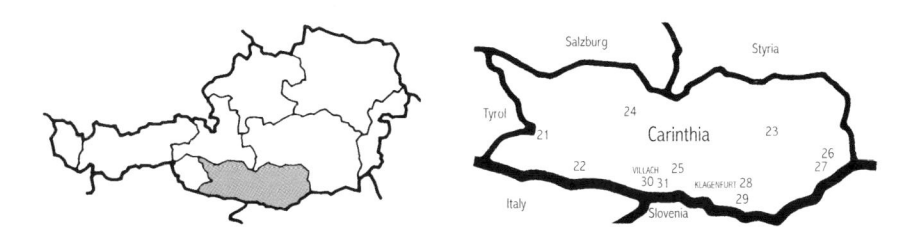

Carinthia, famous for its mountains and lakes, is the most southerly of the Austrian states. Being within the Alps it is surrounded by the ranges of the Carnic Alps, the Karawanken and the Hohen Tauern. Carinthia has borders with the Austrian states of Salzburg and Styria and international frontiers with Italy and Slovenia. Its lakes include the Wörther See, the Millstätter See, the Ossiacher See, and the Faaker See, all major tourist attractions. The main river is the Drau. The capital is Klagenfurt with the next important town being Villach. The inhabitants predominantly speak German with a heavy accent. Carinthia's main industries are tourism, electronics, engineering, forestry and agriculture. The multinational corporations of Philips and Siemens have large operations here. Carinthia enjoys a continental climate with hot and moderately wet summers and long harsh winters. The population is estimated to be 559,881, making it the sixth largest in Austria, resident in an area of 9,535 sq. km (fifth largest).

A class '1044'-hauled train with Italian passenger coaches crosses the River Drau at Oberdrauburg on 17th October, 2007. *Author*

The beautiful Gailtal valley near Hermagor is the setting for this afternoon service to Kötschach-Mauthen on 17th October, 2007. *Author*

# CARINTHIA (KÄRNTEN)

## 21 Drautalbahn

*Location*: Lienz, the midpoint on the line, is 402 km south-west of Vienna, 184 km south of Salzburg and 143 km west of Klagenfurt.
*Michelin map reference*: K8.
*Nearest main line railway station:* Pusarnitz and Lendorf on line 706/806 - the Tauernbahn (*see entry 67*).
*Operated by*: ÖBB.
*Official line number*: 707.
*Timetable number*: 223.
*Last main station in Austria*: Sillian.
*Route*: From Lendorf to San Candido Innichen in Italy via Lienz, a total distance of about 104 km.
*Journey time*: Between 2 hours 12 minutes and about 2 hours 50 minutes according to train service taken.
*Gauge*: Standard by adhesion only. Maximum gradient is 2.6 per cent between Mittewald and Abfaltersbach. Main line - single track.
*Electrified*: Yes, 15 kV AC 16.7 Hz.
*Places to see*: Lienz, the capital of the South Tyrol where Lienz Eisenbahnfreunde organization is based (*see entry 101*).
*Website*: www.oebb.at/en
*Operating dates*: Daily all year round with services every hour.
*Tariff*: An adult 2nd class single from Lendorf to Sillian (a distance of 91 km) is €16.20 (2007).
*Comments*: Follows the beautiful valley of the River Drau (in Italian it is known as the 'Drava').

## 22 Gaitalbahn

*Location*: Arnoldstein is west of Villach and 57 km west of Klagenfurt.
*Michelin map reference*: N9.
*Nearest main line railway station*: Arnoldstein on line 803 - the Pontebbana (*see entry 30*).
*Operated by*: ÖBB.
*Official line number*: 751.
*Timetable number*: 670.
*Route*: From Arnoldstein to Kötschach-Mauthen, a total distance of 61.7 km.
*Journey time*: 1 hour 26 minutes.
*Gauge*: Standard by adhesion only. Local line - single track.
*Electrified*: No.
*Places to see*: Follows the beautiful valley of the River Gail for the entire route. The Arnoldstein Culture Trail is worth walking from the Kreuzkapelle chapel, passing ancient buildings, St Lambert and Andreas Churches, a Benedictine monastery, a local Heritage Museum and a Roman road.
*Website*: www.oebb.at/en
*Operating dates*: Daily all year round every 90 minutes.
*Tariff*: An adult 2nd class single ticket is €12.10 (2007).
*Comments*: Yet another lovely Austrian valley to follow at any time of the year.

The scar up through the woodland to the right of centre of this picture is the route of the Reißeck Funicular. This was the scene on 17th October, 2007 before the snows returned. *Author*

The Reißeck funicular at its base station on 10th July, 2007. *Author*

## 23 Gurktalbahn-Kärntner Museumsbahn (KMB)

*Location*: Treibach-Althofen, 33 km north-east of Klagenfurt.
*Michelin map reference*: P8.
*Nearest main line railway station*: Treibach-Althofen on official line number 813 (Timetables 600 & 601).
*Operated by*: Gurkthalbahn-Kärntner Museumsbahn since 1974.
*Route*: Treibach-Althofen - Pöckstein-Zwischenwässer, a total distance of 3.3 km.
*Journey time*: 25 minutes.
*Gauge*: Narrow (760 mm) by adhesion only. Single track.
*Traction*: Steam-operated.
*Rolling stock*: Steam locomotives - No. UTA 13 and 1941-built No. 898.01, 1944-built 0-8-0T No. 699.101, 1944-built 0-10-0T No. 499.01 and 1926-built 0-8-2T No. 199.02 plus a large collection of passenger and freight rolling stock drawn from narrow gauge lines throughout Austria.
*Contact details*: Gurktalbahn-Kärntner Museumsbahn, Treibach-Althofen A-9330. Telephone: 0664 17 07 136.
*Website*: www.gurkthalbahn.at/
*Operating dates*: 24th June-10th September at weekends and 15th August (public holiday) with departures from Pöckstein at 1125 hours (Sundays only), 1325 hours and 1515 hours. From Treibach trains leave at 1210 hours (Sundays only), 1410 and 1600 hours. There are some extra trains in the late afternoon in August - consult the website for more detail.
*Tariff*: An adult return ticket is €5 and a single €3.6 and fares for children (6-15 years) are half the adult rate. A return family ticket costs €12 and a single €8 (2007).
*History*: The railway first began regular operations in October 1898. It was nationalised at the beginning of 1932. After World War II and into the 1950s the line lost money mainly because the sparsely-populated area could not provide enough business. Notwithstanding, the passenger services continued until late November 1968. Freight continued on a shorter stretch of line (12.7 km) but even that had to stop in 1972. When passenger services stopped a bleak future was envisaged for the line so a number of enthusiasts formed an association later to be named 'Verein der Kärntner Eisenbahnfreunde'. Their objective was to preserve part of the line as a working railway museum. Success came when the heritage railway, the first of its kind in Austria, began tourist services on 1st June, 1974.
*Comments*: The last remaining section of the original narrow-gauge Gurktalbahn, which was originally almost 29 km in length, is this stretch close to Treibach.

## 24 Höhenbahn Reißeck

*Location*: Kolbnitz, 67 km north-west of Villach and 92.4 km west-north-west of Klagenfurt.
*Michelin map reference*: L8.
*Nearest main line railway station*: Kolbnitz on the Tauernbahn (official line number 806 and timetable 220).
*Operated by*: Reißeck Cableways.
*Route*: Schoberboden - Reißeck (the mountain restaurant), a total distance of 3.359 km of which 2.13 km is in the Reißeck tunnel.
*Journey time*: 10 minutes.

*Gauge*: Narrow (600 mm) by adhesion only on a maximum gradient of 3.9 per cent on the Alpine railway and 82 per cent on the funicular.
*Traction*: Diesel.
*Rolling stock*: Diesel locomotives: Jenbach-type Bdm's Nos. 2240 (built 1960) and 2406 (built 1963). There are two enclosed railcars with the locomotive sandwiched between them.
*Places to see*: From the railway there are superb views to enjoy including that of the Großglockner which at 3,798 m is Austria's highest mountain.
*Contact details*: Reißeck Cableways, Zandlach 45, A-9815 Kolbnitz. Telephone: 05 0313/32259. E-mail: reisseck@tauerntouristik.at
*Website*: www.tauerntouristik.at/en/reisseck/
*Operating dates*: 12th May to 14th October daily from 0830 to 1700 hours but check first as the author has experienced unexpected closures, for example, by reasons of heavy snow in July!
*Tariff*: Return ticket for an adult costs €17, for a child (6-15 years) €9 and a dog €5 (2007).
*History*: The funicular was built in three stages to Schütters by March 1950, to Trog in June 1953 and finally reaching Schoberboden, standing at an altitude of 2,236 m, in March 1954. The railway line was built in 1948 specifically to transport materials for the construction of a hydro-electric scheme. However, in 1953 the line was opened to tourist traffic.
*Comments*: The entire journey takes the traveller from an altitude of 719 m to 2,236 m, a height difference of 1,517 m. This is the highest privately-owned narrow gauge railway in Austria which not only transports tourists but maintenance staff as well to the hydro-electric power stations. The journey begins with a 25 minute journey on a funicular, 3,576 m in length, climbing at angles varying between 25 and 82 per cent to the Schoberboden terminal from where the train service runs. On arrival at the Reißeck Mountain restaurant the rest of the journey is on foot. This is the starting point for various mountain hikes and Alpine tours. A very popular walk takes the visitor to the Mühldorf reservoir. There are plenty of helpful information points on the route which provide explanations about the countryside, its geology and vegetation. A particularly popular location is the 'echo spot' near to the reservoir. Operating at an altitude greater than 2,200 m the Höhenbahn claims to be the highest narrow gauge railway in Europe. Weather can be severe here at any time of the year.

## 25 Karawankenbahn

*Location*: Villach, 38 km west of Klagenfurt and 356 km south-west of Vienna.
*Michelin map reference*: N9.
*Nearest main line railway stations*: Villach and Jesenice.
*Operated by*: ÖBB and Slovenian Railways (SZ).
*Official line numbers*: 813 to Gödersdorf (main line twin-tracked) and 706 to Rosenbach and then 806 through the tunnel to Jesenice.
*Timetable number*: 221.
*Route*: Villach to Jesenice in Slovenia, a total distance of 38 km.
*Journey time*: 37 minutes.
*Gauge*: Standard by adhesion only. Main line - single track from Gödersdorf to Rosenbach (last station in Austria before entering Slovenia) then twin-tracked to Jesenice.
*Electrified*: Yes, 15 kV AV 16.7 Hz. The line after Jesenice runs on 3000 V DC.

# CARINTHIA (KÄRNTEN)

Latest in the Siemens-built Taurus class are the '1216s'. Here No. 142-0 emerges into Slovenia from the Karawanken tunnel on 16th October, 2007 on its journey down to Jesenice.
*Author*

*Rolling stock*: Modern ÖBB and Slovenian stock
*Places to see*: The 7.976 m Karawanken tunnel which celebrated the 100th anniversary of its opening on 19th July, 2006.
*Website*: www.oebb.at/en
*Operating dates*: All year round with daily services.
*History*: The tunnel was built 1906 and is the fourth longest rail tunnel in Austria and the longest in Slovenia. It is 112 m longer than the nearby Karawanken road tunnel which was completed and opened in 1991.

## 26 Lavamünde Bahn Betriebs GmbH [LBB]

*Location*: Lavamünd, 62 km east of Klagenfurt.
*Michelin map reference*: Q9.
*Nearest railway station*: St Paul on local line official number 710 - the Lavanttalbahn (*see next entry*).
*Operated by*: Lavamünde Bahn Betriebs GmbH.
*Route*: Bahnstrecke Lavamünd to St Paul, a total distance of 12 km.
*Journey time*: Not known.

Lavamünde Bahn has a strong relationship with the Graz-Köflacher-Bahn (GKB). Here are some of the GKB coaches used by the railway standing at Lavamünd station. *Author*

*Gauge*: Standard by adhesion only.
*Traction*: Diesel
*Rolling stock*: Diesel locomotive No. 383.10 operates here but also NBiK rolling stock sometimes can make visits (*see entry 29*).
*Contact details*: Lavamünde Bahn Betriebs GmbH, Lavamünd 65, A-9473 Lavamünd. Telephone: 0664 1246340 or 04352 2878.
*Website*s: www.nostalgiebahn.at/lavantblitz.php (de) but also try this: www.tiscover.at/at/guide/5,de,SCH1/objectId,SIG692708at,curr,EUR,parentId,RGN17at,season,at2,selectedEntry,sights/intern.html
*Operating dates*: Some Sundays in June, July and August and the public holiday 15th August. Trains leave Lavamünd at 0800 hours and 1600 hours and return from St Paul at 0900 hours and 1645 hours.
*Tariff*: An adult return ticket was €8 and for a single €5. A child's return ticket was €4 and a single €2.50. A family ticket was €20 for a return and €12.50 for a single journey (2006).
*History*: In 2002, Graz-Köflacher Bahn und Busbetrieb GmbH (GKB) along with local authorities collaborated to re-open the line to goods traffic. GKB provides the locomotives.
*Comments*: linked with GKB - Graz-Köflacher Bahn und Busbetrieb GmbH (*see entry 77*) and in conjunction with 'Nostalgiebahn in Kärnten' (Weizelsdorf-Ferlach) (NBiK) (*see entry 29*).

# CARINTHIA (KÄRNTEN)

## 27 Lavanttalbahn

*Location*: St Paul im Lavanttal, 53 km east of Klagenfurt.
*Michelin map reference*: Q8.
*Operated by*: ÖBB.
*Official line numbers*: 710 & 757.
*Timetable number*: 620.
*Route*: From Bleiburg to Zeltweg, a total distance of 86.3 km.
*Journey time*: About 2 hours by a combination of rail and bus services.
*Gauge*: Standard by adhesion only. Single track all the way - local line from Zeltweg to St Paul and main line down to Bleiburg.
*Electrified*: No.
*Places to see*: Lavamünde Bahn Betriebs GmbH operating from St Paul (*see previous entry*).
*Website*: www.oebb.at/en
*Operating dates*: Daily throughout the year, but there is no direct rail service between Bleiburg to Zeltweg. Wolfsberg is a junction between rail and bus services, as is St Paul.
*Tariff*: Bleiburg to Wolfsberg takes 36 minutes by train and a 2nd class adult single costs €4.40 (2007).
*Comments*: Bleiburg is on the route of the new Koralmbahn (*see entry 80*) the planned railway connection between Graz and Klagenfurt.


## 28 Lendcanaltramway

*Location*: Klagenfurt, 317 km south-west of Vienna.
*Michelin map reference*: O9.
*Operated by*: Nostalgiebahn in Kärnten (Weizelsdorf-Ferlach) (NBiK) (*see next entry*).
*Route*: From the edge of the canal into the nearby nature reserve - 'the moss', a total distance of about 1 km. At the end of the journey there is an exhibition on the landscape conservation area 'Lend Spitz'.
*Gauge*: Narrow (metre).
*Traction utilised*: Battery-powered tram sometimes drawn by Haflinger horses.
*Places to see*: The location includes an exhibition 'Klagenfurt - a Journey in Pictures'.
*Contact details*: Nostalgiebahn in Kärnten, Weizeldorf A-9162. Telephone: 0463 740368 or via Klagenfurt Tourist Office or NBiK, A-9028 Klagenfurt, Postfach 27.
*Website*: www.nostalgiebahn.at/museumstramway-klagenfurt-see.php
*Operating dates*: Daily from 5th to 31st August, 2008 with departures at 1500 and 1800 hours and on Saturdays and Sundays every half-hour between 1500 and 1800 hours. Special trains can be arranged for groups by prior appointment.
*Tariff*: An adult ticket is €3, a child €1.50 and for a family €7.50 (2008).
*History*: Has been operating since 1976 with the support of Klagenfurt City Council and other sponsors. Its origins are the former ORF-Mittelwellensendergebäude.
*Comments*: NBiK boasts that it is the biggest of Carinthian trams in modern times - as it happens, it is the only one!

NBiK's locotracteur No. 2016.201 stands at the head of a number of preserved passenger coaches which are kept at Weizelsdorf station. *Author*

The Pontebbana route crosses the Austrian/Italian frontier near to Tarvisio Boscoverde. Further into Italy is the township of Ugovizza Valbruna and here, on 15th October, 2007, a train led by FS locomotive No. E402 044 approaches at speed. *Author*

## 29 Nostalgiebahn in Kärnten (Weizelsdorf-Ferlach) (NBiK)

*Location*: Weizelsdorf, 16 km south-west of Klagenfurt.
*Michelin map reference*: O9.
*Nearest main line railway station*: Weizelsdorf official line number 709 - the Rosenthalbahn (timetable number 660).
*Operated by*: Rosentaler Dampfbummelzug.
*Route*: Weizelsdorf - Ferlach, a total distance of 5.7 km.
*Journey time*: 25 minutes.
*Gauge*: Standard by adhesion only.
*Traction*: Steam- and diesel-powered.
*Rolling stock*: Steam locomotives: 1927-built No. 93.1332 and 1941 WLM-built steam locomotive No. 88.103. Diesel locomotives: Nos. 2061.201 (1969), 383.10 (1957/68), JW 180 (1959), JW 180 (1962), 2060.64 (1957), DGL 30 (1959), DHL 111 (1960) and a Breuer *Locomotor*. Also retained is a 1934-built *Kleinelokomotive* No. X 130.02, draisine Nos. X 614.016 and X 614.030, Schienenbus No. VT 10.01 and *Diesel Electrotriebwagen* Nos. 4042.01 and 4042.02. .
*Contact details*: Nostalgiebahn in Kärnten, Weizelsdorf A-9162. Telephone: 0463 740368. E-mail: nostalgie.bahnen@utnet.at
*Website*: www.dampflok.at/index2.html?/71.htm also www.erlebnisbahn.at/nbik and www.nostalgiebahn.at/willkommen.php
*Operating dates*: 7th July-9th September, 2007 on Saturdays and Sundays leaving Weizeldorf at 1100, 1300, 1500 and 1700 hours and returning from Ferlach at 1230, 1430, 1630 and 1815 hours. Services were also run on Sundays 16th, 23rd and 30th September leaving Weizelsdorf at 1100, 1300 and 1500 hours and returning from Ferlach at 1230, 1430 and 1630 hours.
*Tariff*: A ticket for entry into the museum and a single trip on the train costs an adult €12, a child €6 and a family €30 (2007).
*Comments*: Part of the operation includes a transport museum 'Museum für Technik und Verkehr Historama' ('Historama' for short) located at Ferlach. There is also a shop and restaurant.

## 30 Pontebbana

*Location*: Villach, 355 km south-west of Vienna and 38 km west of Klagenfurt.
*Michelin map reference*: N9.
*Operated by*: ÖBB and Trenitalia.
*Official line number*: 813.
*Timetable number*: 601.
*Route*: From Villach to Pontebba on the Udine route in Italy is a total distance to Pontebba of about 56 km and to Tarvisio just over the border in Italy about 28 km.
*Journey time*: Villach to Pontebba takes 43 minutes with a change at Tarvisio Boscoverde on the Austro-Italian border. Villach to Tarvisio Boscoverde takes 23 minutes.
*Gauge*: Standard gauge by adhesion only.
*Electrified*: Yes, 15 kV AC 16.7 Hz in Austria and after Tarvisio Boscoverde 3000 V DC.
*Website*: www.oebb.at/en
*Operating dates*: Daily all year round but it is understood that there are only three services per day only two of which stop at Tarvisio Boscoverde (2007).
*Tariff*: A 2nd class adult single from Villach to Tarvisio Boscoverde is €5 (2007).
*Comments*: The last railway station in Austria is Thörl-Maglern.

Rosenbach is the last station in Austria before trains enter the Karawanken tunnel on their journey to Slovenia. Not all trains continue into the tunnel; here for example, locomotive No. 1044.275-3 arrives at Rosenbach before running round its train and returning to Villach on 15th October, 2007.
*Caroline Jones*

## 31 Rosenthalbahn

*Location*: Rosenbach, 29 km south-east of Villach and 30 km west-south-west from Klagenfurt.
*Michelin map reference*: O9.
*Operated by*: ÖBB.
*Official line number*: 709.
*Timetable number*: 660.
*Route*: From Klagenfurt to Rosenbach via Weizelsdorf, a total distance of 22.6 km.
*Journey time*: 49 minutes.
*Gauge*: Standard by adhesion only. Local line - single track.
*Electrified*: No, not the section to Klagenfurt, (line 709).
*Places to see*: Karawanken tunnel under the Kahikogel Mountain (1,835 m).
*Website*: www.oebb.at/en
*Operating dates*: Daily all year round but trains are infrequent (one a day each direction departing Klagenfurt 1352 hours and departing Rosenbach at 0625 hours. Services are bus operated in the main or access via Villach.
*Tariff*: An adult 2nd class single is €6.60 (2007).
*Comments*: Many of the services, but not all, on this route are bus-operated. Nostalgiebahn in Kärnten (NBiK) operates steam-hauled tourist trains from Weizelsdorf to Ferlach, where there is also the Historama museum (*see entry 29*).

## Lower Austria (Niederösterreich)

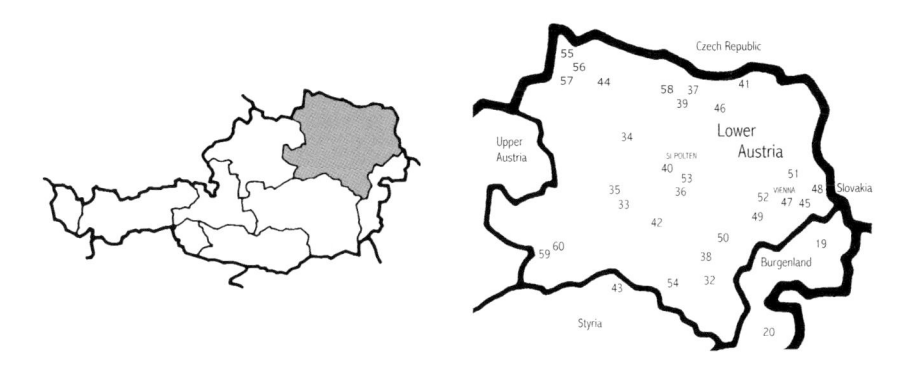

Lower Austria with a geographical area of 19,174 sq. km, is the largest state in Austria and with a population of 1.6 million it is second only to Vienna. Since 1986 the capital of Lower Austria has been St Pölten, prior to that it was Vienna. The state derives its name from the emphasis on 'lower' given its proximity to the low-lying River Danube which flows through. Lower Austria has state borders with Upper Austria, Styria and Burgenland and it surrounds the state of Vienna. Its international frontiers are with Slovakia and the Czech Republic. Lower Austria is divided into four regions: Waldviertel, Mostviertel, Industrieviertel, and Weinviertel and further divided into 21 districts, four chartered *stadts* (towns) and 573 municipalities.

### 32 Aspangbahn leading to the Wechselbahn

*Locations*: Vienna and Friedberg, the latter is in the state of Styria and is 166 km by fast road south-east of St Pölten and 97 km north-east of Graz.
*Michelin map reference*: V4 and U6 respectively.
*Operated by*: ÖBB.
*Official line numbers*: 161 & 167.
*Timetable numbers*: 514 & 520.
*Route*: From Vienna Südbahnhof branching off the Ostbahn at Kledering to Friedberg via Felixdorf and Wiener Neustadt, a total distance of 105 km.
*Journey time*: Vienna to Friedberg takes 1 hour 27 minutes on a direct service.
*Gauge*: Standard by adhesion only. Local line - single track.
*Electrified*: No.
*Website*: www.oebb.at/en
*Operating dates*: Daily all the year round every hour.
*Tariff*: An adult 2nd class ticket is €18.20 (2007). www.erlebnis-bahn-schiff.at
*Comments*: The section of track from Aspang down to Friedberg and through the 2.477 km Gr. Hartberg and 1.212 km Wiesenhöf tunnels is referred to as the Wechselbahn. Friedberg literally means 'peace mountain'. If using satellite navigation this town should not be confused with Friedberg in Hessen, Germany.

The well-tended station at Lunz am See. *Author*

The Donauuferbahn is the non-electrified line north of the River Danube and is the route for the Wachau and the Strudengau Expresses. Here a class '2043' No. 012-0 at Klein Pöchlarn heads towards Emmersdorf on 6th October, 2007. *Author*

## 33 Berstrecke Ybbsthalbahn - 'Ötscherland-Express'

*Location*: Kienberg-Gaming, 120 km west-south-west of Vienna and 63 km south-west of St Pölten.
*Michelin map reference*: R5.
*Nearest railway station*: Kienberg-Gaming on the Erlauftalbahn (*see entry 35*).
*Operated by*: Niederösterreichische Lokalbahnen-Betriebsgelellschaft mnbH (NÖLB) and Österreichische Gesellschaft für Lokalbahnen (ÖGLB).
*Route*: Kienberg-Gaming - Lunz-am-See, a total distance of 16.1 km.
*Journey time*: 1 hour 10 minutes.
*Gauge*: Narrow (760 mm) by adhesion only.
*Traction*: Steam- and diesel-powered.
*Rolling stock*: Three steam locomotives - *StB MOLLN* and Nos. U1 & Uv1, four diesel locomotives - BBÖ 2093.01, BBÖ 2190.01, D7 and V1, seven coaches and five goods wagons.
*Contact details*: Museumsbahn Kienberg-Gaming-Lunz, A-3291 Kienberg. Tel: 07416 52191 55680-0.
*Website*: www.lokalbahnen.at/bergstrecke/
*Operating dates*: June-Sept at weekends.
*Tariff*: An adult ticket is €20 and for a child €10 (2007).
*Comments*: Is also known as Museumsbahn Kienberg-Gaming-Lunz am See.


## 34 Donauuferbahn

*Location*: Krems a.d. Donau, 79 km west-north-west of Vienna and 28 km north of St Pölten.
*Michelin map reference*: S3.
*Operated by*: ÖBB.
*Official line number*: 172.
*Timetable numbers*: 811 & 133.
*Route*: From Krems a.d. Donau to St Valentin, a total distance of about 137 km.
*Journey time*: 1 hour 59 minutes with one change at St Pölten.
*Gauge*: Standard by adhesion only. Local line - single track.
*Electrified*: No.
*Website*: www.oebb.at/en
*Operating dates*: Daily all the year round with services about every hour.
*Tariff*: An adult 2nd class single is €20 (2007). www.erlebnis-bahn-schiff.at
*Comments*: The route, which follows closely the River Danube (Donau), is used for both the Wachau and Strudengau 'Erlebniszug' excursions (*see entries 9 & 10 respectively*).


## 35 Erlauftalbahn

*Location*: Wieselberg a.d. Erlauf, 108 km west of Vienna and 50 km west of St Pölten.
*Michelin map reference*: R4.
*Operated by*: ÖBB.
*Official line number*: 155.

*Timetable number*: 120.
*Route*: From Wieselberg a.d. Erlauf to Kienberg-Gaming, a total distance of 27 km.
*Journey time*: 41 minutes.
*Gauge*: Standard by adhesion only. Local line - single track.
*Electrified*: No.
*Website*: www.oebb.at/en   and www.erlebnis-bahn-schiff.at
*Operating dates*: Daily all the year round with services every two hours.
*Tariff*: An adult 2nd class ticket is €6 (2007).
*Comments*: This line passes through beautiful countryside and is an important connection to the Berstrecke Ybbsthalbahn - 'Ötscherland-Express' (*see entry 33*) operating out of Kienberg-Gaming. Sadly, towards the end of 2007, this line was under threat of closure by ÖBB.

### 36  Feld und Industriebahnmuseum (Museum of Light and Industrial railways)

*Location*: Freiland, 86 km west-south-west of Vienna, 30 km south of St Pölten.
*Michelin map reference*: S5.
*Nearest main line railway station*: Freiland on the Traisentalbahn (ÖBB official line number 151 and timetable 113).
*Operated by*: Feld und Industriebahnmuseum.
*Route*: A total track distance of 500 m in a variety of gauges.
*Gauges*: Narrow (500, 600, 700 & 760 mm).
*Traction*: Steam- and electric-powered.
*Rolling stock*: The collection includes more than 50 locomotives and over 180 various railcars, the majority of which are of 600 mm gauge. Steam locomotives include a 1917-built Henschel & Sohn, Kassel and an 1899-built Orenstein & Koppel build No. 366.
*Contact details*: Feld und Industriebahnmuseum Auwerk 27, A-3183 Freiland. Telephone: 0664 2749113. E-Mail: fim@feldbahn.at
*Website*: www.feldbahn.at (de) (NB: Some summaries are helpfully in English.)
*Operating dates*: The museum was open on the following Sundays in 2007: 27th May, 17th June, 29th July, 26th August, 23rd September, from 1000 hours to 1600 hours. The museum was also open on the public holiday, Monday, 28th May. The August opening usually includes a special parade of rolling stock not normally exhibited and which offers special photographic opportunities. The pattern of opening hours is likely to be similar in future years. Consult the website for more information.
*Tariff*: Adults are charged €5, children €1.80 and a family ticket costs €10. The admission charge includes a guided tour of the museum.
*Comments*: The museum portrays the evolution of light and industrial railways in Austria from the beginning of the 19th century to the present day. Staffed completely by volunteers, it is the museum's aim to preserve and exhibit material for future generations. As well as the guided tour there is the possibility of riding a short distance on a train hauled by the Orenstein & Koppel steam locomotive. There is a shop and a buffet restaurant.

## 37 Franz-Josefs Bahn

Sigmundsherberg is an important station and *Traktion* depot on the Franz-Josefs Bahn. On 4th July, 2007 a mid-afternoon service to be hauled by No. 6020.296-7 awaits its return to Vienna's Franz-Josefs Bahnhof. *Author*

*Location*: Gmünd, Sigmundsherberg (66 km north of St Pölten) and Vienna.
*Michelin map reference*: Q2, T2 & V4 respectively.
*Operated by*: ÖBB.
*Official line number*: 109.
*Timetable number*: 800.
*Route*: North-west from Vienna Franz-Josefs Bahnhof (FJB) to Gmünd, via Tulln and Sigmundsherberg, a total distance of about 167 km.
*Journey time*: 2 hours 17 minutes.
*Gauge*: Standard by adhesion only. Main line - single track.
*Electrified*: Yes, 15 kV AC 16.7 Hz.
*Places to see*: The Waldviertlerbahnen at Gmünd (*see entries 55-57*) and the Waldviertler Eisenbahnmuseum at Sigmundsherberg (*see entry 58*).
*Website*: www.oebb.at/en
*Operating dates*: Daily all the year round with services every half-hour.
*Tariff*: An adult 2nd class ticket is €24.30 (2007). www.erlebnis-bahn-schiff.at
*Comments*: Crosses the border into South Bohemia in the Czech Republic near to Ceské Velenice.

## 38 Höllentalbahn also known as Museumsbahn Payerbach-Hirschwang

The 1926-built railcar No. TW1 approaches Reichenau on 14th October, 2007.   *Author*

***Location***: Payerbach, 88 km south-west of Vienna and Hirschwang, 43 km west of Wiener Neustadt and 82 km south of St Pölten.
***Michelin map reference***: T5.
***Nearest main line railway station***: Payerbach-Reichenau on the Semmeringbahn (Südbahn) (*see entry 50*).
***Operated by and linked to***: Österreichische Gesellschaft für Lokalbahnen (Austrian Light Rail Association).
***Route***: Payerbach-Hirschwang, a total distance of 5 km at a maximum speed of 20 kmh.
***Journey time***: 25 minutes.
***Gauge***: Narrow (760 mm) sometimes referred to as the 'Bosnian gauge'. Operates by adhesion only on a maximum gradient of 2.5 per cent.
***Traction***: Diesel-powered railcar and diesel- and electric-powered locotracteurs. The catenary voltage is 550V DC with an energy supply from rotating and static AC-DC transformers.
***Rolling stock***: 1926-built railcar No. TW1 beautifully liveried in its green and yellow colours, 1903-built electric-powered locotracteur *E-Lok* No. E1, 1943-built diesel locotracteur No. V2; carriages: 1926-built Beiwagen No. BW 11 and 1909-built Beiwagen No. BW 21. There is also a delightful and amusing X3 draisine named *Johann*.
***Contact details***: Höllentalbahn-Projekt Ges.m.b.H. (HPG), c/o ÖGLB, Poschgasse 9, A-1140 Vienna and also Museumsbahn Payerbach-Hirschwang, Hirschwang A-2652 Telephone: 02666 52206. E-Mail: info@lokalbahnen.at
***Website***: www.lokalbahnen.at/hoellentalbahn/info.html links the Südbahn (i.e. the main-line Vienna to Graz) with the Rax ropeway.

*Operating dates*: From 10th June to 14th October on Sundays and public holidays only. Trains leave Payerbach at 0955, 1315, 1440, 1715 and 1840 hours and returning from Hirschwang at 0910, 1105, 1350, 1610 and 1800 hours. The above dates are for 2007 but operating dates and timetables for future years are expected to follow a similar pattern.
*Tariff*: An adult return ticket is €8 and a single €5. A family return ticket is €17 and single €11. There are discounts for groups and it is possible to hire a train for special events (2007).
*History*: The Railway through the 'Hell Valley' as it sometimes referred to, traces its origins back to the beginning of the 20th century. It was decided that a 5 km standard gauge connection should be built from the Semmeringbahn at Payerbach to the little industry village of Hirschwang. The civil engineering company in building this standard gauge line decided to develop a 'construction railway' using 760 mm narrow gauge for material transportation with 1903-built locomotives which had previously been used in the construction of the Karawanken tunnel on Austrian/Slovenian border in Carinthia. After end of World War I, the construction of the standard gauge line was stopped and a planned tunnel was also abandoned. This construction railway, however, continued to support industry in Hirschwang until 1926 when Austria's first gondola ropeway to the Rax was opened. The construction railway was reinforced and extended and what were then ultra-modern four-axle railcars with trailers were purchased. This was the start of the Lokalbahn Payerbach-Hirschwang (LBP-H) which over the following 37 years transported millions of industry workers as well as walkers, skiers and other tourists of all ages. In 1963, the railway was replaced by a bus service which was the way of things in those days! Fortunately, 14 years later the 'Austrian Light Rail Association' (Österreichische Gesellschaft für Lokalbahnen, ÖGLB, for short) was founded and established the museum railway service.
*Comments*: Today, the railway and a narrow gauge museum with its diesel and electric locomotives and railcars is operated and maintained by a small group of volunteers which regrettably limits the service to a few Sundays and public holidays in the summer. Nonetheless, the Höllentalbahn is a delight to thousands of visitors every year and is well worth visiting.

## 39 Kamptalbahn

*Location*: Sigmundsherberg, 85 km north-west of Vienna and 66 km north of St Pölten.
*Michelin map reference*: T2.
*Operated by*: ÖBB.
*Nearest main line station*: Sigmundsherberg on the Franz-Josefs Bahn (line number 109 and timetable number 800).
*Official line number*: 174 (111 between Krems a.d. Donau and Hadersdorf).
*Timetable numbers*: 820 & 810.
*Route*: North-north-east from Krems a.d. Donau to Sigmundsherberg via Hadersdorf, a total distance of 55 km.
*Journey time*: 2 hours 17 minutes.
*Gauge*: Standard by adhesion only. The maximum gradient on the line is 1.7 per cent from Breitenech up to Sigmundsherberg. Local line - single track.
*Electrified*: Yes, 15 kV AC 15.7 Hz but only between Krems a.d. Donau and Hadersdorf.
*Places to see*: The Waldviertler Eisenbahnmuseum at Sigmundsherberg (*see entry 58*).
*Website*: www.oebb.at/en
*Operating dates*: Daily all the year round with services every hour and sometimes more frequently. Some of the rail services operate co-jointly with local bus services.

A single-unit class '5047' leaves Gars-Thunau for Krems a.d. Donau on 4th July, 2007. The River Kamp is in the foreground.
*Caroline Jones*

Obergratendorf station is not the prettiest one on the Mariazellerbahn.
*Author*

*Tariff*: An adult 2nd class return ticket is €10.90 (2007). www.erlebnis-bahn-schiff.at
*Comments*: This is lovely valley down which to travel by train or by car and for the fit, by cycle.

## 40 Die Krumpe also referred to as **Krumpen**

*Location*: Obergratendorf, 70 km west of Vienna and 11 km south-west of St Pölten.
*Michelin map reference*: S4.
*Nearest main line station*: St Pölten on the Westbahn.
*Operated by*: ÖBB.
*Official line number*: 154.
*Timetable number*: 115.
*Route*: Obergratendorf to Mank, a total distance of about 19 km.
*Journey time*: 31 minutes.
*Gauge*: Narrow (760 mm) by adhesion only. Maximum gradient on this line is 2.6 per cent. Local line - single track.
*Electrified*: No.
*Places to see*: The Mariazellerbahn operates through Obergratendorf (*see entry 42*).
*Website*: www.oebb.at/en
*Operating dates*: Daily all round the year with rail services about every hour.
*Tariff*: An adult 2nd class single costs €4.40 (2007).
*Comments*: This line is just about operating albeit the route is supplemented by bus-operated services with journey times shorter by 11 minutes than by *regionalzug* train. The line originally continued on to Wieselberg a.d. Erlauf and is now out of rail service but does have bus-operated services from Mank.

## 41 Lauer Ostbahn (ÖBB)

*Location*: Laa a.d. Thaya, 70 km north of Vienna and 113 km north-east of St Pölten.
*Michelin map reference*: V2.
*Operated by*: ÖBB.
*Official line number*: 116.
*Timetable numbers*: 710 & 901.
*Route*: North from Vienna Floridsdorf to Laa a.d. Thaya, via Mistelbach, a total distance of about 72 km.
*Journey time*: 1 hour 26 minutes.
*Gauge*: Standard by adhesion only. The maximum gradient on the line is 1.1 per cent on the electrified section near Neubau-Kreuzstetten. Main line - single track.
*Electrified*: Yes, to Mistelbach (15 kV AC 16.7 Hz) but not from Mistelbach to Laa a.d. Thaya although it is planned.
*Places to see*: Laa a.d. Thaya, which has a history going back 5,000 years, more recently in the year 1200 was fortified to repel attacks from Bohemia. Parts of the town and its walls date from this time as does the 'tired' castle which now houses a beer museum.
*Website*: www.oebb.at/en and www.erlebnis-bahn-schiff.at
*Operating dates*: Daily all the year round with services about every hour.
*Tariff*: An adult 2nd class single costs €13.50 (2007).
*Comments*: Is one of the four routes from Austria into the Czech Republic eventually reaching Brno (*see entry 164*).

Built by Krauss in Linz in 1909 this electric locomotive No. 1099.02, named *Gosing*, has left Laubenbachmühle and is travelling up the valley, crossing the River Nattersbach, on its way to Unter Buchberg. The gradient at this point is 2.7 per cent. *Author*

## 42 Mariazellerbahn sometimes referred to as 'The Pilgrim's Railway'

*Location*: St Pölten, 65 km west of Vienna and Mariazell in Styria which is 77 km by road to the south.
*Michelin map reference*: S4.
*Nearest main line railway station*: St Pölten on the Westbahn.
*Operated by*: ÖBB in conjunction with Niederösterreichische Verkehrsorganisations-Gesellschaft (NÖVOG).
*Route*: From St Pölten to Mariazell, a total rail distance of 85 km.
*Journey time*: 2 hours 34 minutes.
*Gauge*: Narrow (760 mm) by adhesion only.
*Traction*: Steam- and electric-powered (6500 V 25 Hz).
*Rolling stock*: Steam locomotives: 1898-built 0-6-2T No. 298.54, 1931-built 0-6-2T No. 498.07 (plinthed at Obergratendorf Sportplatz), Mh6 (formerly No. 399.06). Electric-powered locomotives: class '1099s' and modern railcars class '4090' 3/4 car units.
*Contact details*: ÖBB Büro für Sonderreisen, Hauptbahnhof St Pölten A-3100. Telephone: 02742 9300 or 3877. E-mail Ewald.Lienbacher@pv.oebb.at There is also a supporters association for this railway which is: Verein Freunde der Mariazellerbahn, Willingerstraße 5. A-3202 Hofstetten, Telephone: 02723 / 8790 or 8791. E-mail: freunde@mariazellerbahn.at
*Website*s: www.mariazellerbahn.at/en and www.ebepe.com/html/mariazell.html and www.noevog.at
*Operating dates*: The railway operates daily services leaving St Pölten at 0725, 0824, 1327 and 1628 hours. There is an additional service from 1st May to 26th October departing St Pölten at 1024 hours. Trains leave Mariazell at 0747, 1147, 1452, 1647 and 1754 hours (Saturdays and Sundays only). There is an additional service on Mondays to Fridays from 1st May to 26th October departing Mariazell at 1255 hours (2007).
*Tariff*: An adult single ticket from St Pölten to Mariazell costs €22.60 (2007).
*History*: Thoughts on building this railway go back to the mid-19th century about the time the Vienna to Salzburg line was built. However, the thoughts were a long time coming to reality for it was not until 1898 that the first section from St Pölten to Kirchberg was opened. At the same time the branch line from Obergrafendorf to Mank was opened. Owing to the challenging mountainous terrain it was decided that the railway should be narrow gauge and 760 mm was chosen. Incidentally, this gauge was that set by the military authorities. The first trains that ran on this route were steam locomotives of the 0-6-2 'U' class hauling four-wheel coaches with open balconies. The 1899-built 0-6-2T steam locomotive No. U 9 is on static display at St Pölten station. Extending the railway took time; indeed it was eight years before the first train carrying freight arrived at Mariazell and a further six months before the first passengers arrived in May 1907. The principal rolling stock by then became 'Mh' and 'Mv' class locomotives, 0-8-4 Engerth-style articulated engines and eight-wheel bogie coaches. The railway enjoyed immediate success so much so that the then owners, Niederösterreichische Landesbahnen (Lower Austrian Provincial Railways), using steam traction alone could not cope with the demand. Much debate followed as to how to meet the increasing needs and eventually a decision was taken to adopt electrification, then in its infancy. There being no precedents it was decided to install AC current of 6,500V over the entire 90 km route. This was the first main line in Austria to be electrified and subsequently became a model for other

Special steam excursions are run on the Mariazellerbahn during the summer months. The 1908-built locomotive used is No. Mh6 which in former times was referred to as 399.06. There are four other locomotives of this class which have been safeguarded. Mh6 is seen here in her shed at Obergratendorf on 3rd July, 2007.
*Author*

The class '1099' was built between 1909 and 1914 and is still used on the Mariazellerbahn. Here No. 010-9 approaches Steinschall Tradigist on 2nd July, 2007. A huge mural on the side of the station depicting a viaduct on the Mariazellerbahn should be seen if you visit.
*Author*

railways in Austria and elsewhere in Europe. By 1911, tests had shown the viability of the system and operations began in earnest. It is remarkable to note that the railway is today still using much of the original equipment installed by Siemens almost a hundred years ago! Furthermore, the engines, hydro-electric power stations (although since installed with new generators) and many of the catenary poles are still the originals saying much about the quality of craftsmanship of that time. The railway enjoyed continuing success for many decades but during the 1990s freight traffic stopped and more people had by then chosen to use the motor car rather than the train. Declining numbers of passengers put the line under the threat of closure. Fortunately, the struggle to survive did not go unsupported not only by rail enthusiasts but also by the general public. The first success in re-generating interest was achieved by some railway employees who purchased the original steam engine No. 399.06 (now back to its original number Mh 6) and brought it back to the line where it was restored to its original condition. Charged with this success it became quite clear that somebody had to care for the future of the Mariazellerbahn as an everyday means of transport for commuters, students, tourists, and local residents. The answer was the founding of the Verein Freunde der Mariazellerbahn aimed at bringing back regular train services. Matters have since improved in spite of the acquisition of two new 4090 electric-powered railcars which proved to be unreliable. Diesel-driven 5090 railcars had to be brought in not least to preserve the lives of the ageing historic 1099 stock. Help fortunately is at hand. NÖVOG, responsible in the region for local rail and road traffic, is keen to keep the Mariazellerbahn operational. The introduction of the Panoramic 760 service was hoped to re-generate the interest in the line but has not achieved all it set out to do. Nonetheless, the re-introduction of steam for this service has been welcomed as evidenced by growing passenger numbers.

**Comments**:   A branch line (die Krumpen) employing diesel traction runs from Obergratendorf to Mank (*see entry 40*). See also the Mariazell Tram Museum (*see next entry*).

## 43 Mariazell Museum Tramway

*Location*: St Sebastian (Mariazell) 100 km west of Wiener Neustadt and 77 km by road south of St Pölten.
*Michelin map reference*: R5.
*Nearest main line railway station*: St Pölten on the Westbahn.
*Operated by*: IG Museumstramway Mariazell.
*Official line number*: None allocated.
*Route*: St Sebastian station on the Mariazellerbahn to Erlaufsee, a total distance of 2.5 km.
*Gauge*: Standard.
*Traction*: Steam- and electric-powered (600 V DC).
*Rolling stock*: Preserved are: steam powered tram No. 8, steam locomotive No. 31 of Stammersdorf in Vienna, and an electric locomotive and an electric tram from Lokalbahn Wien-Preßburg No. Eg5. Other electric trams include a type 'G2', a 'D' (Vienna), a '7m' der Badner Straßenbahn, a type 'H' No. 2229 from Vienna, a type 'Cmg' No. 1607 of Lokalbahn Wien-Preßburg and a 1939 tram from New York.
*Places to see*: Mariazell is one of the most important sanctuaries in Central Europe for Austrians, Hungarian and Slavs from the former Austro-Hungarian Empire. The focus is a pilgrimage on the 'via sacra' (Holy Road) to the church of *Magna Mater Austriae* (the great mother of Austria). The carved wooden statue of Our Lady of Mariazell dates back to the 13th century. Mariazeller 'Honig-Lebkuchen' spicy honey and ginger bread biscuits must be sampled on a visit to Mariazell.
*Contact details*: IG Museumstramway Mariazell - Die Erlebnis-Tramway, An der Museumsbahn 5, A-8630 St Sebastian/Mariazell. Telephone: 03882 3014.
E-mail: mt-eisenbahn@nextra.at
*Website*: www.museumstramway.at
*Operating dates*: On Saturdays, Sundays and public holidays in the months of July to September with departures from Mariazell at 1030, 1130, 1330, 1530 and 1630 hours. Trams leave Erlaufsee for the return journey at 1100, 1200, 1400, 1500, 1600 and 1700 hours
*Tariff*: An adult single ticket is €5 and a return €8. A child's single ticket is €2 and return €5 (2007).
*History*: The Mariazell Tramway was opened in 1986 connecting the St Sebastian station on the Mariazellerbahn (*see previous entry*) and the Erlaufsee lake 2.5 km to the north-west.
*Comments*: A very interesting collection of over 100 historic trams and other material drawn from Austria and Eastern Europe. Some are run during the summer on a track constructed just over 20 years ago. Others are awaiting restoration.

## 44 Martinsberg Lokalbahnverein

*Location*: Zwettl, 52 km north-west of Krems a.d. Donau and 74 km north-west of St Pölten.
*Michelin map reference*: R3.
*Nearest bus and railway stations*: Zwettl on ÖBB official line number 176 and timetable 830.
*Operated by*: Martinsberg Lokalbahnverein [MLV].
*Routes*: From Zwettl to Martinsberg, a distance of 29 km and Zwettl to Schwarzenau, a distance of 20 km.

## LOWER AUSTRIA (NIEDERÖSTERREICH)

1929-built 2-8-2T steam locomotive No. 93.1434 awaits renovation at Zwettl. Photograph taken on 4th July, 2007.
*Author*

*Journey time*: Not yet determined.
*Gauge*: Standard gauge by adhesion only.
*Traction*: Steam- and diesel-powered.
*Rolling stock*: Steam locomotives: No. 92.2271 built by Krauss & Co in Linz in 1919, No. 93.1434 built by the locomotive factory Wiener Neustadt in 1928; diesel locomotives: Deutz V20 built by Klöckner-Humbold-Deutz in 1940, JW 100 No. V20 built by Jenbacher Werke in 1954, and JW 200 No. V26 also built by Jenbacher Werke in 1960; passenger carriages preserved are a 1915-built BDi No. 47735, a 1914-built Bi No. 38210, a 1918-built Bi No. 39025, a 1915-built Bi No. 39626, a 1915-built CPwi No. 37526; a 1902-built buffet car Bih No. 39790; and, a box car No. G10.
*Places to see*: Zwettl has a *Stadtmuseum* (town museum), a magnificent Cistercian abbey and the baroque *Schloss* (castle) named Rosenau which houses a museum to freemasonry.
*Contact details*: Martinsberg Lokalbahnverein [MLV], Heizhaus Zwettl, Bahnhofstraße 31, A-3910 Zwettl. Telephone: 02822 52343. E-mail: martinsberger@lokalbahnverein.at
*Website*: www.lokalbahnverein.at/index_e.htm
*Operating dates*: Awaiting the completion of the restoration of the 1919-built 0-8-0T steam locomotive No. 92.2271. Monitor the website to discover when excursions will begin. It is possible that some services may begin using the diesel Deutz V20.
*Tariff*: Not yet determined (2007).
*History*: The Martinsberger Regional Railway Club, short MLV, was founded in 1988. The goal of the club is to preserve the Zwettler Regional Railway and to arrange special rides using historic vehicles. Like all private organizations in the heritage railway movement, finance is the critical issue in securing progress.
*Comments*: The re-opening of the tourist service depends on the completion of the class '92' steam locomotive which is currently undergoing a major overhaul. Apparently progress of this work seems to be behind earlier expectations. The Club is located in Zwettl, near to the railway station.

Retz station is the last main station on the Nordwestbahn. From here the Reblaus Express line continues to Drosendorf and the other branch travels to Znojmo in the Czech Republic. *Author*

*Talent* class '4124' No. 005-2 at Ebenfurth on 5th July, 2007 heads for Vienna Südbahnhof via the Pottendorfer Linie. *Author*

## 45 Mattersburgerbahn

*Location*: Sopron (formerly named Ödenburg) in Hungary and is 130 km south-east of St Pölten.
*Michelin map reference*: V5.
*Operated by*: ÖBB/ROeEE-GySEV.
*Official line number*: 108.
*Timetable number*: 524.
*Route*: From Sopron in Hungary to Wiener Neustadt, a distance of 35 km.
*Journey time*: Between 24 and 42 minutes.
*Gauge*: Standard by adhesion only. Main line - single track.
*Electrified*: No.
*Website*: www.oebb.at/en
*Operating dates*: Daily all year round with frequent services every half-hour and sometimes more.
*Tariff*: Not known.


## 46 Nordwestbahn

*Location*: Retz, 81 km north-west of Vienna and 80 km north of St Pölten.
*Michelin map reference*: T2
*Operated by*: ÖBB.
*Official line number*: 112.
*Timetable number*: 940.
*Route*: North-west from Vienna Floridsdorf to Retz, via Stockerau and Hollabrunn, a total distance of about 77 km.
*Journey time*: 1 hour.
*Gauge*: Standard by adhesion only.
*Electrified*: Yes, 15 kV AC 16.7 Hz.
*Website*: www.oebb.at/en
*Operating dates*: Daily all the year round with services every half-hour.
*Tariff*: An adult 2nd class single costs €12.50 (2007).
*Comments*: The Reblaus Express runs from Retz to Drosendorf at weekends in the summer (*see entry 14*).


## 47 Pottendorfer Linie

*Location*: Ebenfurth, 42 km south of Vienna and 100 km south-east of St Pölten.
*Michelin map reference*: V5.
*Operated by*: ÖBB.
*Official line numbers*: 106 & 206.
*Timetable number*: 511 & 512.
*Route*: From Vienna Inzerdorf to Ebenfurth, a total distance of 35 km.
*Journey time*: Between 38 and 42 minutes.
*Gauge*: Standard by adhesion only. Main line single track to Wampersdorf and twin track from there to Ebenfurth.
*Electrified*: Yes, 15 kV AC 16.7 Hz.
*Website*: www.oebb.at/en

*Operating dates*: Daily all the year round with services every half-hour.
*Tariff*: An adult 2nd class single costs €7.60 (2007).


## 48 Pressburgerbahn

*Locations*: Vienna and Wolfsthal, the latter being 133 km east of St Pölten.
*Michelin map reference*: V4 and X4.
*Operated by*: ÖBB.
*Official line numbers*: 291 and 191.
*Timetable number*: 920.
*Route*: From Vienna Südbahnhof east to Wolfsthal, a total distance of 59 km.
*Journey time*: Between 1 hour 2 minutes and 1 hour 17 minutes.
*Gauge*: Standard by adhesion only. Main line - twin track to Flughafen Wien and single thereafter to Wolfsthal.
*Electrified*: Yes, 15 kV AC 16.7 Hz.
*Website*: www.oebb.at/en
*Operating dates*: Daily all the year round with services every half-hour.
*Tariff*: An adult 2nd class single ticket costs €10.90 (2007).
*Comments*: The line continues beyond Wolfsthal to Bratislava in Slovakia, one of the three routes into that country (*see entry 165*).


## 49 Schneebergzahnradbahn also known as Niederösterreichische Schneebergbahn GmbH (NÖSBB)

*Location*: Puchberg am Schneeberg, 80 km south-west of Vienna and 102 km south of St Pölten.
*Michelin map reference*: T5.
*Nearest railway station*: Puchberg on line number 163 and timetable number 522.
*Operated by*: Niederösterreichische Schneebergbahn GmbH.
*Route*: Puchberg to Hochschneeberg, a total distance of 9.85 km.
*Journey time*: using the *Salamander* railcars takes 50 minutes and with steam traction 1 hour 20 minutes.
*Gauge*: Narrow (metre) using a rack/cogwheel system of Roman Abt's design for a maximum gradient of 20 per cent.
*Traction*: 100 year-old+ steam locomotives and modern diesel-powered railcars.
*Rolling stock*: Six steam locomotives of type B1n2zt built between 1896 and 1900 by Krauss & Co. (Munich and Linz). Each steam locomotive can pull two B/sz carriages weighing 8 tonnes each and capable of carrying 50 seated passengers at a maximum speed of 10 kmh. Three *Salamander* diesel-powered railcars built in 1999 by Waagner-Biró - Hunslet Barclay - Swoboda capable of carrying 119 seated passengers at a maximum speed of 15 kmh. These *Salamander* railcars are very eco-friendly in that their diesel engines, being one of the most modern engines in the world, the exhaust fumes are limited by catalytic converter. Their sound absorption systems also keep noise levels down, in fact below 76 decibels.
*Contact details*: Niederösterreichische Schneebergbahn GmbH, Bahnhofplatz 1, A-2734 Puchberg am Schneeberg. Telephone: 0 2636/36 61 Fax: 0 2636/32 62. E-mail: office@schneebergbahn.at
*Website*: www.schneebergbahn.at and www.schneebergbahn.at/front/?language_name=english

*Salamander* No. 2 heads for the summit of the Schneeberg on 5th July, 2007.    *Author*

***Operating dates***:  For the *Salamander* service trains run from 28th April until 29th June and 3rd September until 28th October, outward journeys depart at 0900, 1100, 1330, and 1530 hours with return journeys at 1000, 1200, 1430 and 1630 hours. From 30th June until 2nd September outward journeys depart at 0900, 1000, 1100, 1200, 1330, and 1530 hours with return journeys at 1000, 1100, 1200, 1330, 1430, 1530 and 1630 hours. The steam service also operates from 30th June until 2nd September on Sundays and public holidays leaving at 1015 hours and returning at 1445 hours.  It is possible to travel in one direction by steam and the other by diesel traction. The above dates are for 2007 but operating dates and timetables for future years are expected to follow a similar pattern.
***Tariff***:  An adult ticket costs €29.60 and for a child €14.80. There are a variety of special prices and group rates (2007).
***History***:  The first plans for building a cog railway to climb the Schneeberg began in 1872. In 1885, engineer Josef Tauber secured a licence to build a Lokomotiv-Eisenbahn from Wiener Neustadt to Puchberg am Schneeberg. In 1895 a contract was awarded to build the Schneebergbahn and a groundbreaking ceremony took place on 9th December. April 1897 saw the opening of the standard gauge adhesion railway from Wiener Neustadt to Puchberg am Schneeberg and three months later the first section of the cog railway was opened from Puchberg to Baumgartner. Another three months later the second section of the cog railway to Hochschneeberg was completed. The railway received Royal blessing when in June 1902 Emperor Franz Josef I rode on the Schneebergbahn to visit the Elisabethkirche. In 1937 the railway operation was taken over by the Bundesbahn Österreich (BBÖ) to be succeeded by the Deutsche Reichsbahn (DRB) in 1938. The Schneebergbahn was nationalized in 1940 and incorporated into the assets owned by the Reichsbahn, none of the shareholders receiving compensation. After the end of World War II Österreichische Staatsbahnen (later Österreichische Bundesbahnen - ÖBB) resumed responsibility for the Schneebergbahn, a state of affairs which continued until 1996. At the beginning of 1997 the independent company Niederösterreichische VerkehrsorganisationsgmbH. (NÖVOG) jointly with the ÖBB took over responsibility for the cog railway under its current name. ÖBB still retains ownership of the railway facilities. Also in that year the cog railway celebrated its 100th anniversary.

*Comments*:  Trains leave Puchberg am Schneeberg station and travel at a gentle pace high into the alpine region of the Schneeberg. During the ascent, climbing 1,218 m in just under 10 kilometres, the traveller is able to enjoy an outstanding view of the Alps before finally reaching the terminus which stands at 1,795 m above sea level making it the highest railway station in the whole of Austria.

## 50 Semmeringbahn

Electric locomotive No. 1010.10 crosses the viaduct close to Spital am Semmering on 8th July, 2007. Class '1010s' were built in the late 1950s and two are kept on ÖBB's *Nostalgie* fleet - this one and No. 1010.003. *Author*

*Location*:  Gloggnitz, 85 km south west of Vienna and 126 km south-east by road from St Pölten.
*Michelin map reference*: T5.
*Nearest main line railway stations*:  Gloggnitz or Mürzzuschlag on the Südbahn.
*Operated by*: ÖBB.
*Official line number*: 205.
*Timetable numbers*:  500 and 600.
*Route*:  The route Gloggnitz to Mürzzuschlag via Simmering is a total distance of 41.7 km. The Semmering Pass itself is the highest point with a gradient on the northern side of 2.5 per cent over a distance of 28.4 km to Gloggnitz. The maximum gradient on the southern side is 2.2 per cent over a distance of 13.3 km to Mürzzuschlag. Overall, the difference in height on the route is 459 m with the maximum altitude being 898 m in the centre of the main tunnel.  The distance, 'as the crow flies' between Gloggnitz and Mürzzuschlag, is 21 km but the kilometres the trains travel almost double given the twists and turn the

railway takes to negotiate the challenging mountainous terrain. This is part of the Vienna-Bruck route, a total distance of 160 km taking a journey time of 2 hours.
*Journey time*: From Gloggnitz to Mürzzuschlag takes between 47 minutes and 59 minutes according to which service is taken.
*Gauge*: Standard by adhesion only.
*Traction*: Electric-powered and sometimes steam and diesel specials.
*Rolling stock*: OBB modern and *Nostalgie* rolling stock.
*Infrastructure*: On the route there are 16 viaducts with an overall length of 1,607 m, the longest of which is across the Schwarza near Payerbach with a length of 276 m, and the highest being Kalte Rinne near Breitenstein with a height of 46 m. There are 15 tunnels totalling 5,420 m of which the longest are the two Semmering peak tunnels, one constructed in 1854 is 1,434 m and the other built in 1952 is 1,511 m. The shortest is the Krauselklause tunnel near Breitenstein just 14 m in length.
*Website*: www.oebb.at/en and www.semmeringbahn.at see also www.noe.co.at/partner/trseued/whsemmeringbahn/info_E.htm
*Operating dates*: All year round with departures from Gloggnitz at 0857, 0922, 0957, 1157, 1257, 1357, 1427, 1457, 1557 and 1657 hours. Departures from Mürzzuschlag at 0903, 1103, 1203, 1303, 1403, 1503, 1603, 1605, 1649 and 1708 hours.
*Tariff*: An adult 2nd class ticket between Gloggnitz and Mürzzuschlag costs €8.30 (2007).
*History*: In 1842, an 'Imperial Edict' declared that there should be a railway built over the Semmering Pass. Dr Carl Ritter von Ghega (1802-1860), a mathematician from Vienna, was charged with exploring the feasibility of such a construction, the plans for which he submitted in early 1844. Work began almost immediately and by October of that year the section between Graz and Mürzzuschlag was opened. However, thereafter a delay of four years occurred in the construction project owing to the lack of confidence in the ability to construct the peak tunnel, there being no experience elsewhere to call upon. However, in 1848 - the years of revolutions in Europe including Vienna - work re-commenced and five years later the line was ready for the first trials. Progress had been marred on the way with 14 people killed by falling rocks in 1850 and a cholera/typhoid outbreak between 1850 and 1852 claiming more than 750 lives. In the summer of 1851 four steam locomotives - *Wiener Neustadt*, *Vindobona*, *Seraing* and *Bavaria* - were tested on part of the route to establish whether they could 'pull 140 tons at 11.38 km/h on the steepest gradient'. However, none of these locomotives was convincing enough to justify production which is why Wilhelm Freiherr von Engerth (1814-1884) in co-operation with Fischer von Röslerstamm (1819-1907) was instructed to design and develop the first Semmering locomotives. These steam locomotives, named after Engerth, were ordered in 1852 and built by Kessler in Esslingen (Germany) and Cockerill in Seraing (Belgium). In October 1853 the first trials took place over the entire route and the following July the first scheduled passenger trains crossed the Semmering. It is interesting to note that in the construction of the railway 65 million bricks and 80,000 flag stones were employed. When construction began about 5,000 workers were transported daily to and from Vienna; at the peak of the construction activities a staggering 20,000 people were employed, a real feat of logistics. The next major works took place after the end of World War II which says something for the high quality of the original construction. Problems began to develop with Semmering peak tunnel so in 1949 construction began on a second tube which was completed and opened on 1st March, 1952. In 1956, a programme of electrification was embarked upon which was concluded in May 1959 bringing to an end regular steam operations on the line.
*Comments*: In December 1998 the Semmering Railway was the first railway in the world to be admitted to the UNESCO World Heritage List. This prestigious award was given for meeting two criteria:

The Semmering Railway represents an outstanding technological solution to a major physical problem in the construction of early railways.
With the construction of the Semmering Railway, areas of great natural beauty became more easily accessible and as a result these were developed for residential and recreational use, creating a new form of cultural landscape.

There is no doubt that this railway is a monument to the excellence of the mid-19th century civil engineering. The high standard of workmanship for the construction of the tunnels, viaducts and other buildings has guaranteed the continuing use of the railway to the present day. The line runs through spectacular mountain countryside which, coupled with the plethora of local leisure facilities, makes this railway one of the best 'must-see' and 'must-do' locations in the whole of Austria.
*Tourist information*: Tourismusregion Nö Süd Alpin, Paßhöhe, A-2680 Semmering. Telephone: 02664 2539 Fax: 02664 2335. E-mail: noesued.schabus@aon.at Information about the Semmering Railway World Heritage Site and guided tours on the railway hiking trail can be obtained from Alliance for Nature, Töpfelgasse 2/9, A-1140 Vienna. Telephone/Fax: 01 8939 298.

## 51 Eisenbahnmuseum Strasshof

*Location*: Strasshof, 25 km north-east of Vienna.
*Michelin map reference*: X3.
*Nearest main line railway station*: Silberwald on the Nordbahn (line number 214 and timetable number 930).
*Operated by*: Eisenbahnmuseum Strasshof.
*Gauge*: Standard and narrow.
*Traction*: Steam-, electric- and diesel-powered.
*Rolling stock*: A large collection of locomotives, railcars, carriages and wagons in various states of preservation and, sadly, decay. Steam locomotives kept are: *Licaon* (ex-Nordbahn 1837-1906); ex-Südbahn Nos. 17c372 (*see photographs in entry 16*) 29.852, 32c1665, 109.13, 629.01, & 580.03; ex-Eisenbahn Wien-Aspang No. 21; ex-Niederösterreichische Lokalbahnen No. 1.05; ex-Lagerhaus Wien No. 1; ex-k.k. Österreichische Staatsbahnen Nos. 229.222, 30.33, 178.84 & 180.01; ex-B.B. Österreich Nos. 12.02 & 429.1971; ex-Österreichische Bundesbahnen Nos. 12.10, 15.13, 33.102, 52.7594, 54.14, 55.5708, 156.3423, 57.223, 257.601, 257.605, 58.774, 175.817, 92. 2234, 93.1403, 97.208, 197.301, 986.107 & 999.105; ex-Österreichische Straßenbahn und Eisenbahnllub No. 52.100; ex-Österreichische Staatsbahnen No. 42.2708; and, finally, ex-OMV Nos. 1, 2, 3 & 4. Electric locomotives retained are: ex-k.k. Österreichische Staatsbahnen No. 1060.001; ex-Österreichische Bundesbahnen Nos. 1020.038-4, 1045.14, 1570.01 & 1189.05; ex-Schweitzer Bundesbahn No. Be 6/8II 13257. Diesel locomotives safeguarded are: ex-Österreichische Bundesbahnen No. 2060.004-5; ex-Deutsche Reichsbahn No. Kö 5159; ex-Österreichischer Straßenbahn Nos. X 112.06, X 130.01 & *Martha*. Railcars retained are: ex-B.B. Österreich No. DT 1.07 and ex-Montafonerbahn Bludenz-Schruns No. ET 10 106.
*Places to see*: The village of Deutsch-Wagram is a 1,000-year old village community, 6.5 km west of Strasshof, which owes much of its fame to Napoleon Bonaparte who established his military headquarters here prior to the Battle of Deutsch-Wagram (which he won) in July 1809; the local museum maintains a collection of mementos. Here also is the Marchfeldhof a well-known 'restaurant which provides traditional

Pictured here is the steam locomotive No. 109.13 which was built in 1912 by Wiener Neustadt Lokomotivfabrik for the Südbahn. *Author*

culinary delights set in an outrageously opulent environment'. See also the village and castle/*Schloss* at Wolkersdorf (gateway to the wine country) 12 km north of Deutsch-Wagram (*Source: Insight-Austria page 157.*)
*Contact details*: Eisenbahnmuseum Strasshof, Sillerstrasse 123, Strasshof A-2231. Telephone: 01 603 53 01. E-mail: office@eisenbahnmuseum-heizhaus.com
*Website*: www.mamilade.at/heizhaus/eisenbahn/museum/strasshof/1006620-eisenbahnmuseum_strasshof.html or www.eisenbahnmuseum-heizhaus.com
*Operating dates*: April to October at weekends from 1000 hours to 1600 hours.
*Tariff*: €5.50 for an adult entry (2007). The well-illustrated catalogue (in German) describing the locomotive collection is well worth purchasing at €10 irrespective of whether one understands German (*see Bibliography*).
*Comments*: The largest Austrian railway museum which features Austria's National Collection. There is a small shop where souvenirs, catalogues and other reading material can be bought. There is also a buffet restaurant.

## 52 Südwestbahn

*Location*: The line is south-east of St Pölten, which is 66 km west of Vienna.
*Michelin map reference*: S4.
*Operated by*: ÖBB.
*Official line number*: 107.
*Timetable number*: 113 to Hainfeld and was 513 from Hainfeld to Wittmannsdorf.
*Route*: South and east from St Pölten to Wittmannsdorf via Traisen, a total distance of about 70 km. However, the section to Hainfeld is the only part operational, the distance being 32 km.
*Journey time*: The journey to Wittmannsdorf, much to the locals' disgust, can now only be reached via Vienna and takes about 2 hours.

*Gauge*: Standard by adhesion only. Local line - single track.
*Electrified*: No.
*Places to see*: Berndorf is the cultural focal point for the area with a municipal theatre built in a style more in keeping with the centre of Vienna. Mayerling is not far away where, in 1888, Crown Prince Rudolf first shot his mistress then himself; a Carmelite convent of atonement built by Franz Josef I is located there and can be visited.
*Website*: www.oebb.at/en
*Operating dates*: Daily all the year round every hour to and from St Pölten and Hainfeld.
*Tariff*: An adult 2nd class single ticket from St Pölten to Hainfeld costs €7.60 (2007). www.erlebnis-bahn-schiff.at
*Comments*: The line from Hainfeld down to Weissenbach-Neuhaus via Wittmannsdorf is not now operating but the track and infrastructure is still retained and is used from time to time for ÖBB Erlebnisbahn tourist trains.

## 53 Traisentalbahn

*Location*: St Pölten, 66 km west of Vienna.
*Michelin map reference*: S4.
*Operated by*: ÖBB.
*Official line numbers*: 107 and from Traisen 151.
*Timetable number*: 113.
*Route*: South from St Pölten to Markt St Aegyd, a total distance of 50 km.
*Journey time*: 1 hour 13 minutes.
*Gauge*: Standard by adhesion only. Local line - single track.
*Electrified*: No.
*Website*: www.oebb.at/en
*Operating dates*: Daily all the year round every hour.
*Tariff*: An adult 2nd class single costs €9.30 (2007). www.erlebnis-bahn-schiff.at

## 54 Waldbahnmuseum

*Location*: Naßwald, about 58 km west (by road) from Wiener Neustadt and 68 km south of St Pölten.
*Michelin map reference*: T5.
*Nearest main line railway station*: Some distance away at Payerbach-Reichenau on the Semmeringbahn (*see entry 50*).
*Operated by*: Waldbahnmuseum volunteers.
*Route*: In the centre of Naßwald, a total distance of 800 m.
*Gauge*: Narrow (600 mm) by adhesion only.
*Traction utilised*: Electric- and diesel-powered.
*Rolling stock*: Four diesel-powered locomotives and one electric (accumulators)-powered.
*Contact details*: Museumswaldbahn Naßwald, A-2661 Naßwald. Telephone 0664 4082401. E-mail: office@waldbahn.org
*Website*: www.waldbahn.org (under the course of construction in 2007).
*Operating dates*: Saturdays in the summer months (check with the website).

*Comments*: A museum to record the history of forest railways with a specifically built track but one that was not on the route of an original forest railway. There is a wish to extend the railway track to 2 km but this will require considerable investment for the building of a short tunnel or, alternatively, two bridges.

## 55  Waldviertlerbahn (Gmünd to Litschau)

*Location*:  Gmünd, 97 km north-west of St Pölten.
*Michelin map reference*: Q2.
*Nearest main line railway station*:  Gmünd on the Franz-Josefs Bahn (line number 109 and timetable number 800).
*Operated by*:  Waldviertlerbahn Schmalspurverein (WSV).
*Official line number*: 177.
*Timetable number*: 802.
*Route*:  From Gmünd to Litschau (line 177) a total distance of 25.3 km.
*Journey time*:  1 hour 17 minutes.
*Gauge*:  Narrow (760 mm) by adhesion.
*Traction*:  Steam- and diesel-powered.
*Rolling stock*:  Steam locomotive (Mh series) No. 399.01 built in 1906 by Krauss Linz. Sister locomotives Nos. 399.02 and 399.04 (and possibly 399.05) are also retained at Gmünd but are non-operational. No. 399.01 is operating on the Pinzgauerbahn (*see entry 65*) and No. 399.06 is on the Mariazellerbahn (*see entry 42*). Diesel locomotives retained and operated are 1962-built class '2095' Nos. 12 and 14. There is also a 'snack bar' carriage No. Bi/S 3675, a number of retained carriages and a freight van No. GGD/S 15813 for the carriage of cycles.
*Places to see*: See the bizarre granite formations at the nearby Naturpark Blockheide.
*Contact details*:  Waldviertlerbahn Schmalspurbahnverein, A-3950 Gmünd. Telephone: 0664 358 1099. E-mail: via the website.
*Website*:  www.waldviertlerbahn.at/wvbahn2006/start/index.htm (de en cz jp)
See also some photographs and background information on
 www.ebepe.com/html/waldv_e.html also www.erlebnisbahn.at/wsv/
*Operating dates*:  Various days (mainly Wednesdays and every weekend) from May to October.
*Tariff*: An adult single is €22 and return €37.50 which includes the travel from Vienna to Gmünd. Children travel at half-price and there are discounts for families (2007).
*History*:  The development of the three Walviertlerbahnen lines (*entries 55, 56 and 57*) share a common history. The opening of the Franz-Josefs Bahn in 1870 was the stimulus for the municipal authorities of Gmünd to make plans to connect to other conurbations by building local narrow gauge (760 mm) railways. It was not until April 1899 that construction began on the northern line to Litschau and Heidenreichstein. However, the line was completed incredibly in less than 15 months and opened to traffic in July 1900. Given the success of this construction the building of the line to Groß Gerungs began in May 1901. In August 1902 the connection with Steinbach/Großpertholz was opened and to Groß Gerungs in March 1903. Originally there had been an intention to have a much larger network from Gmünd but in the run-up to what turned out to be World War I the plans were abandoned. After the end of the war the Treaty of Versailles divided the town of Gmünd, the consequence being that Franz-Josefs Bahn station and narrow gauge

stations finished up in České Velenice (sometimes referred to as Gmünd III) in the Czech Republic and the rest remained in Austria. In response, in 1921, the Austrian Federal Railways took over the responsibility for the lines of the Lower Austria State Railways including the Waldviertler and in January 1922 established stations alongside each other for the narrow gauge and standard gauge railways. Over the coming decades this allowed for trains travelling south to remain in Austrian territory but those to the north still had pass through the Czech Republic. In 1950 a new line was constructed and opened between the Gmünd narrow gauge station and the Gmünd Böhmzeil stop and at the same time the narrow gauge connections in České Velenice terminated. Operations continued for another three decades but in 1986 passenger services on the northern railway route were replaced with bus operated services. In 1992, freight was also ended on this route. The southern routes initially fared better. In 1986 new series '5090' railcars were introduced to reduce travel times and encourage greater passenger traffic but the results were disappointing and by May 2001 regular operations ceased. Happily, it was only the next month that limited operations were begun again at weekends for tourists. The number of tourists enjoying the facility was encouraging and has continued since.
*Comments*: A delightful railway which needs your support.

### 56 Waldviertlerbahn (Alt Nagelberg to Heidenreichstein)

*Location*: Alt Nagelberg, 70 km west-north-west of Sigmundsherberg and 108 km north-west of St Pölten.
*Michelin map reference*: R2.
*Nearest main line railway station*: Gmünd on the Franz-Josefs Bahn (line number 109 and timetable number 800).
*Operated by*: Waldviertlerbahn Schmalspurverein (WSV).
*Official line number*: 178.
*Timetable number*: 802.
*Route*: From Alt Nagelberg to Heidenreichstein, a total distance of 13.2 km.
*Journey time*: 40 minutes.
*Gauge*: Narrow (760 mm) by adhesion only.
*Traction*: Steam- and diesel-powered.
*Rolling stock*: See previous entry.
*Contact details*: Waldviertlerbahn Schmalspurbahnverein, A-3950 Gmünd. Telephone: 0664 358 1099. E-mail: via the website.
*Website*: www.waldviertlerbahn.at/wvbahn2006/start/index.htm (de en cz jp) and see also www.weblexikon.de/Waldviertler_Schmalspurbahnen.html (de).
*Operating dates and tariff*: Broadly speaking from June to early September on Wednesdays and at weekends leaving Heidenreichstein at 0930 and 1630 hours and returning from Alt Nagelberg 1035 and 1740 hours. However the operating times and fares can be a little complex so it is worth checking beforehand - www.waldviertlerbahn.at/wvbahn2006/us/timetables/days.htm is helpful in this regard.
*History*: See the History section of entry 55.
*Comments*: Has an operational link with the other two Waldviertlerbahnen (*see entries 55 & 57*).

## 57 Waldviertlerbahn (Gmünd to Groß Gerungs)

Class '2095s' were built in the late 1950s and early 1960s to work ÖBB's narrow gauge lines. Here No. 014-3 crosses a country road near Steinbach-Großpertholz heading for Groß Gerungs on 4th July, 2007. *Author*

*Location*: Gmünd, 97 km north-west of St Pölten.
*Michelin map reference*: Q2.
*Nearest main line railway station*: Gmünd on the Franz-Josefs Bahn (line number 109 and timetable number 800).
*Operated by*: Waldviertlerbahn Schmalspurverein (WSV).
*Official line number:* 179.
*Timetable number:* 801.
*Route:* From Gmünd to Groß Gerungs, a total distance of 43 km.
*Journey time:* 1 hour 20 minutes.
*Gauge:* Narrow (760 mm) by adhesion or rack only.
*Traction:* Steam- and diesel-powered.
*Rolling stock: See entry 55.*
*Contact details:* Waldviertlerbahn Schmalspurbahnverein, A-3950 Gmünd. Telephone: 0664 358 1099 E-mail: via the website.
*Website:* www.waldviertlerbahn.at/wvbahn2006/start/index.htm (de en cz jp). Some good photographs can be found at: www.ebepe.com/html/waldv1_e.html
*Places to see:* Weitra is on this route and is renowned as Austria's oldest brewing town and home to the country's smallest brewery - the Brauhotel. There is also an attractive castle there and a textile museum.
*Operating dates:* Various days (mainly Wednesdays and every weekend) from May to October.
*Tariff:* An adult single for a steam journey is €32 and a return €44 which may seem a little steep but it does include travel from Vienna to Gmünd. Children travel at half price and there are discounts for families. When diesel traction is used the fares are about 10 per cent cheaper (2007).
*History: See entry 55.*

Steam, electric and diesel track can all be found at Sigmundsherberg. Pictured here is early 1950s Floridsdorf-built No. 1040.09 used for *Nostalgie* excursions as is No. 1040.01 kept at Selzthal for the same purpose.                                                                                                            *Author*

Like the Mariazellerbahn, class '2095s' are used on the two Ybbstalbahn routes. Here, on 7th July, 2007 at Waidhofen a.d. Ybbs No. 010-1 is having its batteries re-charged. Class '5090' diesel railcars can be seen in the background.                                                                                *Caroline Jones*

# LOWER AUSTRIA (NIEDERÖSTERREICH)

*Comments:* Regular traffic was cancelled on this line in 2001 due to lack of passengers. Tourist traffic thankfully continues for the Waldviertlerbahnen (*see previous entries*).

## 58 Waldviertler Eisenbahnmuseum

*Location:* Sigmundsherberg, 83 km north-west of Vienna and 66 km north of St Pölten.
*Michelin map reference:* T2.
*Nearest main line railway station:* Sigmundsherberg on the Franz-Josefs Bahn (line number 109 and timetable 800.
*Operated by:* ÖBB.
*Gauge:* Standard.
*Traction:* Steam-, diesel- and electric-powered.
*Rolling stock:* Features a variety of standard gauge rolling stock.
*Contact details:* Waldviertler Eisenbahnmuseum, Bahnhof Sigmundsherberg, Heizhaus, Sigmundsherberg, A-3751 Telephone: 02983 2307 379 E-mail: marktgemeinde@sigmundsherberg.gv.at
*Website:* http://195.58.166.60/volkskultur/noemuseen/mus_ansicht_detail.asp?nr=70
*Operating dates:* Open daily from May to October from 0800 hours to 1600 hours for groups by prior arrangement (2008). Individual access to the site is still possible.
*Tariff:* Not known.
*Comments:* ÖBB *Traktion* is also based here and has a most interesting collection of 'ancient and modern' rolling stock. It well worth calling at the site and museum and combining it with a visit to the Kamptalbahn (*see entry 39*) and for the Waldviertlerbahnen (*see three previous entries*).

## 59 Ybbstalbahn (Waidhofen a.d. Ybbs to Lunz am See)

*Location:* Waidhofen an der Ybbs, 25 km south of Amstetten and 90 km south-west of St Pölten.
*Michelin map reference:* Q5.
*Nearest main line station:* Waidhofen an der Ybbs on official line number 102 and timetable number 130.
*Operated by:* ÖBB.
*Official line number:* 156.
*Timetable number:* 132.
*Route:* Waidhofen an der Ybbs to Lunz am See, a distance of 53.6 km.
*Journey time:* 1 hour 33 minutes.
*Gauge:* Narrow (760 mm) by adhesion only.
*Electrified:* No, diesel-powered traction.
*Rolling stock:* Diesel locomotives: class '2091' No. 009; class '2095' Nos. 010.1, 005.1, 007.7, 009.3 & 008.5. Diesel railcars class '5090' Nos. 009.1, 012.5, 013.3 & 010.9.
*Places to see:* Lunz am See and its beautiful lake - take a picnic or take refreshments at the restaurant at the end of the lake.
*Contact details:* Verein Pro Ybbstalbahn, Südtirolerplatz 1, 3340 Waidhofen a.d. Ybbs. Telephone: 07442 55680-0 Fax: 07442 55680-318. E-mail: verein.pro@ybbstalbahn.at
*Website:* www.ybbstalbahn.at (de) also www.erlebnis-bahn-schiff.at (de).

*Operating dates*: Daily all year round with two-hourly services from Waidhofen a.d. Ybbs from 0530 hours to 1830 hours.
*Tariff*: An adult 2nd class single (1-PLUS-Freizeit-Ticket) costs €10.90 (2007).
*History*: The line originally opened on 15th July, 1896.
*Comments*: This service combines rail operations with bus services. Also operated on this line is the *Nostalgieprogramm-Ybbstalbahn* (enquire locally or visit www.erlebnis-bahn-schiff.at (de) or e-mail bestellung@erlebnis-bahn.at ).

## 60 Ybbstalbahn (Waidhofen a.d. Ybbs to Ybbsitz)

*Location*: Waidhofen an der Ybbs, 25 km south of Amstetten and 90 km south-west of St Pölten.
*Michelin map reference*: Q5.
*Nearest main line station*: Waidhofen an der Ybbs on official line number 102 and timetable number 130.
*Operated by*: ÖBB.
*Official line number*: 157.
*Timetable number*: 132.
*Route*: Waidhofen to Ybbsitz, a distance of 5.7 km.
*Journey time*: 23 minutes.
*Gauge*: Narrow (760 mm) by adhesion only.
*Traction*: Diesel-powered.
*Rolling stock*: *See previous entry.*
*Contact details*: Verein Pro Ybbstalbahn, Südtirolerplatz 1, 3340 Waidhofen/Ybbs. Telephone: 07442 55680-0 Fax: 07442 55680-318. E-mail: verein.pro@ybbstalbahn.at
*Website*: www.ybbstalbahn.at
*Operating dates*: Daily all year round with hourly services from Waidhofen a.d. Ybbs from 0530 hours to 1930 hours.
*Tariff*: A 2nd class adult single (1-PLUS-Freizeit-Ticket) costs €4.40 (2007).
*Comments*: The Ybbstalbahn also operates the 'Nostalgieprogramm-Ybbstalbahn' - see www.erlebnis-bahn-schiff.at (de)

Pair of 1986-built class '5090s' cross the River Ybbs at Gstadt on 8th October. 2007. *Author*

## Salzburg

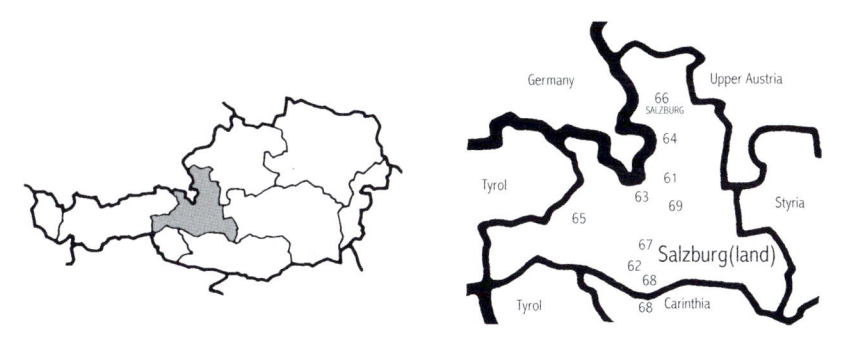

The state of Salzburg has a geographical area of 7,154 sq km (sixth smallest) and a population of 529,085 citizens making it one of the country's least inhabited states, in fact the seventh smallest. It has borders with the states of Upper Austria, Styria, Carinthia and the Tyrol and an international frontier with Germany (Bavaria). The main mountain ranges are the Central Alps including the Hohen Tauern with numerous 3,000 m peaks, the Dachstein Massif and the Berchtesgaden Alps. The capital city is Salzburg, the birthplace of Wolfgang Amadeus Mozart.

### 61 Ennstalbahn

*Location*: Bischofshofen, 57 km south of Salzburg.
*Michelin map reference*: L6.
*Operated by*: ÖBB.
*Official line number*: 302.
*Timetable numbers*: 250, 130 & 131.
*Route*: Bischofshofen-Selzthal, a total distance of 98.8 km and on to Kastenreith a further 76 km.

The route of the Ennstalbahn crosses through some beautiful countryside. Here on 10th July, 2007 the line was closed for track re-laying. Diesel locomotive No. 2043 029-4 is in support of operations. *Author*

*Journey time*: From Bischofshofen to Selzthal takes 1 hour 27 minutes and Selzthal to Kastenreith takes 1 hour 37 minutes. The latter route is also known as the Gesäuse (*see entry 76*).
*Gauge*: Standard by adhesion only. Main line - single track.
*Electrified*: Yes, 15 kV AC 16.7 Hz.
*Places to see*: The station and sheds at Selzthal are worth visiting for there is always interesting rolling stock to be seen.
*Website*: www.oebb.at/en
*Operating dates*: Daily all year round every two hours.
*Tariff*: An adult single ticket 2nd class from Bischofshofen to Selzthal costs €18.20 and from Selzthal to Kastenreith €12.50 (2007).

## 62 Gasteiner Heilstollenbahn

*Location*: Böckstein, 97 km south of Salzburg.
*Michelin map reference*: L7.
*Operated by*: The Gasteiner Heilstollen treatment centre.
*Nearest main line railway station*: Böckstein on the Tauernbahn (line number 806 and timetable number 220) (*see entry 67*).
*Route*: In the Heilstollen caves, a total distance of 2.5 km.
*Journey time*: About 13 minutes at a maximum speed of 8 kmh.
*Gauge*: Narrow (600 mm) underground.
*Traction utilised*: Electric-powered (accumulators). The engine is located at the front of the train, and consists of two single-motor engines, which provide the motive power and illumination. When carrying a full load, the train weighs approximately 25 tonnes.
*Contact details*: Gasteiner Heilstollen, A-5645 Böckstein-Bad Gastein. Telephone: 06434 37530 Fax: 06434 375366. E-mail: info@gasteiner-heilstollen.com
*Website*: www.gasteiner-heilstollen.com
*Operating dates*: All year round.
*History*: The Sonnblick and Ankogel area, about 100 km from the Germany and Italy borders, has since Roman times been considered to be the richest source of metal ores in the Alps. The mining of gold and silver reached its peak in the 16th and 17th centuries but thereafter it declined. About the beginning of World War II, focusing on the Radhaus mountain, attempts were made to revive the gold mining industry but the results were disappointing. Nevertheless, some interesting discoveries were made leading to scientific research in the caves after end of hostilities. It was found that the temperature of some of the rocks reached up to 44°C and that the humidity levels were exceptionally high. Many of the miners who worked in the caves were interviewed about their experiences when working in the caves; many claimed that their rheumatic complaints, as well as problems with joints, asthma, and even skin conditions had been cured. The research found that a combination of high temperature, humidity and levels of radon gas within the mountain were responsible for producing the beneficial effects. The conclusion was that treatment within the caves had a healing effect similar to spa therapies, even surpassing at that time all other modern treatment methods for a significant proportion of patients. In the early 1950s, a company was founded with the first treatment centre being opened in 1954. Extensions to the facilities were added between 1970 and 1971, and again in 1989.

*Comments*: Gasteiner Heilstollen is a treatment centre offering a natural therapy in the *Heilstollen* (Healing Caves). Passengers are transported into and around the treatment area on a train which can carry up to 122 passengers in 14 carriages each with eight seats. Five carriages have two spaces each for patients who need to lie down. There are two drivers. A doctor is always carried on board the train. There are extensive safety precautions and comprehensive emergency procedures in case of an accident with the train service.

## 63 Giselabahn

*Locations*: Zell am See, 97 km by road south-west of Salzburg and Kirchberg near Wörgl in Tyrol which is 67 east-north-east of Innsbruck.
*Michelin map reference*: K7 and I6.
*Introduction*: The main line - known as the Giselabahn - is operated by: ÖBB for normal rail services. However, part of the Giselabahn route is used for *Nostalgie* excursions organized by the local tourist office (see below for contact details).
*Official line number*: 601.
*Timetable number*: 201.
*Route*: From Kirchberg-Hahnenkamm station near Wörgl to Zell am See, a total distance of 60 km.
*Journey time*: 3 hours.
*Gauge*: Standard by adhesion only. The route is on main line - single track.
*Electrified*: Yes, 15 kV AC 16.7 Hz.
*Rolling stock*: Still running on this *Nostalgie* train service is the 1910-built Imperial and Royal post carriage. A special postmark is franked on letters or postcards posted on the train.
*Places to see*: Zell am See and its attractive lake.
*Contact details*: The Tourist Office, Kitzbüheler Alpen-Brixental, Hauptstraße 8, Kirchberg, A-6365 Kirchberg in Tirol. Telephone: 05357 2000 Fax: 05357 3732.
*Website*: www.kitzalps.com/en/nostalgia-train-giselabahn.html
*Operating dates*: On Tuesdays from the end of May to mid-September. (NB: It is necessary to book at the Tourist Office by 1600 hours on the Monday prior to departure.) The excursion train leaves the station at Kirchberg-Hahnenkamm about 0910 hours.
*Tariff*: Adult ticket is €32 and for a child €16 (2007).
*History*: The line was opened by the Imperial and Royal railway company in 1875 and is named after Emperor Franz Josef's eldest daughter, 'Gisela'. The first journey - effectively part of the route of the 'Orient Express' from Paris to Istanbul - took place on 31st July, 1875 in the presence of a member of the Austrian Imperial family, Duke Karl Ludwig. The post carriage, still running today, dates back to 1910 and in an accompanying restaurant car there is a bar and buffet as well as the original post box. Live music is also sometimes played.
*Comments*: This route is ÖBB main line and is worth a journey in its own right as are the special trips on the 'Giselabahn' along the Brixen Valley to Zell am See. The journey is out by train and back by bus. Up to three hours should be allowed for sight-seeing in Zell am See. This route crosses the Salzburg and Tyrol state borders.

A mural depicting salt-mining at the museum at Bad Dürrnberg. *Author*

An 1898-built 0-6-2T No. 298.55 'plinthed' at Mittersill on 27th June, 2007. ÖBB railcar No. 5090.001-8 can be seen in the background. *Author*

## 64  Hallein Salt Mines

*Location*: Bad Dürrnberg, 3 km to the south of Hallein and 19 km south of Salzburg.
*Michelin map reference*: L6.
*Nearest main line railway station*: Hallein on the Westbahn (line 401 and timetable 200). ÖBB offers the 'Salz Erlebnis Ticket' which includes a return rail trip from Salzburg, a bus transfer to the mine and the Salzwelten entrance fee. For details visit Salzburg's main railway station or www.oebb.at/en
*Operated by*: Salinen Austria AG.
*Gauge*: Narrow gauge subterranean railway by adhesion only.
*Visit time*: The guided tour lasts about 1 hour 10 minutes but allow up to three hours for the whole visit. Tours are conducted simultaneously in German and English with Italian, French and Spanish translations available on request.
*Contact details*: World of Salt Information, Salzwelten Reisedienst, Birgit Ellmer, Wirerstraße 10, A 4820 Bad Ischl. Telephone: 043 6132 200 2490 Fax: 06132 200 4400. E-mail: info@salzwelten.at
*Website*: www.salzwelten.at (de en it fr).
*Operating dates*: 1st January to 31st March from 1100 hours to 1500* hours; 1st April to 31st October from 0900 hours to 1700* hours; 1st November to 31st December from 1100 hours to 1500* hours (*time of the last guided tour) (2007).
*Tariff*: An adult ticket costs €15.50, for a child aged 7-15 years €9.30 and for a child aged 4-6 years €7.75. A family ticket (2 adults and one child) costs €32.55 with additional children of any age being charged €7.75 each. Senior citizens are admitted for €13.95. There are discounts for groups (2007).
*Comments*: This is one of the world's oldest mines. The earth beneath the surface of the Dürrnberg Mountain is the source of the wealth of Salzburg's history. Salt or 'white gold' as it is sometimes referred to, has been mined here since Celtic times and was the source of the riches accumulated by Salzburg's elite. Salt played a critical role in the history and economy of Salzburg and its surrounding areas. At the *World of Salt* museum the visitor is transported back in time to experience what it was like to work here searching for that white gold. On arrival the visitor is equipped with a 'miner's uniform' and then is transported by a small train (hence inclusion of this 'railway' in this book) down to the depths of the mine where, on arrival, an explanation is given by a miner of the history of salt mining. Multimedia displays complete the experience. There is a shop where souvenirs can be purchased.

## 65  Pinzgauerbahn

*Location*: Zell am See, 120 km south-east of Linz and 197 km south-west of Salzburg.
*Michelin map reference*: K7.
*Nearest main line railway station*: Zell am See on the Giselabahn (Westbahn) line number 601 and timetable number 201.
*Operated by*: ÖBB.
*Official line number*: 367.
*Timetable number*: 230.
*Route*: Originally from Krimml to Zell am See, a total distance of 52.7 km but unfortunately in 2007 the section from Krimml to Mittersill had to be closed as a consequence of flood damage thereby reducing the journey to almost a half (28.6

km). It is hoped that the full route will be restored in time. In the meantime bus services operate over the damaged section.
*Journey time*: 54 minutes to and from Mittersill and Zell am See.
*Gauge*: Narrow (760 mm) by adhesion rack only.
*Electrified*: No, normally diesel-operated but occasionally with steam-hauled specials.
*Rolling stock*: Single unit class '5090' railcars.
*Preserved rolling stock*: The following are retained on the line: 1906-built steam locomotive No 399.03, diesel locomotive No. 2095 014, diesel railcar No. 5090.001-8, bar carriage *Pinzga Schenke* No. Bi/s 9881000 5902-7 and a 1902-built 32-seater *Nostalgie Reisezugwagen* No. Bi/s 9881000 3641-3 *Gleisalm*, another 12-seater bar carriage No.WRp/s 9881000 5903-5.
*Places to see*: The Krimml Waterfalls (380m high) in the Hohen Tauern National Park.
*Website*: www.pinzgaubahn.at and www.oebb.at/en
*Operating dates*: Daily all the year round with services every hour between about 0600 hours and 1800 hours
*Tariff*: 1-PLUS-Freizeit 2nd class ticket costs an adult €6 (2007).
*Comments*: The narrow gauge line from Zell am See to Krimml service has been disrupted but by late 2007 thoughts were that the line would be recovered over time. *Nostalgie* excursions are operated on the line during the summer months.

### 66 Salzburger Lokalbahn (SLB)

*Location*: Salzburg, 296 km west of Vienna.
*Michelin map reference*: L5.
*Nearest main line railway station*: Salzburg on the Westbahn (official line number 401 and timetable number 101).
*Operated by*: Salzburger Lokalbahn.
*Route*: From Salzburg Lokalbahn (Hbf) to Trimmelkam (31 km) via Zehmemoos (2.6 km), a total distance of about 33.6 km.
*Journey time*: Salzburg Lokalbahn (Hbf) to Trimmelkam takes 53 minutes and Burmoos to Lamprechtshausen, 13 minutes.
*Gauge*: Standard by adhesion only.
*Electrified*: Yes, 750 V DC.
*Rolling stock*: Electric railcars 1908-built No. ET 1 used on the Burmoos to Trimmelkam section, predominantly 1980s-built Nos. ET 41 to ET 54 and 2001/2-built Nos. ET 55 to ET 58 for the rest of the network.
*Preserved rolling stock*: Electric railcars 1908-built No. MBC 3, 1907/8-built Nos. ET 6 & ET 7 and 1951-built No. ET 33.
*Places to see*: See also Salzburger Festungsbahn (*entry number 151*) or enjoy a sight-seeing excursion by boat on the MV *Amadeus Salzburg* which operates each year from around 5th April to 21st October. The boat landing-stage is located at Hanuschplatz/Makartsteg in the heart of the old city. Their website is www.salzburgschifffahrt.at
*Contact details*: Salzburger Lokalbahn, Plainstraße 70, A-5020 Salzburg. Telephone: 0662 44 801 500. E-mail: salzburger.lokalbahn@salzburg-ag.at
*Website*: www.slb.at
*Operating dates*: Daily year-round with services from 0500-0000 hrs - consult timetable at www.salzburg-ag.at/fileadmin/user_upload/verkehr/lokalbahn/Fahrplan_web.pdf

SLB's electric railcar No. ET 57 *Ober Innviertel* awaits departure for Salzburg Lokalbahnhof on 1st July, 2007.  *Author*

*Tariff*: Local fare structure applies.
*Comments*: *Nostalgie* excursions are organized for rail enthusiasts including steam driven traction courtesy of the strong links with ÖGEG (*see entry 118*). Information can be obtained from Heinz Eberhart, Telephone: 043 662 4480 6180. E-mail: heinz.eberhart@salzburg-ag.at Bus-operated services are also run by SLB. See also SETG (*entry number 141*) for brief information about freight services.


## 67  Tauernbahn

*Location*: Bischofshofen, 50 km south of Salzburg.
*Michelin map reference*: L6.
*Operated by*: ÖBB.
*Official line numbers*: 706 and 806.
*Timetable number*: 220.
*Route*: From Bischofshofen to Villach, a total distance of about 140 km including the Tauern rail tunnel from Böckstein to Mallnitz-Hintertal (*see next entry*).
*Journey time*: 1 hour 54 minutes.
*Gauge*: Standard by adhesion only.
*Electrified*: Yes, 15 kV AV 16.7 Hz.
*Website*: www.oebb.at/en
*Operating dates*: Daily all year round every two hours from 0753 to 0216 on the Bischofshofen-Villach route.
*Tariff*: An adult 2nd class single ticket costs €20.70 (2007).
*Comments*: The Tauernbahn tunnel (with car-carrying trains) is an integral part of this route (*see next entry*).

The Tauernbahn, especially between Kölbnitz and Mallnitz is truly magnificent. There are numerous impressive viaducts on the route. This one pictured on 17th October, 2007 is near Oberfalkenstein. *Author*

## 68 Tauernbahn Tunnel

A car-carrying vehicle is being unloaded at Mallnitz-Hintertal on 17th October, 2007.
*Author*

*Location*: Böckstein, 93 km south of Salzburg.
*Michelin map reference*: L7.
*Operated by*: ÖBB.
*Official line numbers*: 707 and 806.
*Route*: From Böckstein to Mallnitz, a total distance in the tunnel of 8.37 km.
*Journey time*: From/to Mallnitz and Böckstein takes 11 minutes.
*Gauge*: Standard by adhesion only.
*Electrified*: Yes, 15 kV AC 16.7 Hz.
*Rolling stock*: Passenger and car-carrying carriages.
*Website*: www.oebb.at/en and www.erlebnis-bahn-schiff.at
*Operating dates*: Daily all year round with services from about 0600 to 2200 hours running every two hours with car-carrying trains leaving Böckstein at 20 minutes past the hour and services leaving Mallnitz-Obervellach at 10 minutes to the hour (2007).
*Tariff*: A car and all its passengers travel the tunnel for a fare of €17 each way (2007).
*History*: The tunnel was built between 1901 and 1906 and electrified in 1925.
*Comments*: The tunnel burrows under the magnificent mountains of the Tauern range, i.e. the Gamskarspitze (2,833 m), the Romantenspitze (2,696 m), the Hohen Tauern (2,459 m), Kreuzkogel (2,686 m) and the Maresenspitze (2,916 m), all of these mountain peaks being within five kilometres or less of the tunnel.

## 69 Tauernbahn Museum

*Location*: Schwarzach St Veit, 63 km south of Salzburg.
*Michelin map reference*: L6/7.
*Nearest main line railway station*: Schwazach St Veit on the Westbahn (line number 401 and timetable numbers 200 and 220).
*Operated by*: Museum Tauernbahn - Salzburger Eisenbahn Museum.
*Gauge*: Standard.
*Traction*: Steam- and electric-powered.
*Rolling stock*: The museum retains a 1938-built Bo-Bo electric locomotive No. 1245.514 (picture of a sister locomotive No. 1245.525 can be seen at *entry 16-08*). A 1927-built 2-8-2T is a static exhibit at Schwarzach St Veit station.
*Contact details*: Museum Tauernbahn, Bahnhofstraße 32, A-5620 Schwarzach im Pongau. E-mail: the custodian of the museum can be contacted michael.koestinger@museum-tauernbahn.com or the webmaster at webmaster@e-gschwendtner.com
*Website*: www.museum-tauernbahn.at/German/indexger.htm (de) The site has not been updated since late 2004, so if contemplating a visit, the advice is to check opening hours beforehand.
*Operating dates*: May to October on Wednesdays and Saturdays between 1300 hours and 1700 hours and on Sundays between 1000 hours and 1700 hours (2004).
*Tariff*: An adult entry costs €3.50, a child (6-12 years) €1.50 and a family ticket €7 (2004).
*History*: Ten railway enthusiasts came together towards the end of 1993 to form the museum.

## 70 Taurachbahn (part of the former Murtalbahn)

*Location*: Mauterndorf, 110 km south-east of Salzburg.
*Michelin map reference*: N7.
*Nearest railway station*: Unzmarkt on the Neumarkt Sattel line (official line number 813 and timetable number 600).
*Operated by*: Club 760 (*see entry 71*).
*Route*: St Andrä-Andlwirt-Mauterndorf, previously the most western section of the Murtalbahn; the total distance is 10 km.
*Journey time*: 35 minutes.
*Gauge*: Narrow (760 mm) by adhesion only.
*Traction*: Steam- and diesel-powered.
*Rolling stock*: Steam: a 1900-built 0-6-2T locomotive known as U6 No. 298.56, a 1944-built 0-8-0 locomotive from the Franco-Belge Locomotive factory No. 699.01, a 1906-built locomotive No. S12 from Krauss Linz operating originally on the Salzkammergutbahn, and locomotive No. Z 6 operating previously on the Thörlerbahn until 1970. Diesel: 1936-built locomotive No. 2091.03, originally No. 2041.03 and operated by the German Reichsbahn as 137.334, and a 1957-built Orenstein & Koppel-built locomotive No. VL 25721, 1942-built locomotive No. D 40 used by the German *Wehrmacht* and later the Salzkammergutbahn. Passenger coaches include Bi 37 *Tamsweg* built in 1906, Bi 38 *Markt Cadolzburg* built in 1925, Bi 39 *Bürgergarde Mauterdorf* built 1892, C 60 built 1892, Ba Nos. 47 & 48, B 3 Nos. 45 & 46 built in 1905 for the Appenzellerbahn in Switzerland, baggage van No. D 83 built in 1894, postal carriage No. F 91 built in 1911 and an 1894-built goods wagon No. G 157.
*Contact details*: Taurachbahn, Bahnhofstrasse 153, Mauterndorf, A-5570. Telephone: 06472 7088 or 06645 751215. E-mail: taurachbahn@club760.at

*Website*: www.club760.at/html/TaurachbahnE.htm (de en)
*Operating dates*: From 10th June until 6th July and from 27th August until 21st September on Saturdays and Sundays operating afternoon services with trains departing Mauterndorf at 1400 hours and returning from St Andrä-Andlwirt at 1540 hours. From 7th July until 26th August operating afternoon services (as described above) on Fridays; and, on Saturdays and Sundays operating both morning and afternoon services. Morning services leave Mauterndorf at 1000 hours and return from St Andrä-Andlwirt at 1140 hours. At the end of the season on 22nd September in 2007 a special steam train was run to Murau and return leaving Mauterndorf at 0900 hours (a special fare applied). This pattern of operating in 2007 is expected to be followed in future years.
*Tariff*: An adult single from St Andrä-Andlwirt to Mariapfarr is €2.50 and a return €5. An adult single from St Andrä-Andlwirt to Mauterndorf is €5 and a return €10. Accompanied children over 6 years and under 15 travel at half-price. Between June and September special steam or diesel trains can be chartered. Arrangements can be made through the Steiermärkische Landesbahnen (StLB) (*see entry 86*) to organize a trip to and/or from Tamsweg and perhaps even further afield (2007).
*History*: The Taurachbahn is located in the Lungau area of the state of Salzburg, on a plateau surrounded by the Radstädter Tauern Mountains to the north, the Hohen Tauern Mountains to the west and the Nock mountains to the south. Originally, what is now the Taurachbahn was the end section of the Murtalbahn (*see entry 81*). This section between Tamsweg and Mauterndorf always had difficulties compared with the rest of the line owing to its isolation from local communities the net effect being that there were consistently low numbers of passengers. This led inevitably to the withdrawal of passenger services in March 1973, albeit some special steam trains did run until 1977. Freight train services continued to run on weekdays but all that came to an end in June 1980. This was not a planned closure rather a result of a road traffic accident. What happened was a road truck too high to pass under a bridge near St Andrä hit it effectively stopping all immediate and future rail traffic from passing over it. The damage was very serious so much so that the cost of repair was seen as too great. The sad consequence was the permanent closure of this section of the line. Club 760 (*see entry 71*), which had anticipated the closure of the line long before the bridge accident, had earlier founded the 'Taurach Railway Study Society'. The aim of the society was to take over the section of line - St Andrä-Andlwirt - Mauterndorf - if, as and when it was closed. It was almost two years after the collision a lease was signed effectively handing over to Club 760 'ownership' of the line. A project was begun and much work followed undertaken mainly by enthusiastic volunteers. Eventually the line between Tamsweg and Mauterndorf was re-constructed and to the west of St Andrä a new route of about a kilometre in length was built. By June 1983, the repair of the damaged railway bridge was completed and then in the August the steam locomotive No. 699.01 passed over the repaired bridge for the first time. Although the list of tasks to make full running on the line possible seemed endless, nonetheless, on 26th October the first steam special train ran the entire line between Tamsweg and Mauterndorf; this marked the re-birth of the Taurachbahn. The Taurach Railway Study Society about that time formally became the 'Taurachbahn' and with an operating licence granted in July 1988 regular operations began. This was a pinnacle of achievement for all the unpaid volunteers who had toiled over the years. For the first few years of operation the rolling stock had to be transferred at the end of each season to Club 760's museum at Frojach. However, this situation improved markedly with the opening of a new shed in 1999 where the rolling stock could be stored in the winter months away from the ravages of the harsh weather. (*Source: Club 760.*)
*Comments*: Well worth visiting not least to lend support to the hard-working volunteers.

## Styria (Steiermark)

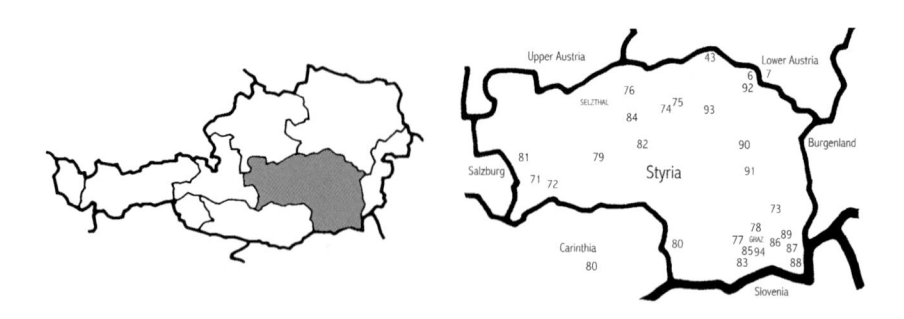

Styria can be found in the south-east of Austria. In geographical area, it is the second largest of the nine Austrian states with 16,388 sq km. It has a population of 1,203,986 making it the fourth largest in Austria. It has state borders with Upper Austria, Lower Austria, Salzburg, Burgenland and Carinthia and an international frontier with Slovenia. The four areas within the state are Upper Styria (*Obersteiermark*), West Styria (*Weststeiermark*), East Styria (*Oststeiermark*) and Lower Styria (*Untersteiermark*). The capital city is Graz. (NB: Mariazellerbahn runs from St Pölten in Lower Austria to Mariazell in Styria. Most of this journey is in Lower Austria where the reference to this railway can be found (*see entry 42*)).

**71 Club 760**

*Location*: Murau, 96 km south-west of Leoben and 131 km by road west of Graz.
*Michelin map reference*: O7.
*Nearest railway station*: Unzmarkt on the Neumarkt Sattel route (line 813 and timetable 600).
*Gauge*: Narrow (760mm) by adhesion only.
*Traction*: Steam- and diesel-powered.
*Rolling stock*: *See next entry.*
*Places to visit*: Murau is known for Nordic sports, woodcarving and the local speciality, Murauer beer. The village contains a number of ancient trees, dating from medieval times.
*Contact details*: Club 760, c/o Eisenbahnmuseum Frojach, P.O. Box 51 Murau, A-8850. Telephone: 06472 7088. E-mail: webmaster@club760.at
*Website*: www.club760.at (de en fr).
*Operating dates*: The museum only opens a few weekends in the summer but visits can be made by groups or individuals by special arrangement.
*History*: In 1969, on the 75th anniversary of the Murtalbahn, the Club 760 - *Verein der Freunde der Murtalbahn* (Society of the Friends of the Murtalbahn) was founded drawing its name from the 760 mm (about 2 ft 6 in.) width of many Austrian narrow gauge railway lines. The aim of the Club was to make the Murtalbahn and its traction and rolling stock better known to the public, the objective being to raise passenger levels in order to keep the Murtalbahn operational for its entire length

from Unzmarkt to Mauterndorf. As nostalgic steam trains excursions became more popular it was found that there was a shortage of passenger coaches; this, therefore, became the Club's next objective of securing more passenger rolling stock. In 1970, the passenger coach No. Bi/s 3665 was bought from the ÖBB and a second coach No. Bi/s 563 (formerly of the SKLGB) was bought from the Zillertalbahn. Both coaches are now in use on the Taurachbahn. In 1973, the Club purchased the steam locomotive No. 699.01, formerly used on the light railways of the German *Wehrmacht* in World War II. During the following years the collection of narrow gauge rolling stock has grown and now forms a very important collection. Today, there is an interesting collection of locomotives on display in the Club's museum at Frojach some of which have been fully renovated and some, the steam locomotive No. U11 for example, can be seen hauling tourist trains. To protect all the rolling stock from the weather, which was originally outdoors, Club 760 rented land near the station of Frojach where a covered narrow gauge museum has since been built. Another important landmark in the Club's history was the opening of the Taurachbahn (*see previous entry*) in July 1988 and since then, steam trains have been regularly operated during the summer months between Mauterndorf and St Andrä. (*Source: Club 760.*)
*Comments*: Like a visit to the Taurachbahn (*see entry 70*, if one can get access to the museum at Frojach, it is well worth visiting as is the nearby Murtalbahn (*see entry 81*).

## 72 Eisenbahnmuseum Frojach

*Location*: Frojach, 123 km west of Graz.
*Michelin map reference*: O7.
*Nearest railway station*: Frojach-Katschtal on the Murtalbahn (*see entry 81*).
*Operated by*: Club 760.
*Gauge*: Narrow (760 mm).
*Traction safeguarded*: Steam- and diesel-powered.
*Exhibits*: A superb exhibition of narrow gauge locomotives including the following steam locomotives (which are all operational): 1900-built No. 298.56 (formerly U6), 1944-built No. 699.01, 1906-built No. S12 (ex-SKLGB), 1893-built No. Z6, 1959-bult JZ SKODA 1932, 1917-built Krauss München (serial No. 7194) CFF No. 764.219, 1890-built No. S5 (ex-SKLGB) and 1909-built JZ 83.076. Steam locomotives not serviceable are: 1930-built Krauss Linz (serial No. 1519) No. Kh111, an 1892-built Krauss Linz (serial No. 2751) No. S7 (ex-SKLGB) and a 1914-built Lokomotivfabr Wien-Floridsdorf (serial No. 2188) No. JZ 9.029. A selection of passenger carriages and wagons are also retained. Also safeguarded is diesel traction all serviceable as follows: a 1963 VL Braubach (diesel) built by Spoorijezer, Delft (serial No. 6008) originally 750 mm but since re-gauged to 760 mm, a 1936-built diesel locomotive No. 2041.02, 1957-built VL No. 25721 and a 1942-built D40/ VL 01.
*Contact details*: Club 760, Eisenbahnmuseum Frojach, P.O. Box 51 Murau, A-8850. Telephone: 06472 7088. E-mail: webmaster@club760.at
*Website*: www.club760.at (de en fr).
*Opening dates*: Mid-July to September some weekends from 1000 to 1600 hours.
*Comments*: A picture of CFF 764.411R, a sister locomotive to CFF No. 764.219 which is retained at Frojach, can be seen at *entry 85*, the Stainzerbahn.

Carriages, lovingly restored by Club 760, are on loan to the Stainzerbahn. *Author*

Club U44's 1949-built 0-8-2 No. 83.180 ex-FTB (Bosnia) crossing the Grub viaduct north of Weiz on 14th October, 2007. *Author*

## 73 Feistritztalbahn Betriebsgesellschaft [FTB]

*Location*: Weiz, 33 km north-east of Graz.
*Michelin map reference*: S7.
*Nearest railway station*: Weiz on StLB's Gleisdorf to Weiz route (*see entry 89*).
*Operated by*: Club U44 and Steiermärkische Landesbahnen (StLB).
*Route*: Steiermärkische Landesbahnen (StLB) operates a freight-only line from Weiz to Oberfeistritz, a distance of 13 km. The preservation society, Club U44, operates on the Weiz-Birkfeld route via Oberfeistritz, Anger and Koglhof, a total distance of 24 km.
*Journey times*: Vary but usually about 1 hour 25 minutes out from Weiz and 1 hour 5 minutes back in from Birkfeld.
*Gauge*: Narrow (760 mm).
*Traction*: Steam and diesel.
*Rolling stock*: Steam locomotives: 1926-built No. Kh101 formerly of the Murtalbahn, a 1949-built 0-8-2 No. 83.180 formerly used in Bosnia, No. 100.13, 1922-built No. U 44 by Krauss (Linz), and two 1894-built 0-6-2Ts Nos. U 8 and U7. Steiermärkische Landesbahnen freight traffic is fulfilled by diesel locomotives: a 1942 Gmeinder-built No. VL 4, 1966 Jung-built No. VL 8, 1967-built Nos. VL 14 to 16 and 1972 Duro Dakovic-built No. VL 22 (fitted with 'radio telecontrol').
*Places to see*: Viaducts on the line include the Nöstl, Peesen, Baz, Bachl, Grub (a 13-arch curved bridge), Hollersbach and Birkfelder. There are three tunnels, one 232 m in length shortly after Hart Puch station, the Frondsberg and the Kirchleiten (106 m).
*Near to here*: Stainzerbahn (*see entry 85*)
*Contact details*: Feistritztalbahn Betriebsgesellschaft, Hauptplatz 13, A-8190 Birkfeld. Telephone: 03174 4507-20 Fax: 03174 4507-60. E-mail: feistritztalbahn@birkfeld.at Friends of the FTB use the name of Club U44, and the can also be contacted at the same address and telephone/fax numbers. Their E-mail is: club-u44@aon.at Steiermärkische Landesbahnen's contact address is at Eggenberger Straße 20, A-8020 Graz. Telephone: 0316 812581-0 Fax: 0316 812581-81. E-mail: office@stlb.at
*Website*: www.feistritztalbahn.at see also www.ingr.co.uk/weiz.html and www.stlb.at The webmaster speaks and writes English.
*Operating dates*: Sundays from 24th June to 26th October trains leave Weiz at 1030 hours and returning from Birkfeld at 1600 hours. On Mondays from 9th July to 3rd September a limited service leaves Weiz at 1310 hours and returns from Anger at 1745 hours. On Thursdays from 21st June to 6th September trains leave Weiz at 0940 hours and 1640 hours and return from Birkfeld at 1330 hours and 1830 hours. On Saturdays from 8th September to 20th October leaving Weiz at 1310 and returning from Birkfeld at 1600 hours. These dates applied to 2007 but operating dates and times are likely to be similar in future years.
*Tariff*: An adult single varies between €15 and €12, children (6-15 years) travel at half-price. A family ticket (two adults and two children) varies between €32 and €26. There are discounts for groups. It is possible to charter a carriage for exclusive use i.e. a 56-seater costs €460 and a 32-seater €310 (2007).
*History*: In 1909, a plan was proposed to build a railway line connecting the town of Weiz with a quarry at Birkfeld. A contract was awarded to construct the line which was opened to traffic on 15th December, 1911. Steiermärkische Landesbahnen took over the running of the line in 1921. Shortly after the original opening, thoughts were given to extending the line a further 25 km to Rettenegg where brown coal deposits had been found. Shortage of funds to build the line meant that a decision was made to use forced labour, this area being under Italian occupation during

World War I. However, construction work eventually stopped and did not resume until a local mining company built the line to Ratten to be used as a siding. However, the lack of professionalism in building the line led to it failing to receive a licence to operate. Notwithstanding this, the line operated illegally carrying miners in dangerous unbraked passenger carriages. Matters improved after AG Weiz-Birkfeld took over and, after undertaking the necessary repairs, received a licence to operate in 1930. Unfortunately it was never profitable and the extended line was eventually closed.

*Comments*: Today freight trains run from Weiz and terminate about 13 km away at Anger. The line from Anger to Birkfeld, where the workshop and engine shed are located, is now only used for steam excursions. The section beyond Birkfeld towards Ratten is used as a green-route cycleway.

*Comments*: An extremely well-run heritage railway utilising interesting and well-maintained traction and rolling stock operated by very friendly staff, many of whom speak and write excellent English. Philatelists who combine their interest with heritage railways may care to know that a stamp depicting one of the railway's steam locomotives has been produced by the Austrian Post Office and is still available from the railway shop.

## 74 Erzbergbahn

*Location*: Vordernberg, 67 km north-west of Graz.
*Michelin map reference*: Q6.
*Nearest main line railway station*: Leoben on the Neumarkt Sattel (line number 813 and timetables 250 & 600).
*Operated by*: Verein Erzbergbahn (Erzberg Railway Association).
*Official line number*: The route still retains ÖBB's number 761.
*Route*: From Vordernberg Markt to Eisenerz, a total distance of 18.1 km.
*Journey time*: 1 hour 20 minutes.
*Gauge*: Standard by adhesion only. Up until 1980 this line had retained its rack rail based on the Roman Abt design.
*Traction*: Diesel railcars.
*Rolling stock*: Railcars class '5081' Nos. 562 to 565 and two *Motorbahnwagen* Nos. X616.003 and X616.084, all are operational.
*Contact details*: Verein Erzbergbahn, Hauptstraße 140, A-8794 Vordernberg. Telephone: 03849 832 Fax: 03849 21995. E-mail: office@erzbergbahn.at
*Website*: www.erzbergbahn.at (de)
*Operating dates*: From 1st July to 16th September on Sundays and on the public holiday 15th August. Departures from Vordernberg at 1030 hours and 1430 hours arriving at Eisenerz at 1140 hours and 1540 hours. Return journeys from Eisenerz at 1150 hours and 1550 hours arriving back at Vordernberg at 1255 hours and 1655 hours. The railway also runs special events throughout the year, the detail of which can be found on the website. (NB the brochure/timetable in English is at www.erzbergbahn.at/fahrplan_2007/fahrplanfolder2007_en.pdf )
*Tariff*: An adult return is €13.50 and single €9 and for a child (under 15 years) €6.75 and €4.50 respectively. For a family (two adults and three children maximum) a return ticket is €33.75 and a single journey €22.50 (2007).
*History*: Whilst the railway between Leoben and Vordernberg opened in 1872 and a year later the section between Hieflau and Eisenerz, the centre section - that which

1967-built diesel railcar No. 5081.563-8 awaiting its Sunday departure from Vordernberg station on 8th July, 2007. *Author*

became to be known as the Erzbergbahn - was not opened as a rack/cogwheel railway until 1891. The prime role was the transporting of iron-ore from the mining area at the Erzberg Mountain over the Präbichl pass to the steelworks in Vordernberg and Leoben-Donawitz. In 1980, the rack was removed making it possible to use diesel locomotives and railcars with strengthened braking systems. In 1988, ÖBB closed the line but fortunately two years later leased the line to an association of local enthusiasts as a museum railway. In 1990 it re-opened for museum traffic. In 2003, the association purchased the railway including the depot at Vordernberg and the station at Erzberg.

*Comments*: There is also a museum (*see next entry*). This journey, on what is said to be the steepest standard gauge adhesion-only railway in Austria, offers the traveller a view of most impressive mountain scenery - not to be missed!

*Further reading*: The UK's Austrian Railway Group has published an excellent book on this railway entitled *Die Erzbergbahn - Austria's Iron Ore Mountain Railways* (2005) (*see Bibliography*).

## 75 Museumsbahn Vordernberg-Eisenerz

*Location*: Vordernberg Markt station.
*Michelin map reference*: Q6.
*Nearest main line railway station*: Leoben on the Neumarkt Sattel (line number 813 and timetables 250 & 600).
*Operated by*: Verein Erzbergbahn (Erzberg Railway Association).
*Traction*: Steam and diesel exhibits.
*Exhibits*: The museum contains interesting railway artefacts including a cogwheel engine and a driver's cab from a steam locomotive. Preserved, but not operational, is steam locomotive No 297.401, said to be one of the world's strongest rack locomotives and which is now plinthed outside the museum at Vordernberg Markt station. It had originally entered service in 1942 and was finally withdrawn in 1968. Its sister locomotive No. 297.402 had a very short life on the railway. It also entered service in January 1942 but was scrapped in 1949 with many of the parts retained to

1941-built 2-12-2T rack locomotive No. 297.401 is 'plinthed' outside the museum at Vordernberg Markt station. *Author*

Running alongside the River Enns the Gesäuse route is very beautiful. Here, on 10th October, 2007, a service from Hieflau runs west near Gesäuse Eingang towards Admont and Selzthal. *Author*

keep 401 going. Steam locomotive No. 97.217 is 'plinthed' in the square of Vordernberg Markt on the approach up to the station.
*Contact details*: Museumsbahn Vordernberg-Eisenerz, Hauptstraße 140, Vordernberg Markt station, A-8794 Vordernberg. Telephone: 03849 832 Fax: 03849 21995.
*Website*: www.erzbergbahn.at (de).
*Operating dates*: From May to October on Sundays when the rail excursions are running. See previous entry for detail of opening hours.
*Tariff*: Included in the cost of the excursion.
*History*: The museum was established at Vordernberg Markt station in 1993.
*Comments*: Shop, museum trains to Eisenerz (*see previous entry*).
*Further reading*: The UK's Austrian Railway Group has published an excellent book on this railway entitled *Die Erzbergbahn - Austria's Iron Ore Mountain Railways* (2005).

## 76 Gesäuse Route

*Location*: Selzthal, 93 km south of Wels and 113 km north-west of Graz.
*Michelin map reference*: O6.
*Nearest main line railway station*: Selzthal on the Ennstalbahn (line numbers 302, 804 and 304 and timetable numbers 250, 130, 131 and 140).
*Operated by*: ÖBB.
*Official line number*: 302.
*Route*: Selzthal-Hieflau, a total distance of 50 km.
*Journey time*: 39 minutes.
*Gauge*: Standard by adhesion only. Main line - single track.
*Electrified*: Yes, 15 kV AC 16.7 Hz.
*Places to see*: The route follows the River Enns through the beautiful Gesäuse valley. The journey is memorable by train or by car.
*Website*: www.oebb.at/en
*Operating dates*: Daily all year round from 0600 hours to 1800 hours about every two hours although some services are train and bus combined making for a much longer journey time.
*Tariff*: A 1-PLUS-Freizeit adult single 2nd class ticket costs €7.60 (2007).
*Comments*: The Gesäuse route is part of the longer Ennstalbahn (*see entry 61*).

## 77 Graz-Köflacher Bahn [GKB]

*Location*: Graz, 243 km south-east of Salzburg and 193 km south west of Vienna.
*Michelin map reference*: S7.
*Nearest main line railway station*: Graz on the Südbahn (line number 805 and timetable number 501).
*Operated by*: Graz Köflacher Bahn.
*Official line number*: The Graz Köflacher Bahn, being a truly independent railway, does not have an official ÖBB line number allocated.
*Timetable number*: 550.
*Routes*: a) Graz to Köflach, a distance of 40.2 km; and, b) Graz - Wies-Eibiswald, a distance of 50.7 km.
*Journey times*: a) 54 minutes; and, b) 1 hour 22 minutes.
*Gauge*: Standard by adhesion only. Local line - single track.

A GKB service approaching Deutschlandberg on 8th July, 2007. *Author*

Built by Bombardier in Vienna, tram No. 656 displaying its 'Sparkasse' livery leaves Graz Hbf for St Peter on 8th July, 2007. *Author*

*Electrified*: No.
*Traction*: Preserved steam and modern diesel-powered railcars.
*Rolling stock*: Steam locomotives: an 1860 StEG-built 0-6-0 No. 671 (this is the oldest locomotive in service on a main line) and a 1914 Floridsdorf-built class '56' 2-8-0 No. 56.3115. Diesel locomotives: 1938 BMAG-built class 'DH 80' No.1, 1978 and 1980 GKB-built class 'DM' 100 Nos. V100 1 & V100 2 used as track maintenance vehicles, class 'DH 600' shunters Nos. 1, 2 & 3, class 'DH 700' shunter No. 1, class 'DH 1100' Nos. 1 & 2, class 'DH 1500' Nos. 1-6 and class 'DH 1700' No. 1. Railcars (diesel powered) class 'VT 10' Nos. 03 and 09 and class 'VT 70' Nos. 001-013. (*Source: Platform 5.*)
*Contact details*: Graz-Köflacher Bahn und Busbetrieb GmbH, Köflacher Gasse 35-41 A-8021 Graz. Telephone: 0316 5987-0 Fax: 0316 5987-16. E-Mail: office@gkb.at
*Website*: www.gkb.at (de).
*Operating dates*: Daily services locally from 0530 hours to 2100 hours. For details of the steam-hauled services contact the railway direct by e-mail at wallner.alois@gkb.at
*Tariff*: Local fare structure applies.
*History*: The construction of the line from Köflach to Graz began in 1857 and was completed by June 1859 when the first train loaded with coal was transported. As a result of lignite being discovered in the Steyeregg-Eibiswald area another line was constructed from Leiboch to Weiz and opened to traffic in 1873. Over the following decades the line had mixed fortunes operating under a number of different companies/regimes. In 1998, Graz-Köflacher Eisenbahn GmbH (GKE) took over responsibility and in 2004 that company became Graz-Köflacher Bahn und Busbetrieb GmbH (GKB)
*Comments*: This railway was originally built for transport of coal from its terminals. Today it is the backbone of public transport, both trains and buses, in the region south and west of Graz. The company provides services for the carriage of passengers as well as freight especially wood. GKB is linked (as a shareholder) with LTE Logistik und Transport GmbH (*see entry 142*). The company operates steam-driven specials during the summer months.

## 78  Graz Trams

*Location*: Graz, 243 km south-east of Salzburg and 193 km south west of Vienna.
*Michelin map reference*: S7.
*Nearest main line railway station*: Graz on the Südbahn (line number 805 and timetable number 501).
*Operated by*: Grazer Verkehrsbetriebe [GVB]
*Routes*: Seven in total as follows: Eggenberg-Mariatrost (Tramway museum is located here); Hauptbahnhof-Krenngasse; Andritz-Liebenau/Stadion; Andritz-Puntigam; Hauptbahnhof-St Peter Schulzentrum; Wetzelsdorf-St Leonhard/Landeskrankenhaus; and, Liebenau/Stadion-Krenngasse. The network totals a distance of 29.7 km.
*Journey times*: Consult local timetables or the 'linienfahrplan' on the website.
*Gauge*: Standard by adhesion only.
*Electrified*: Yes, 600 V DC.
*Rolling stock*: Trams of the following classes are utilised: 1965-built 260 series 2-section cars (i.e. 2-car units); 1978-built 500 series 3-section cars; 1971-4-built 520 series 3-section cars; 1996-7-built 580 series 3-section cars; 1986-built 600 series 3-section cars (adapted to low floor); and, 2000-1-built Cityrunner 650 series 5-section

car (low floor). The livery is green and cream but many now are bedecked in brightly coloured advertising. (*Source: Platform 5.*)
*Contact details*: Grazer Verkehrsbetriebe, Andreas-Hofer-Platz 15, A-8011 Graz. Telephone: 0316 887-8804. E-mail: gvb@gstw.at
*Website*: www.erlebnis-bahn-schiff.atwww.gvb.at
*Operating dates*: Daily all year round - but many routes do not operate after 1930-2000 hours.
*Comments*: Graz was nominated as a UNESCO World Heritage site in 1999.

## 79 Eisenbahnmuseum Knittelfeld

No shortage of ÖBB rolling stock near Knittelfeld Museum on 7th July, 2007. Here are a mixture of types and classes.  *Author*

*Location*: Knittelfeld, 73 km by road north-west of Graz.
*Michelin map reference*: Q7.
*Nearest main line railway station*: Knittelfeld on the Neumarkt Sattel line (line number 813 and timetable 600).
*Exhibits*: On display in the museum are various railway artefacts including a watch collection, a collection of railway staff caps and decorations, a model railway, a driving simulator, a Pullman compartment from the turn of the 19th/20th century and displays depicting railway history of steam, diesel and electric locomotives. Outside there is a collection of electric and diesel locomotives and several trolleys and cranes as well as ÖBB's *Traktion* depot with an equally interesting collection of ancient and modern rolling stock.
*Contact details*: Eisenbahnmuseum Knittelfeld, Ainbachallee 14a, Knittelfeld, A-8720. Telephone: 0676 544 0795.
*Website*: http://members.e-media.at/eisenbahnmuseum-knittelfeld/ (de) See also www.mytrains.at/eisenbahnmuseum_knittelfeld.htm (de)
*Operating dates*: From 1st May to 31st October on Saturdays and Sundays from 0900 hours to 1700 hours. There are also four days around Ascension Day each year when an international 'Steam On' event is held.

*Tariff*: An adult entrance fee is €7 and €3.50 for a child up to 15 years. There are reductions for groups, senior citizens and service personnel (2007). Guided tours for groups of 10 persons or more can be conducted and if required in English all the year round.

*Comments*: Perhaps of equal interest next to the museum and with easy access is an ÖBB Traction maintenance depot complete with roundhouse. There is always an interesting collection of locomotives of varying vintages to see.


80  **Koralmbahn** (under the course of construction)

*Location*: Graz and Klagenfurt
*Michelin map references*: S7 and O9 respectively.
*Operated by*: ÖBB.
*Route*: Graz to Klagenfurt, a total distance of about 140 km.
*Journey time*: Yet to be determined (2007).
*Gauge*: Standard by adhesion only.
*Electrified*: Yes, 15 kV AC 16.7 Hz.
*Website*: www.oebb.at/en
*Opening date*: Hoped to be in 2010.
*Comments*: This is to be an important link between two Austrian cities in the south of the country. At present it is necessary for traveller to go via Bruck a.d. Mur with a regional express (REX) service taking 2 hours 49 minutes and sometimes longer. The linking of these two cities by the Koralmbahn will include the construction of the Koralm tunnel near Deutschlandsberg. The length of the tunnel will be 32.8 km which when it is completed will make it Austria's longest rail tunnel and the world's fourth longest. However, the Brenner Base tunnel, when opened in due course, will eclipse this record with its tunnel between Innsbruck and Fortezza in Italy anticipated to be 56.5 km making it then the longest in the world with the 1988-built Seikan tunnel in Japan being second. However, records are there to be broken and the Gotthard base tunnel when opened may well be the world's winner! The second stage of the Gotthard tunnel will definitely win hands-down with its anticipated 75 km length. As a matter of information, the Channel Tunnel (UK-France) is 50.45 km. There will be a second 6 km tunnel on the Koralmbahn near St Andrä.


81  **Murtalbahn**

*Location*: Unzmarkt, 115 km west of Graz.
*Michelin map reference*: P7.
*Nearest main line railway station*: Unzmarkt on the Neumarkt Sattel line (line number 813 and timetable number 600).
*Operated by*: Steiermärkische Landesbahnen (StLB).
*Official line number*: Not allocated.
*Timetable number*: 630.
*Route*: Unzmarkt to Tamsweg, a total distance of 65.5 km.
*Journey time*: 1 hour 40 minutes.
*Gauge*: Narrow (760 mm) by adhesion only.
*Electrified*: No.
*Traction*: Steam- and diesel-powered.

Railcar No. VS 3 with trailer VT 33 approach Wandritsch near St Ruprecht ob Murau on 7th July, 2007. *Author*

***Rolling stock***: Steam locomotives: Stainz 2 built 1892 by Krauss Linz formerly of the Stainzerbahn and brought to this line in the 1920s, class 'U' built by WrN, Krl Nos. U 11 (1894), U 40 (1908) and U 43 (1913). There is also a 1905-built Krauss (Linz) No. Bh 1. (NB: U 11 and U 43 are not currently operational). Diesel locomotives: 1959 OK-built No. VL 6, 1966-7 ÖAM/BBC-built Nos. VL 12 *Ehrenfried* & VL 13 *Ferdinand*. Diesel railcars: class 'VT 30s' built in 1980/81 by Knotz/BBC Nos. VT 31-34 & VT 35 built in 1999. Platform 5 (*see Bibliography*) also lists 1980/81 class 'VS 40' non-powered railcars Nos. VS 41-44.
***Contact details***: Steiermärkische Landesbahnen, Eggenberger Straße 20, A-8020 Graz. Telephone: 0316 812581-0 Fax: 0316 812581-81. E-Mail: office@stlb.at
***Website***: www.stlb.at (de)
***Operating dates***: Daily services with direct trains between 0800 hours and 2000 hours. Consult the timetable via the website at www.stlb.at/fahrplan/fahrplan.htm
***Tariff***: An adult single ticket for this journey is €10.36 (2007).
***History***: The Murtalbahn's history began in 1892 when the Styrian Parliament granted approval for the building of the line between Unzmarkt to Mauterndorf via Murau, having over the previous 10 years rejected other proposals. Ground-breaking occurred in August 1893 and within an incredible 316 days the 76.23 km line was completed! Included in the construction were 12 stations, 14 halts, offices

and workshop at Murau and engine sheds at Unzmarkt, Murau and Mauterndorf, together with seven water stations variously distributed along the route. Communication was also novel in that telephones were introduced for the first time, the usual means being at that time by morse telegraphy. At first, the operations did not meet planned expectations especially freight and in the particular the movement of felled wood. It seemed that the cheaper option of rafting the timber down the River Mur was the preferred mode of transport. Happily, the fortunes of the railway company improved in the early years of the 20th century. This led to plans to extend the line to Unterweissburg but World War I put a stop to that. The war also seriously affected train services which, because of the shortage of coal supplies, were cut back to one a day, a situation which went on after the end of the hostilities and was only partly resolved by changing to peat burning! In 1921, the Styrian State Railways took over the railway and about the same time matters began to improve and continued to do so over the following decade and until the beginning of the Depression in the early 1930s. Like many others at the time this railway suffered heavy losses. In spite of this, it was decided to experiment with Austro-Daimler-built gas-powered railcars following the lead of the Salzkammergutbahn (*see entry 121*). Enthusiasm for these soon waned when the railway suffered a number of accidents as well as technical difficulties requiring a great number of repairs, coupled with a general shortage of gas supplies. By 1939 the 'experiment' was ended and steam returned as the main means of propulsion. During World War II, surprisingly perhaps, passenger numbers increased so much so that a goods wagon had to be modified to become a passenger carriage. In 1943, steam locomotive No. Kh111 (still preserved today by Club 760) was transferred from the Feistritztal Railway to help out. Fortunately, the railway suffered no destruction during the war and was able to continue its services unhindered. The situation was not so pleasing after the end of the war with the growth of motor transport on the roads both for passengers and freight. By the end of the 1950s the situation was desperate. The response was to invest heavily in a modernisation plan and so over a six year period new rolling stock was acquired and diesel traction was taken on with the purchase of three diesel-electric locomotives. This led directly to the demise of steam power in 1967. Fortunately, local enthusiasts as well as representatives of the railway management itself were reluctant to abandon steam altogether, so much so that steam excursions were maintained and have been an important part of the annual timetable ever since. They have been proved to be most popular and have become a helpful source of revenue to sustain all services. At the end of March 1973, passenger services on that section of line between Tamsweg and Mauterndorf were ended, yet another casualty of the growth in the use of the automobile. This problem took two forms; firstly, the obvious preference by car owners not to use the railway and secondly, and bizarrely, in 1980, a truck hit a bridge near St Andrä rendering the line at that point impassable. The whole section was finally closed at the beginning of September 1982. (For the history of this section of line which has now become the Taurachbahn *see entry 70.*) Notwithstanding, the remainder of the route has flourished especially after the acquisition of modern railcars in the 1980s and a little later the installation of equipment at Unzmarkt to ease the transfer of freight from narrow gauge to standard gauge rolling stock. It is estimated that in excess of 430,000 people are transported every year and which with timber and other freight has made today's Murtalbahn a viable concern (*Source: Club 760*).
**Comments:** This railway links to the Taurachbahn which runs from Tamsweg to Mauterndorf (*see entry 70*). Club 760 also operates on this line (*see entry 71*).

A class '4024' railcar set crosses the River Mur at Preg on 7th July, 2007. *Caroline Jones*

Approaching Wald am Schoberpass is a mid-morning service to Bruck a.d. Mur via St Michael on 10th October, 2007. *Author*

## 82 Neumarkter Sattel Route

*Location*: Bruck a.d. Mur, 145 km south-west of Vienna and 55 km north of Graz.
*Michelin map reference*: R6.
*Nearest main line railway station*: Bruck a.d. Mur on the Südbahn (line number 805 and timetables 500, 501 and 600).
*Operated by*: ÖBB.
*Official line number*: 813.
*Timetable numbers*: 250 and 600.
*Route*: From Bruck a.d. Mur to Villach, a total distance of 212 km.
*Journey time*: 2 hours 38 minutes on the Intercity service and 3 hours 22 minutes on the REX service.
*Gauge*: Standard by adhesion only. Main line - twin-tracked.
*Electrified*: Yes, 15 kV AC 16.7 Hz.
*Website*: www.oebb.at/en
*Operating dates*: Daily all year round a few minutes after each hour.
*Tariff*: An adult 2nd class single costs €30.20 and €50.20 for first class travel (2007).
*Comments*: This is part of the route which has to be taken from Graz to Klagenfurt, a situation which will prevail until the new Koralmbahn (*entry 80*) is opened.

## 83 Radkersburgerbahn

*Location*: Spielfeld-Straß, 54 km south of Graz.
*Michelin map reference*: S8.
*Operated by*: ÖBB.
*Official line number*: 762.
*Timetable number*: 560.
*Route*: From Spielfeld-Straß to Bad Radkersburg in Austria and on to Gornja Radgona in Slovenia, a total distance of 33.4 km.
*Journey time*: 42 minutes to Bad Radkersburg.
*Gauge*: Standard by adhesion only. Local railway - single track.
*Electrified*: No.
*Traction utilised*: Diesel-powered.
*Website*: www.oebb.at/en
*Operating dates*: Daily all year round with rail services about every two hours.
*Tariff*: An adult 2nd class single ticket is €6.60 (2007).
*Comments*: Bus services also operate on this route taking three to four minutes longer for the journey. This is one of the four routes into Slovenia (*see entry 170*).

## 84 Schoberpass

*Location*: Selzthal, 113 km north-west of Graz.
*Michelin map reference*: O6.
*Nearest main line railway station*: Selzthal on the Ennstalbahn (line number 302).
*Operated by*: ÖBB.
*Official line number*: 804.
*Timetable number*: 250.
*Route*: Selzthal to St Michael, a total distance of 63 km.

Former Romanian steam locomotive No. 764.111R seen here undergoing routine maintenance at Preding-Wieseldorf on 8th July, 2007. *Author*

The distinctive red, white and green livery of the Steiermärkische Landesbahnen. *Author*

*Journey time*: Between 40 and 49 minutes.
*Gauge*: Standard by adhesion only. Main line - twin track.
*Electrified*: Yes, 15 kV AC 16.7 Hz.
*Website*: www.oebb.at/en
*Operating dates*: Daily all year round with Intercity services every two hours and REX services every four hours
*Tariff*: An adult 2nd class single ticket costs €12.10 (2007).


## 85 Stainzerbahn also known as Museumsbahn Stainz

*Location*: Stainz, 33 km south-west of Graz.
*Michelin map reference*: R8.
*Nearest railway station*: Preding-Wieseldorf on GKB's line (*see entry 77*) from Lieboch to Wies-Eibiswald (timetable number 550).
*Operated by*: Museumsbahn Stainz.
*Route*: Preding-Wieseldorf to Stainz, a total distance of 11.3 km.
*Journey time*: Not known.
*Gauge*: Narrow (760 mm) by adhesion only. Single track.
*Traction*: Steam.
*Rolling stock*: A CFF (Romanian Forest Railways) steam locomotive No. 764.411R with a maximum speed of 30 km/h. Surprisingly, perhaps, when you look at it this locomotive was built as late as 1986. There are some excellent passenger carriages dating from the 1890s, many being on loan from Club 760. A sister locomotive to 764.411R is held by Club 760.
*Contact details*: Museumsbahn Stainz, A-8510 Stainz. Telephone: 03463 2203 12. E-mail: zug@stainz.steiermark.at
*Website*: www.stainz.at/stainz/zug.htm
*Operating dates*: From April to August on Saturdays, Sundays and Public Holidays at 1500 hours. In September and October on Fridays, Saturdays and Sundays at 1500 hours.
*Tariff*: An adult single ticket is €7 and for a child (6-15 years) €3.50 and return tickets for an adult are €11 and for children €5 (2007).
*Comments*: Another narrow gauge branch line in the south of Austria. It is here the grapes of *Schilcher* wine grow. As well as the museum and the railway line there is a shop and a buffet restaurant.


## 86 Steiermärkische Landesbahnen (StLB)

*Location*: Graz, 193 km south-west of Vienna.
*Michelin map reference*: S7.
*Operated by*: Steiermärkische Landesbahnen.
*Routes*: Six separate routes are operated by this company as follows: a) Feldbach-Bad Gleichenberg (*see entry 88*); b) Gleisdorf-Weiz (*see entry 89*); c) Mixnitz-St Erhard (*see entry 90*); d) Peggau-Übelbach (*see entry 91*); e) Unzmarkt-Tamsweg, known as the Muratalbahn (*see entry 81 earlier*); and, f) Weiz-Oberfeistritz - the Feistritztalbahn (*see entry 73 earlier*).
*Gauges*: Standard and narrow (760 mm) by adhesion only. Steiermärkische Landesbahnen operates on a total of 47 km of standard and 120 km of narrow gauge track in the region.
*Traction*: Steam-, diesel- and electric-powered. Electricity power supplies vary according to route - see individual entries.

*Rolling stock*: See individual route entries.
*Contact details*: Steiermärkische Landesbahnen, Eggenberger Straße 20, A-8020 Graz. Telephone: 0316 812581-0 Fax: 0316 812581-81. E-Mail: office@stlb.at
*Website*: www.stlb.at
*Operating dates & tariff*: Daily all year round - consult Steiermärkische Landesbahnen's timetables and tariffs at local stations or on-line at www.stlb.at/fahrplan/fahrplan.htm
*Comments*: Steiermärkische Landesbahnen operates the largest private network in Austria.

### 87 Steirische Ostbahn

*Location*: Graz, 193 km south west of Vienna.
*Michelin map reference*: S7.
*Operated by*: ÖBB.
*Official line number*: 714.
*Timetable number*: 530.
*Route*: From Graz to Szentgotthárd on the Hungarian border, a total distance of 78 km.
*Journey time*: 1 hour 35 minutes.
*Gauge*: Standard by adhesion only.
*Electrified*: No, diesel traction is operated.
*Places to see*: Route passes through Feldbach from where Steiermärkische Landesbahnen (StLB) operates the service to Bad Gleichenberg (*see entry 88*).
*Website*: www.oebb.at/en and www.erlebnis-bahn-schiff.at
*Operating dates*: Daily all the year round with services every 75 minutes from about 0600 to 1800 hours (2007).
*History*: The route was opened between Graz and Jennersdorf (the last major railway station in Austria) in May 1873.
*Comments*: For much of the journey the line follows the Raab (Hungarian: Rába) and the Laßnitz rivers. The line connects with Hungary's Westbahn travelling on to Szombathely.

### 88 StLB - Feldbach to Bad Gleichenberg Route

*Location*: Feldbach, 45 km east of Graz.
*Michelin map reference*: T8.
*Operated by*: Steiermärkische Landesbahnen.
*Official line number*: None allocated.
*Timetable number*: 532.
*Route*: From Feldbach to Bad Gleichenberg, a total distance of 21.2 km.
*Journey time*: 35 minutes.
*Gauge*: Standard by adhesion only.
*Electrified*: Yes, 800 V DC. Diesel traction is also deployed.
*Rolling stock*: Electric locomotive - Graz/AEG 1930-built No. E 41; electric railcars: 1930-built (re-built in 1979 and 1990) Graz/Elin Nos. ET 1 & ET 2; and, diesel locomotive 1963-built JW No. RT 1.
*Contact details*: Steiermärkische Landesbahnen, Eggenberger Straße 20, A-8020 Graz. Telephone: 0316 812581-0 Fax: 0316 812581-81. E-Mail: office@stlb.at
*Website*: www.stlb.at
*Operating dates & tariff*: Daily all year round - consult Steiermärkische Landesbahnen's timetables and tariffs at local stations or on-line at www.stlb.at/fahrplan/fahrplan.htm

# STYRIA (STEIERMARK)

## 89 StLB - Gleisdorf - Weiz Route (sometimes referred to as the **Weizer Bahn**)

Weiz station with a morning service awaiting departure for Gleisdorf.   *Author*

*Location*: Gleisdorf, 30 km east of Graz.
*Michelin map reference*: T7.
*Operated by*: Steiermärkische Landesbahnen.
*Official line number*: None allocated.
*Timetable number*: 531.
*Route*: From Gleisdorf to Weiz, a total distance of 15.2 km.
*Journey time*: 1 hour 5 minutes.
*Gauge*: Standard by adhesion only.
*Electrified*: No. Diesel traction is deployed.
*Rolling stock*: Diesel locomotives 1964-65 ÖAM/BBC-built Nos. DE 1 & DE 2; 1993 Käble/Gmeinder No. D 3; Gmeinder-built Nos. D 4 (1999) and D 5-6 (2002); 1970 U23A-built No. D 45; Elin-built No V 60; class '2016' Nos. 901-7 & 902-5; and, diesel railcars 1987 JW-built Nos. VT 51-52. There are four shunting robots.
*Contact details*: Steiermärkische Landesbahnen, Eggenberger Straße 20, A-8020 Graz. Telephone: 0316 812581-0 Fax: 0316 812581-81. E-Mail: office@stlb.at
*Website*: www.stlb.at
*Operating dates & tariff*: Daily all year round - consult Steiermärkische Landesbahnen's timetables and tariffs at local stations or on-line at www.stlb.at/fahrplan/fahrplan.htm

## 90 StLB - Mixnitz - St Erhard Route

*Location*: Mixnitz, 41 km north of Graz.
*Michelin map reference*: S6.
*Operated by*: Steiermärkische Landesbahnen.
*Route*: From Mixnitz to St Erhard, a total distance of 10.4 km.
*Journey time*: Not published.
*Gauge*: Narrow (760 mm) by adhesion only.
*Electrified*: Yes, 800 V DC. Diesel traction is also deployed.
*Rolling stock*: Diesel locomotives: 1956-built Gebus No. VEL 1, 1967-built JW No. VHL 2, 1913-built AEG Nos. E 1 & E 2; and, 1957/63-built ÖAM/BBC Nos. E 3 & E 4.

*Contact details*: Steiermärkische Landesbahnen, Eggenberger Straße 20, A-8020 Graz. Telephone: 0316 812581-0 Fax: 0316 812581-81. E-Mail: office@stlb.at
*Website*: www.stlb.at and www.erlebnis-bahn-schiff.at
*Operating dates & tariff*: This is a freight only line. However, occasionally some tourist specials may run but information about such operations is scarce. Consult Steiermärkische Landesbahnen's timetables and tariffs at local StLB stations or on-line at www.stlb.at/fahrplan/fahrplan.htm or ask!
*Comments*: It was thought that Steiermärkische Landesbahnen may introduce passenger services again on the Mixnitz - St Erhard route after the success of special trains for the 90th anniversary of the line in 2003. By 2007 this had not materialised on a regular basis although there was a special excursion during the year on this line.

### 91 StLB Peggau-Übelbach route

The lovely church at Übelbach Vormarkt provides the backdrop for a morning (train) service from Peggau. Seen here is diesel railcar No. ET 15 with trailer ES 25 on 12th October, 2007. *Author*

*Location*: Peggau, 21 km north of Graz and 20 km south of Mixnitz.
*Michelin map reference*: S7.
*Nearest main line railway station*: Peggau-Deutschfeistritz on the Südbahn (line number 805 and timetable numbers 250 and 501)
*Operated by*: Steiermärkische Landesbahnen.
*Route*: From Peggau-Übelbach, a total distance of 10.25 km.
*Journey time*: 28 minutes.
*Gauge*: Standard by adhesion only.
*Electrified*: Yes, 15 kV AC 16.7 Hz.
*Rolling stock*: 1955-built SWS/MFO electric-powered railcars Nos. ET 14 (formerly BDe 4/4 91) & ET 15 (formerly BDe 4/4 593) with non-powered railcars Nos. ES 24 (ex-Bt 191) & ES 25 (ex-Bt 994). These vehicles were second-hand acquisitions from Switzerland and in October 2007 were still carrying SZU livery and BDe 4/4 & Bt

designations. (NB: SZU - Sihltal-Zürich-Uetliberg-Bahn - ran a tram-like service as part of the Zürich city S-Bahn network to the top of Ütliberg mountain).
*Contact details*: Steiermärkische Landesbahnen, Eggenberger Straße 20, A-8020 Graz. Telephone: 0316 812581-0 Fax: 0316 812581-81. E-Mail: office@stlb.at
*Website*: www.stlb.at
*Operating dates & Tariff*: Daily all year round - consult Steiermärkische Landesbahnen's timetables and tariffs at local stations or on-line at www.stlb.at/fahrplan/fahrplan.htm

## 92 Südbahn Kulturbahnhof

*Location*: Mürzzuschlag, 57 km south-west of Wiener-Neustadt and furthermost station from Vienna on the Semmeringbahn and 93 km north of Graz.
*Michelin map reference*: S6.
*Nearest main line railway station*: Mürzzuschlag on the Südbahn (line 805 and timetables 500 and 600).
*Operated by*: ÖBB.
*Gauge*: Standard.
*Traction*: Steam-, diesel- and electric-powered.
*Exhibits*: Preserved is the 1900-built former 'Neuberger' 2-6-0T steam locomotive No. 91.32, a 1943-built 2-10-0 JZ No. 33.329 and an early 1950s-built electric locomotive No. 1040.010-9. There is a fascinating collection of draisines and other departmental stock including an interesting ÖBB *kranwagen* No. 916824.
*Places to see*: A visit here can easily be combined with a trip to or on the Semmeringbahn (*see entry 50*) either by one's own arrangement or by joining in on the organized 'hiking trail'. The trail is 17.2 km in length and takes three to four hours under a local guide. It starts at the railway station at Semmering and goes to the station at Steinhaus a. Spital and terminates at the station at Mürzzuschlag. The level of difficulty is said to be 'easy and suitable for families'.

The former Yugoslavian Railways 1943-built 2-10-0 No. 33.329 displayed in the Kulturbahnhof museum. *Author*

*Contact details*: Südbahn Kulturbahnhof, Mürzzuschlag am Semmering, Heizhausgasse 2, A-8680 Mürzzuschlag. Telephone: 03852 2530 326 or 0664 910 820 1 Fax: 03852 2530 326. E-mail: info@kulturbahnhof.at
*Website*: www.kulturbahnhof.at (de en).
*Operating dates*: Daily from 1st May to 31st October from 1000 hours to 1700 hours and from 1st November to 31st March on Saturdays and Sundays from 1000 hours to 1600 hours.
*Tariff*: An adult ticket is €6.90 and for a child €2.50. A family ticket (2 adults and 1 child) costs €13.80. There are reductions for seniors and students as well as group discounts (2007).
*Comments*: Since June 2007 the museum at Mürzzuschlag has been extended with the opening of an additional exhibition hall - the Roundhouse. This roundhouse was originally built in the late 19th century and is classed as being of historical interest and is the last of its type in Austria, hence the preservation order made in 2006. The roundhouse contains the largest collection of Austrian rail trolleys (draisines) and motor rail vehicles which were in use on the Südbahn from 1838 to 1970. There are also some historical Südbahn locomotives. The large hall is available for special events and is particularly suitable where the theme is transportation and railways in particular. Mürzzuschlag is also an important ÖBB *Traktion* depot and there is always interesting rolling stock to see in the yard or passing through the main station opposite.

## 93 Thörlerbahn

*Location*: Kapfenberg, 5 km north-north-east of Bruck a.d.Mur and 62 km north of Graz.
*Michelin map reference*: R6.
*Nearest main line railway station*: Bruck a.d. Mur and also at Kapfenberg itself on the Südbahn (line number 805 and timetable numbers 500, 501 and 600).
*Operated by*: Steiermärkische Landesbahnen (StLB).
*Route*: From Kapfenberg to Au Seewiesen, a total distance of 22.7 km.
*Gauge*: Narrow (760 mm) by adhesion only for the maximum gradient of 2.5 per cent.
*Website*: www.passion-metrique.net/pagesweb/manifestations/Autriche/Thorlerbahn.html (fr) is well worth visiting to see the scenery of the beautiful Thörl valley and what is now left of the railway.
*History*: Operated by the Steiermark Landesbahnen (StLB) from 1st July, 1922 until its complete closure in 1999. The section between Seebach-Turnau and Au-Seewiesen was closed on the last day of 1964 and from Kapfenberg to Seebach-Turnau in 1998. A tourist service did continue to operate on the line but this also ended its life in 1999.
*Comments*: The line used to leave the ÖBB station at Kapfenberg on Semmering route and head due north up the gorges of the Thörl sharing its route along the way with the river - the Thörlerbach - and the main road. After the large village of Thörl (the former station is well-worth seeing) the route of the railway diverted due east passing picturesque meadows alongside another river - the Stübming, a tributary of the Thörl. A vast plateau is reached on which the old station of Seebach-Turnau, about 3 km from Turnau, can be found. Heading north for a further 6.5 km, the line reached the foot of the Col d'Alfenzer Seeberg at the terminus at Au Seewiesen. This railway unfortunately is discontinued and the route now serviced by buses operated

by Steiermärkische Landesbahnen. It is included here, however, as the route of the old railway and much of its infrastructure still exists, some in an extraordinary state of good repair. It will be of interest to those who care for Austrian railway history and to those who want to walk or cycle in outstandingly attractive countryside. Sadly, there are no plans, and unlikely ever to be so, to resurrect the railway for regular or tourist use.

## 94 Tramway Museum - Graz

*Location*: Graz, 193 km south-west of Vienna.
*Michelin map reference*: S7.
*Nearest main line railway station*: Graz on the Südbahn (line number 805 and timetable 501). The museum can be found at Mariatrosterstraße 204, at the end of Line 1 on the Graz Tram network.
*Operated by*: Grazer Verkehrsbetriebe (GVB).
*Exhibits*: An interesting collection of trams and buses dating back over 100 years. The exhibits include trams from the territory once ruled by the Austrian monarchy (the countries now of Hungary and Croatia, and the cities of Vienna and Innsbruck). The oldest item on display is a trailer built in 1873 by the 'Imperial Carriage Works' in Graz.
*Contact details*: More information about the museum and its activities can be obtained by contacting the administration at Grazer Verkehrsbetriebe, Steyrergasse 114-116, A-8010 Graz. Telephone: 0316 887 401 Fax: 0316 887 788. E-mail: l.steinhöfler@gstw.at or gvb.sonderverkehre@gstw.at
*Website*: www.gvb.at/home/unsere_dienstleistungen/tramwaymuseum.php (de) and also www.gstw.at/home/verkehr/unsere_dienstleistungen/tramwaymuseum.php (de).
*Opening dates*: From July to September on the following Sundays in 2007 - 1st, 15th & 29th July, 12th & 26th August and 9th & 16th September from 1400 hours to 1800 hours. (NB: The pattern of opening hours is likely to be followed in future years.)
*Tariff*: Adults are charged €1 for a visit with children under 15 being admitted free (2007).
*History*: In 1971 the then Building Officer for the City of Graz, Herr Erwin Franz, one of whose ancestors built the first electric tramway in Styria, founded the Graz Tramway Museum Association. The objectives of the Association were to collect, restore and maintain in working order historic trams. In 1983, the museum was established in its present home, the former Grazer Verkehrsbetriebe tram shed at Mariatrost built originally in 1898. In 1999, the museum celebrated the centenary of electric trams in Graz. In 2003, the City of Graz became 'The Cultural Capital of Europe'. To celebrate this important accolade the Grazer Verkehrsbetriebe re-established the former No. 2 tram line. Since then, trams have operated on this route which has since become known as 'The Culture Line' offering travellers the opportunity to see the historic sights of the city from the comfort of the tram.
*Comments*: The museum houses over 40 vintage trams drawn from Graz as well as elsewhere, numerous smaller exhibits such as tickets, ticket-cancelling machines, uniforms and many other items, including historic documents and photographs. There is also a model tramway. Overall the museum usefully charts the technical development and history of the Graz tramways from their beginnings in 1878 to the present day. It is well worth a visit.

## Tyrol (Tirol)

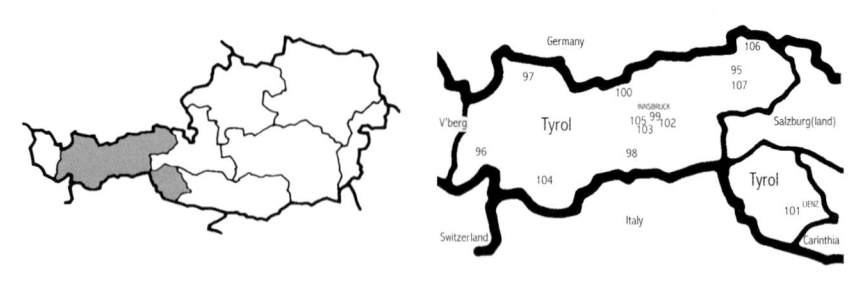

Tyrol is located in the west of Austria and is divided into North Tyrol and East Tyrol by a 20 km-wide strip of territory belonging to the state of Salzburg. The Tyrol has borders with the Austrian states of Salzburg, Vorarlberg and Carinthia and international frontiers with Germany, Switzerland and Italy. The highest mountain in the state and in Austria is the famous Großglockner (alt. 3,798 m) in the Hohen Tauern. The population of Tyrol is 698,472 (fifth greatest of the nine states in Austria) living in an area of 12,648 sq km (third greatest). The capital is Innsbruck situated in the River Inn valley where it meets the River Wipptal which runs down a valley from the Brenner Pass. Innsbruck is perhaps best known for its winter sports facilities with good skiing to be had at resorts such as Kitzbühel, Ischgl and St Anton. There are two universities in the capital, one being the Medical University which has a Europe-wide reputation for excellence, perhaps not unsurprisingly, in the treatment of skiing injuries. (NB: The Giselabahn begins and or ends its journey near Wörgl in Tyrol and Zell am See in the state of Salzburg. The entry for this route has been recorded in the latter state at *entry 63*.)

### 95 Achenseebahn

*Location*: Jenbach, 39 km east-north-east of Innsbruck.
*Michelin map reference*: H6.
*Nearest main line railway station*: Jenbach on the Westbahn (line number 601 and timetables 201 and 301).
*Operated by*: Achenseebahn AG.
*Route*: From the ÖBB Bahnhof at Jenbach to the bahnstation at Seespitz, a total distance of 6.78 km.
*Official line number*: None allocated.
*Journey time*: 45 minutes
*Gauge*: Narrow (metre) by adhesion combined with rack/cogwheel assistance based on the Riggenbach design.
*Traction*: Steam and diesel.
*Rolling stock*: Three steam locomotives were built at Floridsdorf (near Vienna) in 1899. They are No. 1 *Eben am Achensee*, No. 2 *Jenbach* and No. 3 *Achenkirch*. No. 4 was constructed in the mid-1990s with newly cast cylinders, replacement boiler and other parts recovered from an earlier steam locomotive No. '704'. There is also a 1948-built Schöma/Deutz diesel locomotive, No. D1.

No. 2 *Jenbach* running round its carriages in preparation for the next departure to Achensee on 27th June, 2007.   *Author*

**Places to see**: The railway links to the Achensee-Schiffahrt which operates sailings on the Achensee from Seespitz to Scholastika (Achenkirch), an outward or inward voyage each taking about 55 minutes. The sailings are linked to train arrival and departure times. Achensee-Schiffahrt GMBH operate the services and can be contacted by telephone on 05243 5253 0, by fax on 05243 6273 or by e-mail info@tirol-schiffahrt.at A website is maintained at www.tirol-schiffahrt.at (de) The Zillertalbahn also operates from Jenbach station (*see entry 107*).

**Contact details**: Achenseebahn AG, Bahnhofplatz 1-3, A-6200 Jenbach. Telephone: 05244 62243 Fax: 05244 62243-5. E-mail: info@achenseebahn.at

**Website**: www.achenseebahn.at (de en it fr es pt nl ru sv ja zh kr).

**Operating dates**: May to October with seven services each way with departures from Jenbach at 0840, 1015, 1055, 1210 1345, 1455 and 1645 hours and from the Achensee landing stage at 0930, 1110, 1225 1400, 1510, 1555 and 1736 hours. There are reduced services (three each way) in May and October. The rail services are timed to link with boat sailings on the Achensee.

**Tariff**: An adult single ticket costs €22 and a return €28. Children under-6 travel free and 6-15 year olds travel at half the adult fare. From May to October on Sundays those aged 60 years and over can enjoy a return journey for the price of a single ticket. There are reductions for groups of 10 persons or more. It is also possible to hire a train to celebrate a special event (2007).

**History**: In 1886, the k.k. Consul Theodor Friedrich Freiherr von Dreifuß sought a concession from Emperor Franz-Josef I to build a railway connecting Jenbach with the southern tip of the Achensee. The Emperor gave his consent in August 1888 and a month later the construction of the railway began. (Incidentally the Emperor's document awarding the consent partly handwritten is still in the possession of the owners.) It took less than a year to build the line to within 400 metres of the steam

124 THE ESSENTIAL GUIDE TO AUSTRIAN RAILWAYS AND TRAMWAYS

Two Class '1116s', seen here from the tiny village of Laguz near to Braz on 12th July, 2007, double head a service towards Innsbruck. *Author*

The Trisanna-Brucke viaduct on the late afternoon of 23rd October, 2007 with Railjet class '1216' No. 200-6 *Spirit of Wien* Heading a train for Bregenz. *Author*

boat landing stage. This stopping short of the landing stage was deliberate as the local monastery saw an opportunity to earn income by providing an escalator - a moving walkway - to transport luggage and other goods to and from the steam boats. The escalator ran until 1916 when it was removed by the military and tracks then extended to the landing stage. The line was officially opened in June 1889 and at that time used four Floridsdorf-built steam locomotives with inclined boilers capable of driving both the wheels and the cogs. These locomotives and their accompanying carriages were equipped with rack braking systems. Siemens experimented with electrification during 1913 as did Brown Boveri & Cie (BBC) in 1915. However, World War I disrupted further development and the overhead catenary was later dismantled. The railway has had an interesting history. The main purpose of the railway was originally to transport felled wood but during World War II it played a vital role in the transportation of 141,000 refugees escaping from the Allied bombings. Prisoners of war were also conveyed at various times on the trains. In 1950 the Tirolean Water Power Company (TIWAG) acquired the majority of the shares but much later, in 1979, these were distributed to the community authorities in the surrounding villages. Since that time Jenbach, Achenkirch and Eben have been the principal shareholders. (*Source: The Achenseebahn's excellent website.*)

*Comments*: This steam-worked rack railway from Jenbach to Achensee is well worth visiting and combining it with a trip on the next door's Zillertalbahn (*see entry 107*). The Achenseebahn truly believes in catering for the international traveller which is best evidenced perhaps by the fact that their website is written in 12 languages!

## 96 Arlbergbahn

*Location*: Innsbruck and Feldkirch.
*Michelin map reference*: G7 and A7 respectively.
*Nearest main line railway stations*: Innsbruck, Feldkirch and Bludenz.
*Operated by*: ÖBB.
*Official line numbers*: This is part of the Westbahn and here is allocated numbers 601 and 501.
*Timetable numbers*: 400 and 401.
*Route*: Feldkirch to Innsbruck, a total distance of 159 km. Twin-tracked main line except for the sections between Bludenz and the Arlberg tunnel and from the Kronburg tunnel to Ötztal which are both single track.
*Journey times*: Vary between 1 hour 46 minutes and 2 hours according to the service taken but it is planned for the connection to be much faster when the Railjet service using the new *Taurus* class '1216s' is introduced on a regular basis sometime in 2008.
*Gauge*: Standard by adhesion only.
*Electrified*: Yes, 15 kV AC 16.7Hz.
*Places to see*: There are many attractive sights on the route of this railway but not to be missed is the Trisanna-Brucke viaduct near Landeck.
*Website*: www.oebb.at/en
*Operating dates*: Daily all year round with regular services every two hours from early morning to late evening.
*Tariff*: An adult single 2nd class ticket from Innsbruck to Feldkirch costs €23.30 (2007).
*Comments*: An important feature on the line is the Arlberg tunnel near St Anton which is 10.648 km long. It was built in 1883 and electrified in 1923.

## 97 Außerfernbahn

A *die Bahn* railcar crossing the River Lechbrücke at Unterletzen travelling to Reutte on the Außerfernbahn on 23rd October 2007.  *Caroline Jones*

*Location*: Reutte, 93.4 km north-west of Innsbruck by road.
*Michelin map reference*: E6.
*Operated by*: ÖBB and Germany's die Bahn (DB).
*Official line number*: 552.
*Timetable numbers*: 410 (ÖBB) and 976 (DB).
*Route*: From Garmisch-Partenkirchen in Germany to Kempten also in Germany but through Austria (near Schober to near Schönbichl im Tirol), a total distance 30.4 km.
*Journey time*: 1 hour 22 minutes from Garmisch-Partenkirchen to Schönbichl im Tirol and 2 hours 45 minutes with one change to Reutte.
*Gauge*: Standard by adhesion only. Main line single track.
*Electrified*: Yes, but only between Garmisch-Partenkirchen and Reutte at 15 kV AC 16.7 Hz. From Reutte to Kempten services are provided by diesel traction.
*Places to see*: The peak of the highest mountain in Germany - the Zugspitze at an altitude of 2,962 m - is actually on the Austro-German border near to Griesen on the Außerfernbahn. The Zugspitze can be accessed by a rack railway from Garmisch-Partenkirchen (*see entry 162*).
*Website*: www.oebb.at/en or www.db.de/site/bahn/en/start.html
*Operating dates*: Daily all the year round with services every two hours.
*Tariff*: Not published on the website - enquire locally.
*Comments*: Garmisch-Partenkirchen is the terminus of the Karwendelbahn (also known as the Mittenwaldbahn) from Innsbruck (*see entry 100*). Running along the German border this part of the North Tyrol is not well served by many roads or railways. Having said that, it is a very attractive and popular area for summer pursuits such as hiking and cycling. Much of it being over 700 m in altitude the area is popular for winter sports, snow usually arriving early in the season.

## 98 Brennerbahn

*Location*: The Brenner Pass, 38 km south of Innsbruck.
*Michelin map reference*: G7.
*Nearest main line railway stations*: Innsbruck and Fortezza Franzensfeste in Italy.
*Operated by*: ÖBB and Trenitalia/Ferrovie dello Stato (FS) the Italian State Railways.
*Official line number*: 602 in Austria.
*Timetable numbers*: 300 (ÖBB) and 50 (Trenitalia).
*Route*: Innsbruck to Bozen (Bolzano) a total distance of 125 km and a distance of 240 km to Verona. Innsbruck to Fortezza Franzensfeste is 93 km.
*Journey time*: 36-40 minutes from Innsbruck to the Brenner station, 1 hour 22 minutes to Fortezza and 3 hours 33 minutes to Verona.
*Gauge*: Standard by adhesion only. Main line - twin track.
*Electrified*: Yes, 15 kV AC 16.7 Hz in Austria and 3000 V DC in Italy.
*Website*: www.oebb.at/en
*Operating dates*: Daily all year round with frequent services running about every half-hour.
*Tariff*: An adult 2nd class single ticket without a vehicle from Innsbruck to the Brenner station is €6.60 (2007).
*Comments*: The Brenner Pass (alt. 1,375 m) is the lowest route across the Alps and the only one by a main railway line in the open. However, that will change when eventually the Brenner Base tunnel is opened in due course. It is anticipated that this tunnel between Innsbruck and Fortezza will be 56.5 km making it the longest in the world. The second longest will then be the 1988-built Seikan tunnel in Japan. This route is always very busy moving heavy goods vehicles (HGVs) to and from Innsbruck. The cost of an ascent or descent for an HGV is about €150. Over the

The Brennerbahn at the St Jodok loop on 26th June, 2007 with, on the left, an auto-carrying train loaded with heavy goods vehicles heading for the Brenner Pass and on the right a passenger train travelling down to Innsbruck. *Author*

Snow came early on the Brenner Pass in 2007. Here on 20th October, No. 1144 202 leaves Brenner for Innsbruck fully loaded with heavy goods vehicles. The drivers are carried in the front passenger carriage and not in their vehicles. *Author*

Bombardier-built tram No. 53 departs the depot at Wilthen on 20th October, 2007. *Author*

relatively short distance of 38 km from Innsbruck to the Pass the altitude rises 789 m (2,564 feet) making for a steep gradient for road vehicles to travel. The ascent is further compounded by serious weather problems for much of the year. In 2006 the number of trucks transported by rail on the Brenner route more than doubled thus achieving a rate of use of about 70 per cent of capacity.

**99 Innsbruck Tramways [IVB]**

*Location*: Innsbruck.
*Michelin map reference*: G7.
*Nearest main line railway station*: Innsbruck on the Westbahn (line number 601 and timetable numbers 201 and 300).
*Operated by*: Innsbrucker Verkehrsbetriebe und Stubaitalbahn GmbH.
*Route*: There are three city tram line routes, which, with the former Stubaitalbahn, provide a network totalling 35.8 km.
*Journey time*: Vary according to the journey taken.
*Gauge*: Narrow (metre) by adhesion only.
*Traction*: Electric-powered at 600V DC.
*Rolling stock*: 11 x Series 31 two-section cars built by Duewag/Kiepe in 1957 and between 1962-3 again for Bielefeld in North-Rhine - Wesphalia Nos. 31 and 33 - 42, Series 51 three-section cars also built by Duewag/Kiepe between 1962-3 for Bielefeld Nos. 51 - 53, Series 71 two-section cars built by Lohner/Kiepe in between 1966-7 and delivered new to Innsbruck Nos. 71 - 77 (*source: Platform 5*).
*Places to see*: The interesting city of Innsbruck.
*Website*: www.ivb.at
*Operating dates*: Daily services throughout the year - consult local timetables.
*Tariff*: Local fare structure applies.
*Comments*: The depot is located at Wilthen. The livery is red and beige although many are now gaily coloured with advertising material. The Tiroler Museum safeguards a large collection of trams and related material (*see entry 105*).

**100 Karwendelbahn** also known as the **Mittenwaldbahn**

*Location*: Innsbruck in the heart of the Tyrol in Western Austria.
*Michelin map reference*: G7.
*Nearest main line railway station*: Innsbruck on the Westbahn (line number 601 and timetable numbers 201 300).
*Operated by*: ÖBB and Germany's *die Bahn*.
*Official line number*: 551.
*Timetable number*: 410.
*Route*: Innsbruck to Garmisch-Partenkirchen via Scharnitz (last station in Austria before the German border) a total distance of 60 km. The route continues on to Munich.
*Journey time*: Innsbruck to Scharnitz takes 49 minutes and on to Garmisch-Partenkirchen in a total of 1 hour 21 minutes.
*Gauge*: Standard by adhesion only. Main line - single track.
*Electrified*: Yes, 15 kV AC 16.7 Hz with no change of type of voltage supply when entering into Germany.

A *die (Deutsche) Bahn* service crossing a bridge near Kranebitten on its way to Innsbruck on 21st October, 2007. *Author*

Lienz Bahnhof in the South Tyrol is the home to Verein der Eisenbahn Freunde-Lienz. Here at the bahnhof on 17th October, 2007 is the multi voltage class '1216' No. 148. *Author*

*Places to see*: Roßhutte-Bahn at Seefeld (*see entry 157*).
*Website*: www.oebb.at/en
*Operating dates*: Daily all year round with services every two hours.
*Tariff*: An adult 2nd class single ticket to Scharnitz is €6.60 (2007).
*Comments*: Connects Innsbruck to the Außerfernbahn at Garmisch-Partenkirchen (*see entry 97*).

## 101  Lienz - Verein der Eisenbahnfreunde

*Location*: Lienz, 107 km west of Villach and 177 km south-west of Innsbruck.
*Michelin map reference*: K8.
*Nearest main line railway station*: Lienz on the Drautalbahn (line number 707 and timetable number 223).
*Operated by*: Verein der Eisenbahnfreunde.
*Gauge*: Standard and narrow gauge (760 mm).
*Preserved material*: Steam- and electric-powered traction some of which is in operational order and used on excursions from time to time including: steam locomotive standard gauge No. 52.3816 (ex-ÖBB and built in 1944) and 760 mm gauge Sulm B1 0-6-0T No. 290c (built 1907). Preserved electric locomotives include Nos. 1020.018 (built 1940), 1020.023 (also built 1940), 1161.20 (also built 1940) and 1245.522 (built 1938). Diesel locomotive No 2045.015 (built 1954) is also safeguarded together with a variety of other material from ÖBB, Linzer Lokalbahn and others.
*Places to see*: It is not far from Lienz to reach the Großglockner, Austria's highest mountain.
*Contact details*: Verein der Eisenbahnfreunde, Bahnhofsplatz 10 (Heizhaus), 9900 Lienz. Telephone: 04852 64457.
*Website*: See www.privat-bahn.de/Lienzer_Eisenbahnfreunde.html

## 102  Mittelgebirgsbahn

*Location*: Innsbruck.
*Michelin map reference*: G7.
*Nearest main line railway station*: Innsbruck on the Westbahn (line number 601 and timetable numbers 201 and 300).
*Operated by*: Innsbrucker Verkehrsbetriebe (IVB).
*Route*: From the southern side of Innsbruck to the popular skiing and hiking resort of Igls, a total distance of 8.3 km.
*Journey time*: 25 minutes.
*Gauge*: Narrow (metre) by adhesion only.
*Electrified*: Yes, 800 V DC.
*Rolling stock*: 31 series 2-section cars, 51 series 3-section cars and 71 series 2-section cars (*source: Platform 5*).
*Places to see*: Kofel Cable Car operates from Igls to the summit of Patscherkofel (2,250m) where one can enjoy the Jochleitensteig circular hiking route (1 hour 30 minutes).
*Contact details*: Innsbrucker Verkehrsbetriebe und Stubaitalbahn GmbH, Pastorstraße 5, A-6010 Innsbruck. Telephone: 0512-5307-0.
*Website*: www.ivb.at (de en).

132  THE ESSENTIAL GUIDE TO AUSTRIAN RAILWAYS AND TRAMWAYS

On it way up to Igls high above Innsbruck on 26th June, 2007 is tram No. 52 which was built between 1962 and 1963. The tram is ex-Bielefeld, Eastern Westphalia. *Author*

The Stubaitalbahn is part of the Innsbruck tram service (IVB). Pictured here is 1960/61-built Tram No. 88 which, when it previously operated in Bielefeld (Westphalia), carried the number 68/802. *Author*

*Operating dates*: Daily all the year round with frequent services leaving Innsbruck 10 minutes past the hour and leaving Igls at 15 minutes before the hour.
*Tariff*: Local fare structure applies.
*History*: The Mittelgebirgsbahn was originally opened to the public in the mid-summer of 1900. From the outset and for the following 36 years the trains were steam-hauled using Krauss-built 0-6-2T tank engines. Four of the carriages used during that time have been preserved - Nos. 104, 105, 108 and 111 - and all can be seen in the Tiroler Museumsbahnen (*see entry 105*) which is located in the former Stubaitalbahn depot or even better occasionally on tracks in the summer months on local excursions. Steam came to an end when the line was electrified in June 1936 adopting an 800 V DC power supply. The line was subsequently amalgamated into the Innsbruck Tramways (IVB) network as Route 6 (*see entry 99*). By the mid-1990s the line had become under-utilised and therefore unprofitable leading to a threat of closure. Fortunately, there was reprieve for three years but at the cost of a reduced service effectively denying a connection with the nearby Hungerburgbahn funicular (*see entry 155*). Since then, there has been another reprieve which has been rewarded with an increase in passenger traffic especially with museum excursions operating during the summer holidays.
*Comments*: Being part of the Innsbruck Tramways it is also linked to the Tiroler Museumsbahnen (*see entry 105*).

## 103 Stubaitalbahn

*Location*: Innsbruck.
*Michelin map reference*: G7.
*Nearest main line railway station*: Innsbruck on the Westbahn (line number 601 and timetable numbers 201 and 300).
*Operated by*: Innsbrucker Verkehrsbetriebe.
*Route*: From Innsbruck to Fulpmes, a total distance of 18.2 km.
*Journey time*: 60 minutes.
*Gauge*: Narrow (metre) by adhesion only. Local line - single track.
*Electrified*: Yes, 800 V DC.
*Rolling stock*: Series 81 three-section cars built jointly by Duewag and the electric parts are believed by Kiepe in 1960-1 for Bielefeld and Hagen in Germany, Nos. 81 (formerly 89) and 82 - 88 came to the Stubaitalbahn between 1976 and 1981 (*source: Platform 5*).
*Contact details*: Innsbrucker Verkehrsbetriebe und Stubaitalbahn GmbH, Pastorstraße 5, A-6010 Innsbruck
Telephone: 0512-5307-0.
*Website*: www.ivb.at (en de) see also www.stubai-tal.at/Bahn.htm (de).
*Operating dates*: Daily all year round with frequent services - consult the local timetable.
*Tariff*: Local fare structure applies.
*History*: Absorbed into the Innsbruck Tramway services in 1997.
*Comments*: Innsbrucker Verkehrsbetriebe (*see entry 99*) operate this service as well as the tram service Innsbruck-Igls formerly known as the Mittelgebirgsbahn (*see previous entry*).

A view of the traffic-free village of Serfaus with the entrance to the 'underground' by the tower on the right. *Author*

1907-built ex Zurich tram No. 19 is used frequently for the Tiroler museum excursions around the city centre of Innsbruck. It was photographed here on 20th October, 2007 having just passed St Anne's Column on the Maria-Theresien Strasse and heading towards Herzog Friedrich Strasse where the famous landmark of the city can be found, the Goldenes Dachl. *Author*

## 104 Serfauser Alpen U-bahn also known as Dorfbahn Serfaus

*Location*: Serfaus, 28 km south of Landeck and 94 km west-south-west of Innsbruck.
*Michelin Map reference*: D7.
*Nearest main line railway station*: Landeck on the Westbahn (line number 601 and timetable number 400).
*Operated by*: Dorfbahn Serfaus.
*Route*: Seilbahn (cable car) to Parkplatz (car park) with stops at Raika (bank) and Kirche (Church), a total distance of 1,280 m (4199.5 feet). The maximum gradient is 5.3 per cent.
*Journey time*: 7 minutes.
*Contact details*: Serfaus-Fiss-Ladis Marketing GmbH, Untere Dorfstraße 13, A-6534 Serfaus. Telephone: 05476 6239 Fax: 05476 6813. E-mail: info@serfaus-fiss-ladis.at
*Website*: www.serfaus-fiss-ladis.at
*Operating dates*: All year round with services between 0800 hours and 1800 hours in winter and 0930 hours and 1730 hours in summer.
*Tariff*: Free of charge (2007).
*Comments*: The Dorfbahn Serfaus is a unique underground railway. The name literally means Serfaus Village Railway. Serfaus is a busy Tyroleon ski resort which in the winter months caters for large numbers of skiers. The ski slopes are accessed by a cable car as well as a gondola lift. The lower ski stations are located at the far end of the village's main street with the Dorfbahn Serfaus operating a shuttle service to and from the large car park at the other end, the only arrival point to the village from Landeck and elsewehere. This railway allows the narrow village streets to be car-free, a situation similar to that which applies in Zermatt in Switzerland. The line, built in 1985 by the Freissler-Otis company, consists of a single, 1,280 m (4,199.5 ft) long, one-track line, with a single train operating on a regular shuttle basis. The train comprises two cars which are carried on an air cushion and moved by a funicular haulage system. The tunnel is 10 feet wide and 11 feet high. The train can carry up to 270 people at any one time and travels at speeds of up to 40 kmh (25 mph).

## 105 Tiroler Museumsbahnen

*Location*: Innsbruck.
*Michelin map reference*: G7.
*Nearest main line railway station*: Innsbruck Hauptbahnhof on the Westbahn (line number 601 and timetables 201, 300 and 400).
*Operated by*: Innsbrucker Verkehrsbetriebe.
*Route*: A tour of the city centre is included in the visit to the museum. The 'oldtimer' trams leave the museum at 1100, 1300 and 1500 hours and return just under an hour later to the museum and depot. It is possible to leave the tram anywhere on the route. This is an enjoyable (and cheap) way of seeing the city before later discovering it on foot.
*Journey time*: 50 minutes.
*Gauge*: Narrow (metre) by adhesion only.
*Electrified*: Yes, 600 V DC.
*Exhibits*: The following trams originally delivered to Lokalbahn Innsbruck-Hall in Tirol (LBIHTiT) have been preserved: 1891-built Nos. 120 and 124 (not in service); 1892-built No. 16 (a superb open carriage in service); a 1905-built No. 54 (in service on loan from Zeughaus Ibk); 1906-built Nos. 142 (out of service) and 143 (in service); 1909-built Nos. 53 (not restored), 1 (in service), 4 (in the course of restoration), SK100 (snow-sweeping tram on loan from Zeughaus Ibk but not in service) and 1907-17-built No. 147 (in service).

Trams originally delivered to Innsbrucker Mittelgebirgsbahn are: 1900-built Nos. 104 (in service), 105 (in service) and 111 (in service); 1900-36-built No. 262 (an overhead wire maintenance vehicle in service) and a 1904-built baggage car No. 263 (not in service). The following trams originally delivered to Innsbrucker Verkehrsbetriebe (IVB) and preserved are: a 1942-built tram-motorcar No. 60 in the course of restoration; a 1907/55 ex-Zurich tram No. 19 and ready for service and a 1960-built 4-axle tramcar No. 61 and ready for service. The following trams originally delivered to the Stubaitalbahn and preserved are: 1904-built trams Nos. 11 (in course of restoration) and 2 (not in service); 1905-built No. 4 (not in service but used as the Society's library); 1905-65 carriage No. 14 (not in service); 1904-built goods wagons Nos. 22 & 22 (both in service); and, 1905-built No. 34 (in the process of restoration). The following tram originally delivered to the Rittnerbahn (Bozen in Italy) and preserved is: a 1909-built 2-axle tram No. Lok 4 ready for service and on loan from Zeughaus Ibk. (*Source: Tiroler Museum.*)

*Places to see*: The excellent glass exhibition at the Swarovski™ shop in the city centre is well worth a visit (NB: Factory tours are no longer possible - see http://kristallwelten.swarovski.com ).

*Contact details*: Innsbrucker Verkehrsbetriebe und Stubaitalbahn GmbH, Pastorstraße 5, A-6010 Innsbruck. Telephone: 0512 3445-71.

*Website*: www.tmb.at (de en fr it) http://members.aon.at/tmb/ (de en fr it).

*Opening dates*: beginning of May to the end of October on Saturdays only from 0900 hours to 1700 hours.

*Tariff*: Adults €3 and children (6-14 years) €1.50 (2007). The entry ticket also includes a tour of the city centre on an 'oldtimer' tram. It is possible to rent a tram exclusively for a special event.

*History*: The museum was founded in 1983 as a non-profit making society. It set its goals to collect, restore and preserve trams and other light railway vehicles, to use the trams for tours from time to time, to safeguard historical documentation and to make all this material accessible to the general public for educational and cultural purposes. One of the main motivating factors which drove enthusiasts to establish the society was the fact that Stubaitalbahn (*see entry 103*) had chosen in 1983 to convert its electricity supply from 3000 V AC 50Hz to 850 V DC which meant that the former trams could no longer be used because of the differing power supply. This was not the only obstruction for it was found that the length of the old vehicles and their distance between axles had the effect of damaging the track. Had the society not been established this important collection of old trams would have been scrapped and lost forever.

*Comments*: This excellent museum engaged in the preservation of historic trams can be found in the former Stubaitalbahnhof in Innsbruck on 4, Pater-Reinisch-Weg next to Innsbruck Trams' (IVB) current main depot. The workshop is also accessible. The society also publishes an informative journal but only in German.

### 106 Wachtl-Express

*Location*: Kiefersfelden, in Bavaria, Germany on the border with Austria's Tyrol region. Kiefersfelden is 85 km north-east of Innsbruck and 104 km driving distance west of Salzburg.

*Michelin map reference*: I6.

*Nearest main line railway station*: Kufstein on the Westbahn (line number 602 and timetable 300) and Kiefersfelden in Bavaria.

*Operated by*: Rohrdorfer Cement Company which is part of the Heidelberg Cement Group.

*Route*: From Kiefersfelden, Bavaria to Thiersee-Wachtl, Tirol, a total distance of 5 km.
*Journey time*: 20 minutes.
*Gauge*: Narrow (900 mm) by adhesion only.
*Electrified*: Yes, 1200 V DC.
*Rolling stock*: Two Krokodil-type electric-powered locomotives built in 1929 and 1930 and three 1912-constructed passenger carriages obtained from the Wendelsteinbahn in Brannenburg, 18 km to the north of Kiefersfelden.
*Places to see*: The Wendelsteinbahn just over the border in Germany is another railway worth visiting if one is in this area - see www.wendelsteinbahn.de (de).
*Contact details*: 'Wachtl-Express', Dorfstraat 23, D-83088 Kiefersfelden and Pendlingstr. 6, D-83088 Kiefersfelden, Telephone: 08033 3048-13 or 08033 9765-27 Fax: 08033 9765-44. E-mail: info@kiefersfelden.de
*Website*: www.kiefersfelden.de/freizeit/wachtl.php (de).
*Operating dates*: Eight weekends (until recently seven) are arranged during the summer for passenger tourist traffic i.e. in 2007 - 30th June-1st July, 14th-15th July, 28th-29th July, 11th-12th August, 25th-26th August, 8th-9th September, 22nd-23rd September and 6th-7th October. Trains leave Kiefersfelden at 1420 hours and 1620 hours and return from Wachtl/Tirol at 1510 hours and 1710 hours. On the Sundays only there is an extra service leaving Kiefersfelden at 1220 hours and returning from Wachtl/Tirol at 1310 hours. These dates and times were those for the time of the research but the schedule of operating dates and times is likely to be repeated in future years.
*Tariff*: An adult single ticket is €3 and €5 with children (6-14 years) travelling at half-price. A family return ticket costs €12 (2007).
*History*: The association which operates this tourist service with the blessing and support of the cement company and the local government authority was formed in 1994. It began operations the same year.
*Comments:* This line is an 'international' industrial railway used daily with between 12 and 14 journeys transporting quarried limestone to the Kiefersfelden works for the production of cement. The tourist service is known locally in the German language as *Nostalgie Express Wachtlbahn*.

## 107 Zillertalbahn

*Location*: Jenbach, 39 km north-east of Innsbruck.
*Michelin map reference*: H6.
*Nearest main line railway station*: Jenbach on the Westbahn (line number 601 and timetable numbers 201 & 300).
*Operated by*: Zillertaler Verkehrsbetriebe AG.
*Official line number*: None allocated.
*Timetable number*: 310
*Route*: Jenbach to Mayrhofen, a total distance of 31.7 km.
*Journey time*: 56 minutes for general services and 1 hour 20 minutes for steam-hauled services.
*Gauge*: Narrow (760 mm) by adhesion only for very little gradient over the 31 km.
*Electrified*: No, but operates diesel-powered modern railcars as well as steam and diesel locomotives.
*Rolling stock*: Five steam locomotives: 1900-built Krauss Linz No. 2 *Zillertal*, 1902-built Krauss Linz No. 3 *Tirol*, 1909-built Krauss Linz No. 4 (belonging to Club 760), 1930-built Krauss Linz No. 5 *Gerlos* and 1916-built Krauss München No. 6 *Hobbylok*

The Zillertalbahn's 1902-built Krauss (Linz) No. 3 *Tirol* has not long crossed the River Ziller and heading for Zell am Ziller on 27th June, 2007. *Author*

Steam is not used exclusively on the Zillertalbahn. Regular services are delivered using diesel-powered VT railcars. Here, VT4, named *Raimund Rainer* leads the way near Gagering towards Mayrhofen on 27th June, 2007.  *Author*

There are six diesel locomotives Nos. 8-13; six powered railcars Nos. VT3-VT8 (VT4 is named *Raimund Rainer* and VT5 *Adolf Trappmair*); two non-powered railcars Nos. VS3-VS4; and, one wagon BD No. 4/49. One can drive to the Krimml Falls from the Zell am Zeller along the Gerlos valley and on to the Pinzgauerbahn (*see entry 65*).
**Places to see**: The Achenseebahn also operates from Jenbach station (*see entry 95*).
**Contact details**: Zillertaler Verkehrsbetriebe AG, Austrasse 1, Jenbach A-6200. Telephone: 05244 606 0 Fax: 05244 606 39. E-mail: office@zillertalbahn.at
**Website**: www.zillertalbahn.at
**Operating dates**: General rail and bus services run all the year round from 0605 hours to 2105 hours from Jenbach to Mayrhofen and from 0530 hours to 1910 hours from Mayrhofen to Jenbach. Morning steam-hauled services operate over Easter and from 5th May running daily until 21st October leaving Jenbach at 1047 hours and returning from Mayrhofen at 1248 hours. Afternoon steam-hauled services operate from 2nd June to 9th September leaving Jenbach at 1516 hours and returning from Mayrhofen at 1705 hours. Some other steam services run at Christmas and in the winter months - consult the website. The above dates are for 2007 but operating dates and timetables for future years are expected to follow a similar pattern.
**Tariff**: Fares for steam-hauled trips vary according to length of journey taken. The maximum adult single fare for the journey from Jenbach to Mayrhofen is €10.70 with a return ticket costing €15.50 (2007). (NB: Verkehrsverbund Tirol (VVT) the Tirolean Travel Network links 21 transport providers in the region and offers favourable tariffs for train and bus services. However, VVT network tickets are not valid on the Nostalgic Steam Trains.)
**History**: The line first opened to traffic on 31st July, 1902.
**Comments**: Provides hourly general services between Jenbach and Mayrhofen. Steam trains operate in the summer months.

## Upper Austria (Oberösterreich)

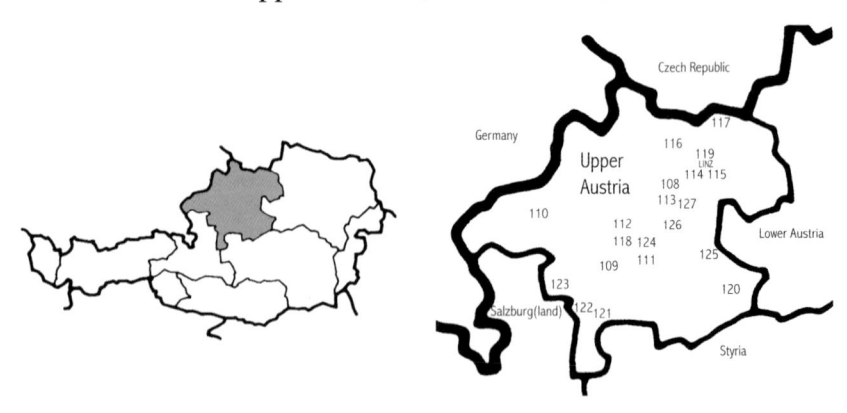

Upper Austria is located north of the centre in Austria and is divided into four regions: Hausruckviertel, Innviertel, Mühlviertel and Traunviertel and further divided into 15 districts and three *statutarstädte* (cities declared by statute) of Linz, Wels and Steyr. Upper Austria has borders with the other Austrian states of Lower Austria, Styria, and Salzburg and international frontiers with Germany and the Czech Republic. It has a geographical area of 11,980 sq. km making it the fourth largest of Austria's nine states and a population of 1.4 million (third largest). Its capital is Linz which is the third largest city in Austria. Adolf Hitler, born nearby, saw the city as his home town.

### 108 Almtalbahn

*Location*: Wels, 34 km south-west of Linz.
*Michelin map reference*: O4.
*Nearest main line railway station*: Wels on the Westbahn (line number 401 and timetable number 101).
*Operated by*: ÖBB.
*Official line number*: 352.
*Timetable number*: 153.
*Route*: From Wels to Grünau im Amtal via Sattledt, Pettenbach and Steinbachbrücke, a total distance of 42 km.
*Journey time*: 1 hour 3 minutes.
*Gauge*: Standard by adhesion only. Local line - single track.
*Electrified*: No.
*Website*: www.oebb.at/en
*Operating dates*: Daily throughout the year with services every two hours.
*Tariff*: A '1-PLUS-Freizeit' adult 2nd class single ticket costs €9.30 (2007).

## UPPER AUSTRIA (OBERÖSTERREICH)

### 109 Attergaubahn

ET 26 No. 111 having left St Georgen in Attersee is heading down to Attersee on 28th June, 2007.
*Caroline Jones*

*Location*: Vöcklamarkt, 54 km north-east of Salzburg and 88 km south-west of Linz.
*Michelin map reference*: M5.
*Nearest main line railway station*: Vöcklamarkt ÖBB station on the Westbahn (line number 401 and timetable number 101).
*Operated by*: Stern & Hafferl.
*Official line number*: None allocated.
*Route*: Attersee to Vöcklamarkt via St Georgen im Attergau, a total distance of 13.3 km on a maximum gradient of 4.7 per cent.
*Journey time*: 28 minutes.
*Gauge*: Narrow (metre) by adhesion only. Local line - single track.
*Electrified*: Yes, 750 V DC.
*Rolling stock*: A 1913-built electric-powered railcar ET 20 No. 104. Also operated are ET26s Nos. 109, 110, 111 and 112; a special children's car Bi 26 No. 201 and a 1914-built buffet car which are all used in summer to provide the *Nostalgie* service.
*Places to see*: Enjoy a 'cruise' on Attersee's lake operated by Stern und Hafferl (*see website*).
*Contact details*: Stern & Hafferl Verkehrsgesellschaft m.b.H., Kuferzeile 32, A-4810 Gmunden. Telephone: 07612 795  200 Fax: 07612  795  202. E-mail: sekretariat@stern-verkehr.at The telephone number for the bahnhof at Attersee is 07666 7805 and at St Georgen im Attergau is 07667 6264.
*Website*: www.stern-verkehr.at/sverkehr/de
*Operating dates*: From about 1st May to 9th September each year with 12 daily services in each direction from about 0600 hours to 1845 hours.
*Tariff*: Local fare structure applies.
*History*: The concession to build this railway was granted in April 1912 and the line was opened on 14th January, 1913.
*Comments*: Stern & Hafferl also operate ships on the lake from Weyregg to Schörfling, Seewalchen and Attersee.

**110 Club Florianerbahn** also known as the **Museum-tram St Florian**

*Location*: St Florian, 17 km south-east of Linz.
*Michelin map reference*: P4.
*Nearest main line railway station*: Asten-St Florian on Westbahn (line number 401 and timetable number 100).
*Operated by*: Club Florianerbahn (CFB).
*Route*: From Markt St Florian to Pichling, a total distance of 4.7 km.
*Journey time*: Not known.
*Gauge*: Narrow (900mm) by adhesion only.
*Electrified*: Yes, 600 V DC.
*Rolling stock*: The depot is on a stretch of line in St Florian where a small historic collection is retained. Safeguarded are: 1913-built trams Nos. EM 1, EM 2 and EM 3 all originally used locally; 1907-built No. TW 7 from Gmunden Tramway; 1951-built No. TW11 ex-Linz; 1953-built TW XIII ex-Postlingbergbahn; 1920-built Nos. 16 & 17 ex-Linz; Nos. TW 21 (1956), TW 30 (1958), TW (1961) and TW 41 (1914) all ex-Linz. Also retained is a 1977 (rebuilt 1997) draisine and 1913-built carriages Nos. EP 1, EP 2, EP 3, EP 4 and EP 5 all previously operated locally. Also retained is a 1903-built goods wagon formerly on the Stubaitalbahn.
*Places to see*: Visit the baroque abbey - *Stift St Florian* - built in 1686 where the composer Anton Bruckner gained fame and where he is now buried. The magnificent ceiling paintings in the abbey - the *Marmorsaal* - should not be missed.
*Contact details*: Club Florianerbahn, Alter Bahnhof, St Florian A-4490. Telephone: 0664 820 84 81.
*Website*: www.florianerbahn.at (de).
*Operating dates*: From May to September on Sundays but the service is believed to have been suspended in 2007.
*Tariff*: Not declared.
*History*: The Florianerbahn originally opened in 1887 as an independent tramway serving small villages to the south-west of Linz. The line, ran for many years by Stern und Hafferl (*see entry 124*) was never very profitable, a difficulty compounded by improvements to the local road network in the 1960s which brought better bus services. The line was finally closed to passenger traffic on the last day of 1973. The track fortunately was not removed at that time which allowed enthusiasts in 1982 to re-open part of the route, i.e. from St Florian to Pichling See. It has always been the intention, however, to re-connect Pichling See with Ebelsburg and thus be able to link with the modern Linz tramway network, but at the time of writing that looks a long way off.
*Comments*: The Museumsbahn operations are believed to be suspended, principally because large sections of the route are not accessible or in a poor state of repair. However, the Club Florianerbahn continues to offer technical assistance to other tramway systems in Europe, including planning and maintenance services. Whether and when the tram operations will be resumed is unclear; however, on a positive note, the museum's collection at St Florian can be viewed by prior appointment. Club Florianerbahn has strong links with nearby ÖGEG (*see entry 118*).

## 111 Gmunden Tramway (Straßenbahn)

*Location*: Gmunden, 73 km south-west of Linz.
*Michelin map reference*: N5.
*Nearest main line railway station*: Gmunden on the Salzkammergutbahn (line number 306 and timetable number 170).
*Operated by*: Stern & Hafferl.
*Route*: From the station by the Traunsee (Franz-Josef Platz) up the hill to Gmunden station (Hauptbahnhof), a total distance of 2.33 km.
*Journey time*: 10 minutes
*Gauge*: Narrow (metre) by adhesion only on a maximum gradient of 10 per cent.
*Electrified*: Yes, 600 V DC.
*Rolling stock*: *Nostalgie* stock comprises: a 1911-built closed tram No. GM 5 *Jugendstiltriebwagen* offering 32 seats and 18 standing, and a second tram, No. 100, which is owned by Gmunden Municipal authorities. It is described as an open-sided 'toast-rack' vehicle built by Graz Lokomotiv in 1898 for the Pöstlingbergbahn (*see entry 119*). It was bought by the Gmunden authorities in 1995 to celebrate the tramway's 100th anniversary. Three other trams deliver general services all built by Lohner - No. 8 (1962) and Nos. 9 & 10 (built 1951-2). The tram livery is red and cream and one does carry the ubiquitous McDonald's advertising.
*Contact details*: Stern & Hafferl Verkehrsgesellschaft m.b.H., Kuferzeile 32, A-4810 Gmunden, Telephone: 07612 795-200 Fax: 07612 795-202.
*Website*: www.stern-verkehr.at/sverkehr/
*Operating dates*: Daily all year round with services every half-hour in each direction from about 0600 hours to about 2100 hours. *Nostalgie* services are also run on seven Saturdays during the year. The 2007 dates were: 17th February, 18th March, 11th, 25th & 26th August, 8th and 15th December. Trams operated on these dates were at 1400, 1500, 1600, 1700 and 1800 hours. Dates and times are likely to be similar in future years.

Tram No. 8 'McDonald's' having a wash down at the Gmunden tram depot on 29th June, 2007. *Author*

*Gisela* operated by Stern and Hafferl on the Attersee seen here at Gmunden on 29th June, 2007.
*Author*

ÖGEG's 1935-built steam locomotive No. 638.1301 approaching Ampflwang on 1st July, 2007.
*Author*

*Tariff*: For normal tram services an adult single is €1.60 (a child €0.80), an individual daily ticket is €2.50 and a family day ticket €3 (2007).
*History*: The tramway opened on 13th August, 1894.
*Comments*: Even though more than 300,000 passengers use the service annually, it is said to be the smallest tramway service in the world. Stern & Hafferl also operate pleasure boat cruises on the nearby Traunsee.
*Further reading*: *The Railways of Stern und Hafferl GmbH* published by the UK's Austrian Railway Group, 2006.


## 112 Kohlebahn

*Location*: Ampflwang, 80 km south-west of Linz.
*Michelin map reference*: M4.
*Nearest main line railway station*: Timelkam on the Westbahn (line number 401 and timetable number 101).
*Operated by*: ÖGEG.
*Route*: From Ampflwang to Timelkam, a total distance of 10.4 km.
*Journey time*: 25 minutes.
*Gauge*: Standard by adhesion only.
*Electrified*: No, steam- and diesel-powered.
*Rolling stock*: Listed on the entry for ÖGEG (*see entry 118*).
*Things to do*: Ampflwang has developed the reputation as an equestrian centre and the whole village is dedicated to the sport all year round. There will be no difficulty for the novice or the experienced rider to find activities to suit.
*Contact details*: Museumsbahn Ampflwang-Timelkam, A-4843 Ampflwang. Telephone: 0664 5087 664 or 0664 4344 666 on Mondays-Fridays from 1900 hours to 2100 hours. E-mail: ampflwang@oegeg.at
*Website*: www.oegeg.at (de).
*Operating dates*: From July to September at weekends. The museum at Ampflwang is open from 1st April to 31st October on Wednesdays to Saturdays from 1000 hours to 1700 hours. These hours are extended from 0900 hours to 1800 hours in July, August and the first week in September.
*Tariff*: Entry to the museum only is €7 for an adult and €3 for a child (6-15 years). A return trip on the Kohlebahn is €10 for an adult and €5 for a child. A single trip on the Kohlebahn is €6 for an adult and €3 for a child. A combined ticket for the museum and a return journey on the train is €14 for an adult and €6 for a child. There are discounts for families and for groups (2007).
*History*: ÖGEG has been in existence since 1974.
*Comments*: Is also known as Eisenbahnmuseum Ampflwang. The depot and museum at Ampflwang is a railway enthusiast's mecca and should not be missed. The newly revised facilities include a shop and a restaurant.


## 113 Lambach-Haag (LH) also referred to as **Haager-Lies**

*Location*: Lambach, 92 km north-east of Salzburg and 50 km south-west of Linz.
*Michelin map reference*: N4.
*Nearest main line railway station*: Lambach on the Westbahn (line number 401 and timetable number 101).

Stern and Hafferl's Bombardier-built ET 25.104 awaiting departure from Lambach station on 29th June, 2007. *Author*

*Operated by*: Stern & Hafferl.
*Official line number*: 300.
*Timetable number*: 162.
*Route*: Lambach to Haag am Hausruck, a total distance of 26.3 km.
*Journey time*: 43 minutes.
*Gauge*: Standard by adhesion only operating on a maximum gradient of 3 per cent.
*Electrified*: Yes, dual voltage - 750 V DC & 15 kV AC 16.7 Hz. Two transformer units - dual voltage transformer units Nos. EGL 25.051 & 25.052 - which are attached and detached to allow the 750 V DC electric traction to travel the 4.2 km section of the Westbahn to and from Lambach and near Neukirchen. Diesel traction is also operated.
*Rolling stock*: Electric locomotive No. E 20.007 built in 1956 by SGP, Graz & BBC; diesel locomotives: Nos. V 20.011 (built 1982) and V 20.012 (built 1992) and electric railcars Nos. ET 24.104 (built 1950), ET 25.102 (built 1932), ET 25.103 and 25.104 (both built by Bombardier in 1989). (*Source: Platform 5.*)
*Contact details*: Stern & Hafferl Verkehrsgesellschaft m.b.H., 4810 Gmunden, Kuferzeile 32. Telephone: 07612 795-200 Fax: 07612 795-202.
*Website*: www.stern-verkehr.at/sverkehr/ (de).
*Operating dates*: Daily throughout the year with nine services each way between 0500 and 1900 hours.
*Tariff*: Local fare structure applies.
*History*: In 1875 the plan was to build a railway line from Lambach on the Westbahn to Pram on the Reid im Innkreis - Neumarkt im Hausstruckkreis route. It took almost 25 years to obtain the permission of the principal landowner to build the line but nonetheless when agreed construction work began in earnest and the route as far as Haag was opened to traffic within the following two years. Unfortunately, the further section of seven kilometres to Pram never materialised. The railway did not fare well in the first two decades of the 20th century to such an extent that the company went into liquidation in 1930 and the line was taken over by the Federal Railways. In 1932, the Federal Railways handed the line to Stern & Hafferl to operate. Stern & Hafferl decided upon electrification for the route which they implemented in April 1933. They chose to install a system operating on 750 V DC and began running services using two railcars Nos. ET 25.101 & ET 25.102, the latter still operating today and is used from time to time

for *Nostalgie* excursions. Stern & Hafferl's decision to use the DC power supply later presented problems of compatibility with the Federal Railways AC system introduced in 1949 particularly because the Lambach-Haag railway shared a short section of main line track with the Federal Railways before reaching its own metals. The answer was to build two dual-voltage transformer units. The idea was as the 750 V DC train approached the 15 kV AC supply, the transformer vehicle was inserted between the locomotive and its train and the AC power then taken off the catenary and 'transformed' to DC supply, the current then passing by cable from transformer vehicle to locomotive. In 1950 this worked well with the first transformer vehicle built and to such an extent that a second one was built in 1952. These units have continued to work efficiently even up until today. However 39 years later, modernisation came in the form of two Bombardier dual-voltage railcars which, with their automatic switching, have speeded up the whole service. Freight is still run on the line using diesel-powered locomotives. In 2005, a proposal was presented to close the service from December of that year. Fortunately, the local government in the form of the Niederösterreich Land intervened with a subsidy to keep the service running for a further 12 months whilst a solution was found. In late 2007 the railway was still operating but the threat of closure remained. (*Sources: Stern und Hafferl, Platform 5 and ARG.*)
*Comments*: Special events are offered during the summer months.
*Further reading*: *The Railways of Stern und Hafferl GmbH* published by the UK's Austrian Railway Group (ARG), 2006.

## 114 Linz Tramways

*Location*: Linz, 135 km north-east of Salzburg.
*Michelin map reference*: O-P4.
*Nearest main line railway station*: Linz on the Westbahn (line number 401 and timetable number 100).
*Operated by*: Linz AG Linien.
*Routes*: From Bergbahnhof via Hauptbahnhof to Auwiesen, to Solar City and finally to Universität, a total network of 15.3 km.
*Journey times*: Vary according to route taken.
*Gauge*: Narrow (900 mm) by adhesion only.
*Electrified*: Yes, 600 V DC.
*Rolling stock*: 2002-5-built Cityrunner 7-section cars Nos. 001-021; 1985-6-built Third Series 4-section cars Nos. 41 - 56; and, 1977-built Second Series 4-section cars (converted from 3-section) Nos. 68 -79. The livery is white with an orange lower body side band (NB: only 012 to 021 carry this livery - the rest carry various multi-coloured advertising). All these trams are unidirectional. (*Source: Platform 5.*)
*Historic stock*: The following bi-directional historic trams are safeguarded: Nos. 6 (1950), 12 (1962), 23 (1902), 25 (1957), 32 (an 1880-built 2-axle horse car) and the following 2-axle trailers: 109 & 111 (both 1950) and 140 & 141 (both 1954).
*Contact details*: Linz AG Linien GmbH, Wiener Straße 151, A-4021 Linz Telephone: 0732 3400-4000. E-mail: info@linzag.at
*Website*: www.linzag.at
*Operating dates*: Daily all year round.
*Comments*: Linz AG Linien is a huge transport undertaking. Annually, it carries about 93 million passengers on their overall 180 km-long transport network. The Postlingbergbahn also operates a tram service in Linz (*see entry 119*).

148 THE ESSENTIAL GUIDE TO AUSTRIAN RAILWAYS AND TRAMWAYS

Linz tram No. 70, not carrying advertising livery when photographed, in heavy traffic in the centre of Linz on 29th June, 2007. *Author*

The 2000-built Stadler/Bombardier-built ET 22.158 arriving at Linz Hbf on 29th June, 2007.
*Author*

## 115 Linzer Lokalbahn [LILO]

*Location*: Linz, 100 km west of Vienna.
*Michelin map reference*: O-P4.
*Nearest main line railway station*: Linz on the Westbahn (line number 401 and timetable number 100).
*Operated by*: Stern & Hafferl.
*Routes*: a) Linz-Peuerbach; and, b) Waizenkirchen-Niederspaching-Neumarkt-Kalham, a combined total distance of 58.9 km making the Linzer Lokalbahn the largest of Stern & Hafferl's individual operations.
*Journey times*: a) 1 hours 31 minutes; and, b) 19-24 minutes.
*Gauge*: Standard by adhesion only for a maximum gradient of 2.7 per cent.
*Electrified*: Yes, 750 V DC.
*Rolling stock*: Electric locomotives: 1915 Ganz-built No. E 22.001, 1915 Ganz/SSW-built No. E 22.002, Ganz-built Nos. E 22.004 (1915) & E 22.005 (1926) and 1912 Maffei/SSW-built No. E 22.006. Electric railcars: 1951 Graz/AEG-built No. ET 22.105 (described as a museum exhibit), 1951 SGP Graz/Elin-built Nos. ET 22.106 & ET 22.107, 1952 SGP Graz/BBC No. ET 22.108, 1908 Graz/AEG-built No. ET 22.109 (a historic exhibit used for excursions), 1953-4 Westwaggon/Kiepe-built Nos. ET 22.134 (with unpowered railcar ES 22.234) ET 22.135 (with ES 22.235) & ET 22.137 (with ES 22.237), 1954-56 Westwaggon/SSW-built Nos. ET 22.141 to 143, 2000 Stadler/Bombardier-built Nos. ET 22.151 to 158 and 2005 Stadler/Bombardier-built Nos. ET 22.159 to 164. Trailers: 1950 SGP-built B 22.209 & 22.254. (*Source: Platform 5*.)
*Places to see*: Linz city itself and take a boat trip on the River Danube.
*Contact details*: Stern & Hafferl Verkehrsgesellschaft m.b.H., 4810 Gmunden, Kuferzeile 32, Telephone: 07612 795-200 Fax: 07612 795-202. E-mail: sekretariat@stern-verkehr.at
*Website*: www.stern-verkehr.at/sverkehr/
*Operating dates*: Daily with services from 0600 hours to 0130 hours.
*Tariff*: Local fare structure applies.

MV *Stadt Linz* one of the many pleasure cruise boats operating on the Danube. On 29th June, 2007 the 'Blue' Danube was not so blue! *Author*

*History*: The routes were opened to traffic in stages, i.e. Neumarkt-Waizenkirchen-Peuerbach (NWP) in December 1908; Linz-Eferding in March 1912; and, Eferding-Waizenkirchen in December 1912. NWP and the Linz-Waizenkirchen were operated as separate units until they were amalgamated in 1998. Now the Linz-Lokalbahn is jointly owned by Stern & Hafferl with the City of Linz together with the townships of Eferding, Leonding and Peuerbach.
*Comments*: *Nostalgie* excursions are run from time to time using primarily their 1908-built railcar No. ET 22.109 originally numbered as NWP's 21.150.
*Further reading*: *The Railways of Stern und Hafferl GmbH* published by the UK's Austrian Railway Group (ARG), 2006.

## 116 Mühlkriesbahn

*Location*: Linz, 100 km west of Vienna.
*Michelin map reference*: O-P4.
*Operated by*: ÖBB.
*Official line number*: 358.
*Timetable number*: 142.
*Route*: North-north-west from Linz (Urfahr station is near to the Postlingbergbahn terminus, *see entry 119*) to Aigen-Schlägl, via Rottenegg, Neufelden, Haslach and Rohrbach-Berg, a total distance of about 57.6 km.
*Journey time*: 1 hour 44 minutes by Regional Express (REX).
*Gauge*: Standard by adhesion only negotiating a maximum gradient of 4.6 per cent between Haslach and Rohrbach-Berg.
*Electrified*: No, diesel-operated. Local line - single track.
*Website*: www.oebb.at/en
*Operating dates*: Daily all year round with services every two hours.
*Tariff*: 1-PLUS-Freizeit 2nd class ticket for an adult is €10.90 (2007). www.erlebnis-bahn-schiff.at
*Comments*: Aigen-Schlägl is close to the border of the Czech Republic near to the Moldaustausee.

Two class '5047' railcars (Nos. 070-7 and 072-3) standing at Linz Urfahr station on 29th June, 2007.
*Author*

# UPPER AUSTRIA (OBERÖSTERREICH)

## 117 Museums Pferde-Eisenbahn Kerschbaum (Horse-drawn railway)

*Location*: Kerschbaum, 48 km north east of Linz on the Czech border.
*Michelin map reference*: P3.
*Nearest main line railway station*: Summerau at the end of the ÖBB line number 321 from Linz (timetable number 141). Kerschbaum is 5.6 km north-east by road from Summerau Bahnhof.
*Operated by*: Museumspferdebahn Kerschbaum.
*Route*: Originally the route went from Linz to Budweis (Ceské Budûjovice), a total distance of about 129 km.
*Journey time*: Not known.
*Gauge*: Narrow (1106 mm).
*Electrified*: No, operates on oats, bran and hay!
*Infrastructure preserved*: Given that nearly the whole Czech part of the railway was taken over by steam operations in 1870, not much of the original 1106 mm gauge track remains. Just a few aspects have been preserved, i.e. the station house in Ceské Budûjovice, part of the railway between stations in the small villages of Suchdol and Rybník, the bridge and the horse changeover station in the village of Holkov near the small town of Velesín.
*Contact details*: Can be obtained through the Tourist Office, Nam Premyslaotakara 11 2T38 Ceské Budûjovice, Czech Republic. Telephone: +420 (0) 680 1413. This 'railway' is linked to the European Route of Industrial Heritage (ERIH) whose e-mail is: info@erih.net
*Website*: http://en.erih.net/index.php?pageId=109&anchor=309&filter= (en) www.ckrumlov.cz/uk/region/histor/t_kondra.htm (en cz)
*Operating dates*: Summer weekends but enquire locally for precise dates and times.
*Tariff*: Not known (2007).
*History*: Salt, sometimes referred to as 'white gold' was transported long ago on the Travna and Dunaj rivers to Linz. There, the commodity was transferred to carts drawn by teams of horses to take it across the Sumava ridges to Ceské Budûjovice and on to the River Vltava. In 1807, Frantisek Josef Gerstner examined the feasibility of connecting the Vltava and Danube rivers with a canal. However, he rejected the idea and proposed the building of a railway, the construction of which was subsequently directed by his son Frantisek Antonín Gerstner. Building of this railway began in 1828 and, with the advantage of the first part having already been completed in Bohemia in 1827, was opened to traffic in June 1830. The transport of goods began in 1832 and later passenger traffic was added. The 'train' comprised two horses in line which were regularly changed on the route. Overall the route was 129 km in length and it took 14 hours to complete the journey. The passenger trains left daily from each terminus at 0500 hours and they met and crossed over at Kerschbaum station where an hour's lunch break was enjoyed in what was at that time the first railway restaurant in Europe. The horse railway became redundant in 1872 when a line was opened for steam-hauled trains. However, 19 stations still remain intact on the Austrian and Czech parts of the route, and the passenger and freight terminals at Ceské Budûjovice have been preserved. Today, a way-marked path for walkers follows this route.
*Comments*: Close to the Czech border, short stretches of tracks have been re-built and rides in horse-drawn carriages are offered. In 1970 what remains of this horse-drawn railway were designated as an item of historical and cultural interest.

## 118 Österreichische Gesellschaft für Eisenbahngeschichte (ÖGEG)

Yet another of ÖGEG's well restored locomotives – this one is a new acquisition No. 657.2770 which originally operated as '50.770' on the Romanian Railways (CFR). Photograph taken at Ampflwang on 1st July, 2007. *Author*

*Location*: Ampflwang, 250 km west of Vienna and 82 km west-south-west of Linz.
*Michelin map reference*: M4.
*Nearest main line railway station*: Timelkam on the Westbahn (line number 401 and timetable number 101).
*Operated by*: Österreichische Gesellschaft für Eisenbahngeschichte (ÖGEG).
*Route*: ÖGEG also operates the Kohlebahn heritage railway from Timelkam to Ampflwang. The total distance of this route is 10.4 km (*see entry 112*).
*Gauges*: Standard and narrow (760 mm).
*Traction*: Steam-, diesel- and electric-powered locomotives.
*Rolling stock*: Much, but not all, is in full operational order as follows: Standard gauge - steam locomotive 2-10-0 1944-built Jung No 52.3316; other steam locomotives all 2-10-0s - Nos. 52.1198 92 (1943-built), 52.3517 (1943-built), 52.4552 (1944-built); and also 1920-built 4-6-2T No. 77.28, 1938-built 4-6-4T No. 78.618, 1927-built 0-8-0Ts Nos. 392.2510 & 392.2530, 1927-built 2-8-2Ts Nos. 93.1326, 93.1394 & 93.1455, 1913-built 0-10-0T No. 694.503. There are also a further 23 steam locomotives from other non-ÖBB railways. Also preserved is diesel locomotive 1954-built Brown Boveri No. 2045.012; diesel-powered railcar 1955-built SGP No. 5046.214; other diesel railcars ÖGEG retains include class '5145' No. 009, class '5046' Nos. 204, 214 & 215, class '5146' Nos. 207 & 208 and class '5081' No. 208. Electric locomotives retained are: 1939-built Floridsdorf/AEGU No. 1018.002; class '1010' Nos. 004, 005, 013, 014, & 015; class '1110' Nos. 008, 025, 522, 526, 528 & 529; class '1018' Nos. 007 & 008; class '1020' Nos. 012, 014, 022, 024 & 038; class '1040' No. 015; class '1041' Nos. 005 & 006; class '1141' No. 020; class '1245' Nos. 516 & 518; class '1046' No. 001; class '1061' No. 02; class '1161' No. 019; class '1062' No. 012; class '1067' No. 004; class '1670' No. 012; class '1670' No. 102; class '1073' Nos. 03 & 20; class '1080' No. 011; class '1180' No. 004; and, class '1280' No. 14. Narrow gauge (760 mm) steam locomotive 0-6-2T 1898-built Krauss Linz No. 298 52 is also safeguarded. (*Source: Platform 5.*)

*Contact details*: Österreichische Gesellschaft für Eisenbahngeschichte (ÖGEG) Postfach 11, A-4018 Linz. Telephone: 0664 5087 664. E-mail: sonderzuege@oegeg.at and Oberösterreichisches Eisenbahn & Bergbaumuseum, Bahnhofstraße 29, A-4843 Ampflwang. Telephone: 0664 5987 664. E-mail: ampflwang@oegeg.at
*Website*: www.oegeg.at
*Operating dates*: The museum at Ampflwang is open from 1st April to 31st October on Wednesdays to Saturdays from 1000 hours to 1700 hours. These hours are extended to 0900 hours to 1800 hours in July, August and the first week in September.
*Tariff*: Entry to the museum only is €7 for an adult and €3 for a child (6-15 years). A return trip on the Kohlebahn is €10 for an adult and €5 for a child. A single trip on the Kohlebahn is €6 for an adult and €3 for a child. A combined ticket for the museum and a return journey on the train is €14 for an adult and €6 for a child. There are discounts for families and also for groups (2007).
*Comments*: ÖGEG has strong links with the Steyrtal Museumsbahn (*see entry 125*) and the Club Florianerbahn (*see entry 110*). This in the author's opinion is the best museum and heritage railway in Austria and because of its presentation and varied activities offers something for all the family. The Ampflwang Museum and the Kohlebahn should not be missed.

## 119 Pöstlingbergbahn

*Location*: Linz, 135 km north-east of Salzburg.
*Michelin map reference*: O-P4.
*Nearest main line railway station*: Linz on the Westbahn (line number 401 and timetable number 100).
*Operated by*: Linz AG Linien.
*Route*: Linz (Urfahr station) to Pöstlingberg, a total distance of 2.9 km.
*Journey time*: 16 minutes.
*Gauge*: Narrow (1000 mm) by adhesion only to negotiate the 10.5 per cent gradient (1 in 9.5) without rack assistance. The gradient for this adhesion-only rail/tramway is the second steepest in the world. As a matter of information the AFAIK Lisbon tram has short sections of 14.5 per cent (1 in 7) and is the steepest. However, the Guinness Book of Records claims that the Postlingbergbahn holds the world record, probably because of the overall distance involved.
*Electrified*: Yes, 600 V DC.
*Rolling stock*: All rolling stock is four-wheeled and bi-directional and the livery is cream with Roman numerals to distinguish them from the Linz trams. Operational are: 1898-built Nos. I, II, III, VI & VIII; 1912-built No. X; 1948-50-built Nos. XI & XII; and 1954-58-built Nos. XIV & XVIII.
*Contact details*: Linz AG Linien GmbH, Wiener Straße 151, A-4021 Linz/ Telephone: 0732 3400-4000. E-mail: info@linzag.at
*Website*: www.linzag.at Of interest is: www.linz.at/english/tourism/default_9222.asp and see also http://website.lineone.net/~tramscape/Linz/Linz2003.htm
*Operating dates*: Daily all the year round with very frequent services.
*Tariff*: An adult single is €2.40 and a return €4 and for child €1.20 single and €2 return (2007).
*Comments*: Platform 5 reports that there are plans to re-gauge this line to 900 mm (in keeping with the Linz Trams proper) and replace the 'museum pieces' with modern trams. What a shame if and when that happens!

Postlingbergbahn's tram No. XVIII heading for the terminus near Linz's Urfahr station on 29th June, 2007.

*Author*

## 120 Pyhrnbahn

*Location*: Linz, 100 km west of Vienna.
*Michelin map reference*: O-P4.
*Operated by*: ÖBB.
*Official line numbers*: 404 and 304.
*Timetable number*: 140.
*Route*: From Linz to Selzthal, a total distance of about 104.2 km.
*Journey time*: 1 hour 42 minutes with no changes by Regional Express (REX).
*Gauge*: Standard by adhesion only. Main line - single track.
*Electrified*: Yes, 15 kV AC 16.7 Hz.
*Places to see*: The Wurzeralmbahn operates from Spital am Pyhrn (*see entry 158*).
*Website*: www.oebb.at/en
*Operating dates*: Daily all the year round with hourly trains supplemented by EuroCity and ÖBB InterCity services (2007).
*Tariff*: An adult 2nd class single ticket is €18.20 (2007).
*Comments*: Passes through the 4.76 km Bosruck tunnel north of Ardning near Selzthal.

## 121 Salzkammergutbahn

*Location*: Attnang-Puchheim, 81 km east of Salzburg, 235 km west of Vienna and 73 km south-west of Linz.
*Michelin map reference*: N4.
*Operated by*: ÖBB.
*Official line number*: 306.
*Timetable number*: 170.
*Route*: From Attnang-Puchheim to Stainach-Irdning, via Bad Ischl, a total distance of 107.6 km.
*Journey time*: 2 hours 3 minutes.
*Gauge*: Standard by adhesion only. Main line - single track.
*Electrified*: Yes, 15 kV AC 16.7 Hz.
*Places to see*: There is a museum specialising in transport matters including railways located at Bad Ischl which is open from the beginning of April to the end of October (0900 hours-1800 hours). The museum can be found at Sulzbach, 178 at Bad Ischl and their telephone number is 06132 266 58. A website is maintained at www.fahrzeugmuseum.at Of considerable pictorial interest as the train follows its route are the Traunsee and the Hallstätter See lakes.
*Website*: www.oebb.at/en
*Operating dates*: Daily all the year round with Regional Express (REX) services operating every two hours.
*Tariff*: An adult single 2nd class ticket is €18.20 (2007).
*Comments*: This is a particularly scenic route. At Stainach-Irdning the Salzkammergutbahn meets the Ennstalbahn (*see entry 61*). The Hallstätter Salzburgerbahn is on this route (*see entry 148*).

Locomotive No. 1116 175-9 leads a service on the Pyhrnpass route. Photograph taken near to Windischgarsten on 10th October, 2007. *Caroline Jones*

The station at Obertraun-Dachsteinhöhlen is visited by a train led by No. 1142 549-3 on its way to Bad Ischl and Attnang-Puchheim from Stainach-Irdning on 30th June, 2007. *Author*

## 122 Schafbergbahn

*Location*: St Wolfgang, 49 km east-south-east by road from Salzburg and 120 km south-west of Linz.
*Michelin map reference*: M5.
*Nearest main line station*: Bad Ischl on the Salkammergutbahn (line number 306 and timetable number 170).
*Operated by*: Salzkammergutbahn GmbH (formerly ÖBB).
*Official line number*: 373.
*Route*:   Schafbergbahn St Wolfgang to Schafbergspitze via the stations at Mittelstation and Schafbergalpe, a total distance of 5.85 km.
*Journey time*: Up to 45 minutes.
*Gauge*:   Narrow (metre) by adhesion and rack/cogwheel of Roman Abt's design negotiating a maximum gradient of 26 per cent.
*Traction*: Steam- and diesel-powered.
*Rolling stock*:   Four 1992-built diesel locomotives, four heritage steam locomotives built between 1893 and 1894, two powered railcars built in 1964, nine passenger carriages and three goods wagons.
*Places to see*: The view from the summit of the Schafberg mountain, at 1,783 m, is considered to offer one of the most beautiful in the whole of the Salzkammergut region of Austria. Sailings are also organized by the same company and other enterprises on the Wolfgangsee between St Gilgen, Fürberg, Ried-Falkenstein, the Schafbergbahn station, St Wolfgang, Gschwendt Parkplatz and Strobl. Services operate all year round but are limited in number in the winter months.
*Contact details*: Salzkammergutbahn GmbH, Markt 35, A-5360 St Wolfgang. Telephone: 06138 22 32-0 Fax: 06138 2232-12. E-mail: berg.schiff@schafbergbahn.at
*Website*: www.schafbergbahn.at
*Operating dates*:   From the beginning of May to the end of October (weather permitting) trains leave Schafbergbahn St Wolfgang at 0825, 0900, 1000, 1100, 1200, 1300, 1400, 1500, 1600, 1700 and 1800 hours and leave Schafbergspitze at 0910, 1010, 1110, 1210, 1310, 1410, 1510, 1610, 1710, 1810 and 1910 hours. Steam trains operate between 7th July and 9th September leaving Schafbergbahn St Wolfgang at 1007 and 1307 and returning from Schafbergspitze at 1146 and 1446 hours. Each train carries a maximum of 20 passengers with two trains ascending or descending together at busy times. The above dates are for 2007 but operating dates and timetables for future years are expected to follow a similar pattern.
*Tariff*: An adult single ticket is €14 and return €24. Children aged 6-14 years travel at half the adult fares. A family return ticket is €59.40. There are discount rates for groups (2007).
*History*: The railway began operations in 1893.
*Comments*: Schafbergbahn claims to be the steepest steam rack/cogwheel railway in Austria. There is a hotel at Schafbergspitze at which one can stay overnight but it can only be reached by way of the cog railway. Another part of this operation is to offer boat trips on the Wolfgangsee using the 1873-constructed paddle steamer *Franz-Josef I* steaming between the ports of Kurs, Strobl, Gschwendt Parkplatz, St Wolfgang, the station at Schafbergbahn, Ried-Falkenstein, Fürberg and St Gilgen. Consult the website for details of sailing times and tariffs. Special offer tickets combine boat and train trips.

In the foreground rack locomotive No. Z 14 built by SLM (Winterthur) is waiting its turn at St Wolfgang to push its train up the Schafberg. Immediately behind it is locomotive Z 12 with its train which will follow its leader, 30th June, 2007. *Author*

## 123 Salzkammergutbahn-Lokalbahn-Museum (SKGLB) Mondsee

The 'old' shed at SKGLB museum at Mondsee. *Author*

*Location*: Mondsee, 30 km east of Salzburg.
*Michelin map reference*: M5.
*Nearest main line railway station*: Salzburg on the Westbahn (line number 401 and timetable number 101).
*Operated by*: SKGLB Museum.
*Exhibits*: There are preserved narrow gauge steam locomotives, carriages and goods wagons including former Salzkammergut Lokalbahn (SKLGB) steam locomotives Nos. S4, S5 and S9. An 'Imperial' coach, which was used by Emperor ('Kaiser') Franz-Josef I when he was visiting the region by train, is also safeguarded.
*Places to see*: In the local church in Mondsee the wedding scene in the film *The Sound of Music* was filmed.
*Contact details*: SKGLB Museum, Seebadstraße 2, Mondsee A-5310. Telephone: 06232 4270. E-mail: info@mondsee.at
*Website*: www.mondseeland.org/mondseeland.html
*Operating dates*: June to September at weekends from 1000 hours to 1200 hours and 1400 hours to 1700 hours.
*Tariff*: An adult entry is €3 (2007).
*Comments*: A small but nonetheless interesting museum focusing on the history of the Salzkammergut Lokalbahn which also features model railways and has a shop where new and second-hand books can be purchased. The Attergaubahn is not far away at Attersee (*see entry 109*).
*Further reading*: See *Railways of Salzburg and the Salzkammergut Region* (*on page 41*) published by the UK's Austrian Railway Group (ARG), 2002.

## 124 Stern und Hafferl (StH)

*Location*: Gmunden and Linz areas.
*Michelin map reference*: N4-5.
*Nearest main line railway station*: Lambach or Vöcklamarkt on the Westbahn (line number 401 and timetable number 101).
*Services*: operated by Stern & Hafferl are the Attergaubahn (*see entry 109*), the Traunseebahn (*see entry 126*), the Vorchdorferbahn (*see entry 127*), Haager Lies or Lambach-Haag (*see entry 113*), the Linzer Lokalbahn (*see entry 115*) and the Gmunden Straßenbahn (*see entry 111*). Stern & Hafferl also operate the Attersee-Schifffahrt which provides passenger sailing services on the Attersee lake.
*Routes and journey times*: See individual entries. For special events visit the website.
*Contact details*: Stern & Hafferl Verkehrsgesellschaft m.b.H., Kuferzeile 32, A-4810 Gmunden, Telephone: 07612 795200 Fax: 07612 795202. E-mail: info@stern-ver.at
*Website*: www.stern-verkehr.at
*Operating dates and tariffs*: Vary according to service taken - consult locally.
*History*: The company was founded by Josef Stern and Franz Hafferl in 1883 initially as an electricity supply company to provide to organizations and homes in the Upper Austria region. However, it was not long before the company became involved in railways. In 1891 an office was set up in St Wolfgang and it was from there that the building of the Schafbergbahn and the Salzkammergut Lokalbahn were managed. In 1894, the Gmunden Tramway followed as did many other transport projects which still exist today. In 1924 Josef Stern died and was succeeded by his son, Karl. In 1925, Franz Hafferl also died but this time the family chose to sell off their share in the business. The company, however, has continued to prosper and today Stern Hafferl Holdings comprises five main divisions: Stern Hafferl Bau, Stern Hafferl Verkehr, GEG Elektrobau, GEG Werburg and Wintereder. Nearly 500 employees are engaged in these businesses and the annual turnover is said to be in the region of €40 million.
*Comments*: Stern & Hafferl also provide a comprehensive programme of special excursions throughout the year including heritage services referred to as 'Nostalgiefahrten' as well as combined rail and lake trips. Stern & Hafferl also provide local bus services.
*Further reading*: *The Railways of Stern und Hafferl GmbH* published by the UK's Austrian Railway Group (ARG), 2006.

Stern und Hafferl's livery on a carriage at Attersee station.
*Author*

## 125  Steyrtal Museumsbahn

*Location*: Steyr, 166 km west of Vienna and 38 km south of Linz.
*Michelin map reference*: P4.
*Nearest main line railway station*: Steyr (on line number 303 and timetable number 131).
*Operated by*: Steyrtal Museumsbahn.
*Route*: From Steyr Lokalbahnhof to Grünburg, a distance of 17.6 km. (NB: Steyr Lokalbahnhof is 1.8 km from Steyr's ÖBB Bahnhof and can be reached by crossing the River Enns by way of the Schönauer Brücke.)
*Journey time*: Not known.
*Gauge*: Narrow (760 mm) by adhesion only for a maximum gradient of 2 per cent.
*Traction*: Steam and diesel traction.
*Rolling stock*: The Museumsbahn retains the following former ÖBB rolling stock, all 760 mm gauge: 1898-built 0-6-2T Nos. 298.52 & 298.53, 1888-built 0-6-2T No. 298.102, 1914-built 0-6-2T No. 298.106, 1929-built 0-6-2T No. 498.04, and 1944-built 0-8-0T No. 699.103 (or at the Waldviertler Schmalspurbahnverein - *entry 58*). Also preserved are 1957-built 0-8-0T No. 764.480 (ex-CFF) and 1954-built 0-8-0T No. 764.007 (ex-CFI). Ex-ÖBB diesel departmental stock includes Nos. X616.901 & 903.
*Places to see*: The railway hugs the banks of the River Steyr (a tributary of the River Enns) for the entire route. Steyr is an old iron town and offers interesting Gothic architecture - see the *Bummerlhaus* on the *Stadtplatz* and the parish church.
*Contact details*: Steyrtal Museumsbahn, Steyr Lokalbahnhof, Redtenbachergasse 14, A-4400 Steyr. Telephone: 07252 46569 Fax: 07257 7102. E-Mail: Karl.Mader-Steyr@aon.at
*Website*: www.steyrtalbahn.at   www.ooemuseumsverbund.at/de_museum_30.html (de) also see http://schmalspur.bahnen.at/strecke11.php (de).
*Operating dates*:   From the beginning of June until the end of September at weekends. Advent weekends in December up until the last day of the month.
*Tariff*: An adult return ticket is €10 and €6 for a single ticket. Children (under 15) travel at half-price. A family ticket is €20. There are discounts for groups and it is possible to charter a train for a special event (2007).
*History*: The Steyrbahn was opened in 1889 and is said to be the oldest narrow gauge steam railway in Austria.
*Comments*: One of many rail routes in Austria that was closed to regular traffic, after a comparatively light land-slide damaged the tracks. The connection on former ÖBB line (number 351) from Pergern to Rohr-Bad Hall was closed in 2004. The Museumsbahn has a shop selling books, CDs and videos. There is also a buffet restaurant.

## 126  Traunseebahn also known as Gmunden-Vorchdorf Lokalbahn

*Location*: Vorchdorf-Eggenberg, 78 km east of Salzburg and 51 km south-west of Linz.
*Michelin map reference*: N4.
*Nearest main line railway station*:  Attnang-Puchheim and Lambach on the Westbahn (both line number 401 and timetable 101) and Gmunden on the Salkammergutbahn (line number 306 and timetable 170).
*Operated by*: Stern & Hafferl.

ET 23.112 built in 1954 by SWS/BBC approaches Kirchham on 29th June, 2007 on its way to Vorchdorf-Eggenberg. *Author*

*Official line number*: Not allocated.
*Timetable number*: 161.
*Route*. Gmunden Seebahnhof to Vorchdorf-Eggenberg, a total distance 14.918 km.
*Journey time*: 30 minutes.
*Gauge*: Narrow (1000 mm) by adhesion only. The maximum gradient is 4.3 per cent.
*Electrified*: Yes, 750 V DC. (Originally the power supply was 600 V DC but over time this was gradually increased to reach its present level).
*Rolling stock*: Electric railcars: 1921-built No. ET 23.103 (a museum unit), 1954-built Nos. ET 23.105, 106, 111 and 112 plus trailers 20.224 (1916), 20.225 buffet car (1926), 20.227 (1942) and 23.221 (1899). The maximum speed on the line is 50 kmh.
*Places to visit*: Gmunden offers a variety of watersport facilities as well as salt water baths offering traditional cures. There is a famous porcelain factory here offering its distinctive green-glazed china.
*Contact details*: Stern & Hafferl Verkehrsgesellschaft m.b.H., Kuferzeile 32, A-4810 Gmunden. Telephone: 07612 795200 Fax: 07612 795202. E-mail: info@stern-ver.at
*Website*: www.stern-verkehr.at/sverkehr/
*Operating dates*: Daily throughout the year and hourly between about 0500 hours and 1800 hours with more services at busy times. The timetable can be found at www.stern-verkehr.at/sverkehr/Fahrplan/Fpl_2007GV.pdf
*Tariff*: Local fare structure applies.
*History*: The route was first opened in March 1912.
*Further reading*: *The Railways of Stern und Hafferl GmbH* published by the UK's Austrian Railway Group (ARG), 2006.


**127 Vorchdorferbahn** also known as **Lambach-Vorchdorf Lokalbahn**

*Location*: Lambach, 95 km east of Salzburg and 50 km south-west of Linz.
*Michelin map reference*: N4.
*Nearest main line railway station*: Lambach on the Westbahn (line number 401 and timetable number 101).
*Operated by*: Stern & Hafferl.
*Official line number*: Not allocated.

*Timetable number*: 160.
*Route*: From Lambach to Vorchdorf, a total distance of 14.7 km.
*Journey time*: 25 minutes.
*Gauge*: Standard by adhesion only.
*Electrified*: Yes, 750 V DC.
*Rolling stock*: 1910-built Maffei electric locomotive No. 24.010; 1953-built electric railcars Nos. ET 20.109 and 111, ET 22.133 & 136, ET 24.101 (built 1931 and a museum item) and ET 24.103 (built 1912 and also a museum item).
*Places to visit*: Lambach Abbey (*Stift Lambach*) a Benedictine Abbey monastery, founded in about 1040 by Bishop (Saint) Adalbero of Würzburg, houses some unique treasures including the Romanesque St Adelbero's Chalice, an unusual rococo theatre and a series of extremely well-preserved Romanesque frescoes which go back to the 11th century and are believed to be the oldest in Southern Germany and Austria. (*Source: Insight-Austria*.)
*Contact details*: Stern & Hafferl Verkehrsgesellschaft m.b.H., Kuferzeile 32, A-4810 Gmunden. Telephone: 07612 795200 Fax: 07612 795202. E-mail: info@stern-ver.at
*Website*: www.stern-verkehr.at/sverkehr/
*Operating dates*: Daily with 17 services from Lambach to Vorchdorf-Eggenberg, the first leaving at 0529 hours and the last at 1920 hours. The same number of services operate in the opposite direction with the first leaving at 0453 hours and the last at 1849 hours (2007).
*Tariff*: Local fare structure applies.
*History*: The railway began operations in 1903.
*Comments*: Special excursions using historic material are run on this line throughout the year. At Vorchdorf-Eggenberg the Vorchdorferbahn meets Stern & Hafferl's narrow gauge service from Gmunden - the Traunseebahn (see *previous entry*).
*Further reading*: *The Railways of Stern und Hafferl GmbH* published by the UK's Austrian Railway Group (ARG), 2006.

Standing at Vorchdorf-Eggenberg on 29th June, 2007 is electric railcar No. ET 20.109. This 1953-built railcar was acquired from the German Extertalbahn and first used on the Burmoos-Trimmelkam line of the Salzburger Lokalbahn. *Author*

## Vienna (Wien)

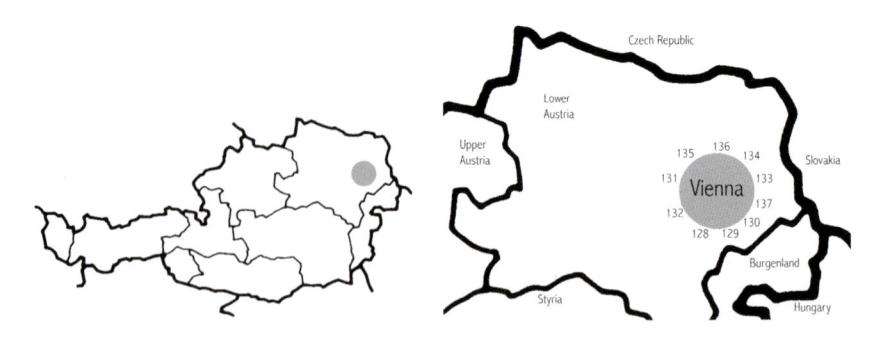

Vienna is the capital city of Austria, and also the capital of one of the nine states of Austria. Vienna has the largest population of all the states with 1.66 million which grows to 2.26 million when one takes into account the metropolitan area. The state and city has 23 districts and occupies an area of 414.9 sq km making it the smallest geographically in the country. It is completely surrounded by its only neighbour the state of Lower Austria and has no international frontiers although it is very close to the Czech Republic, Slovakia and Hungary. It is renowned for its cultural assets. In 2001, the centre was designated a UNESCO World Heritage Site. The Economist Intelligence Unit which is part of the US Economist Group made a study of 127 world cities and ranked it third for 'quality of life' after Vancouver and Melbourne.

Der Graben is probably one of the most famous streets in Inner Vienna. There one can find the *Pestsäule* monument which was built to commemorate the Great Plague of Vienna, 1682-1692.
*Author*

## 128 Donauländebahn

*Location*: Vienna.
*Michelin map reference*: V4.
*Operated by*: ÖBB.
*Official line numbers*: 224 and 124/133.
*Route*: From Wien Meidling to Wien Zentralverschiebebf, a total distance of about 15 km.
*Gauge*: Standard by adhesion only.
*Electrified*: Yes, 15 k V AC 16.7 Hz.
*Website*: www.oebb.at/en
*Comments*: A connecting line to the south of Vienna between the Südbahn and the Ostbahn mainly used for freight transfer.

## 129 Liliputbahn Prater Wien

*Location*: Vienna (Wien).
*Michelin map reference*: V4.
*Nearest main line railway station*: Vienna Nord (Liliput Prater is behind the Fractenbahnhof close to the Danube).
*Operated by*: Liliputbahn im Prater GmbH.
*Route*: A circular route in the amusement park with a total distance of 3.9 km.
*Journey time*: 20 minutes.
*Gauge*: Narrow (381 mm - 15 inches) by adhesion only.
*Traction*: Steam- and diesel-powered. The maximum power delivered by both the steam and diesel locomotives is 22 kW which can deliver maximum speeds of 22 kmh.
*Rolling stock*: Comprises the following: Steam: No. Da 1 *Grete* (built by Krauss, Munich, manufacturer type 8441) & No. Da 2 *Brigitte* (also built by Krauss Munich, manufacturer type 8442) and diesel traction: 1958-built D1 *Bernhard*, circa 1960-built No. D2 *Harry* & 1964-built No. D3 *Michael*.
*Places to see*: The Prater - the amusement park itself - allow a full day and perhaps the evening as well.
*Contact details*: Liliputbahn Prater, Schrotzberggasse 7/8, Vienna A-1120. Telephone: 01 726 8236 Fax: 01 7268236-4. E-mail: info@liliputbahn.com
*Website*: www.liliputbahn.com (de).
*Operating dates*: From March to October daily from 1000 hours to 2200 hours. It can be opened outside these months/times by special arrangement.
*Tariff*: An adult return ticket is €3.50 and for a child (2-12 years) €2.20. Dogs on leads are admitted to the park and are permitted to travel free of charge on the trains (2007).
*History*: The Liliputbahn began life in 1923 and has run continuously ever since.
*Comments*: The railway is just one of the attractions of the Prater amusement park. The Prater boasts more than 250 attractions including a Giant Ferris Wheel (*Riesenrad*) ghost trains, merry-go-rounds, go-cart rinks, arcades, stands for games of skill, ultra-modern rides, restaurants, cafés, snack bars, and beer gardens. One of these attractions - the Liliputbahn featured here - is said to be too big to be a toy and too small to be a proper railway. Having said that if one takes the railway away from its background thus removing the scale, the locomotives look for all intents and purposes like the real thing! Picnics, including the supply of food and beverages, are offered in the park.

## 130 Eisenbahnmuseum Schwechat

*Location*: Schwechat, 11 km south-east of the centre of Vienna.
*Michelin map reference*: V4.
*Nearest railway station*: Schwechat on the S-Bahn.
*Operated by*: Eisenbahnmuseum Schwechat (Verband der Eisenbahnfreunde - VEF).
*Exhibits*: Material from narrow (600 mm) to standard gauge including steam, diesel, diesel-electric traction and an interesting selection of carriages some dating back to 1882 and a *postwagen* of 1899 vintage.
*Contact details*: Eisenbahnmuseum Groß Schwechat, Groß Schwechat station, Hintere Bahngasse 2B, A-2320 Schwechat. Telephone: 01 368 15103 Fax (01) 369 13 58. E-mail: is from their website in the *kontaktformular* section.
*Website*: www.eisenbahnmuseum-schwechat.at (de).
*Operating dates*: From 1st May to 26th October on Saturdays from 1300 to 1800 hours and on Sundays from 1000 hours to 1700 hours.
*Tariff*: An adult entry costs €6 (seniors €5) and a child €3. A family ticket costs €15 (2007).
*Comments*: The exhibition is located in a 1200 sq. metre hall. It has a shop and features a short (1.5 km) narrow gauge line with working steam locomotives.


## 131 Verbindungbahn

*Location*: Vienna.
*Michelin map reference*: V4.
**Operated by**: ÖBB.
*Official line numbers*: 222 with 224 branching off on to the Donauländebahn (*entry 128*) beyond Wien Speising.
*Timetable numbers*: 700 and 900.
*Route*: From Wien Penzing to Wien Meidling, a total distance of about 6 km.
*Gauge*: Standard by adhesion only. Main line - twin track and four track.
*Electrified*: Yes, 15 kV AC 16.7 Hz.
*Website*: www.oebb.at
*Comments*: One of ÖBB's Vienna connecting lines carrying both passengers and freight.


## 132 Vorortlinie

*Location*: Vienna.
*Michelin map reference*: V4.
*Operated by*: ÖBB.
*Official line number*: 220.
*Timetable number*: 111.
*Route*: From Wien Penzing to Wien Heilingenstadt on the Franz-Josefs Bahn (*see entry 37*) a total distance of 8.4 km.
*Journey time*: 17 minutes.
*Gauge*: Standard by adhesion only. Main line - twin track.
*Electrified*: Yes, 15 kV AC 16.7 Hz.
*Website*: www.oebb.at/en
*Operating dates*: Daily all the year round with frequent services about every 15 minutes.
*Tariff*: A 2nd class adult ticket is €4.40 (2007).

*Comments*: An ÖBB connecting line between the Franz-Josefs Bahn and the Westbahn. There are four tunnels on this short route - Breitensee (813 m), Kleine Türkenschanz (245 m), Grand Türkenschanz (705 m) and the Unterdöblinger (71 m).

## 133  Vienna Tramway Museum (Wiener Straßenbahnmuseum)

*Location*: Vienna. The Vienna Tramway Museum is located in the Erdberg coach-house of the Vienna Public Transport system (the 'Wiener Linien' - *see next entry*) in the third district of Vienna. The entrance is on the Ludwig-Koeßler-Platz near to Stadionbrücke.
*Michelin map reference*: V4.
*Nearest railway station*: Schlachthausgasse on the U-Bahn line U3 and Tram Line 18.
*Operated by*: Wiener Straßenbahnmuseum (WTM).
*Exhibits*: An extensive collection of streetcars and trams from the beginnings of the service in Vienna up until today.
*Contact details*: Wiener Tramwaymuseum, Holochergasse 24, Vienna A-1150. Telephone: 01786 03 03 Fax:  0198 24 124. E-mail:  info@tram.at
*Website*: www.wiener-tramwaymuseum.org  (de) see also www.tram.at (de).
*Opening dates*: From first week in May to the end of the first week in October on Saturdays, Sundays and public holidays from 0900 to 1600 hours. For those interested in having a nostalgic sightseeing tour of the city on a vintage tram, rides are offered from May until early October. The tour takes one hour on a tram dating back to 1929. It starts from Otto Wagner Pavilion at Karlsplatz leaving at 1130 hours and later at 1330 hours on Saturdays and at 0930, 1130 and 1330 hours on Sundays as well as the public holiday on 15th August each year.
*Tariff*:  €3 (2007).
*History*: The museum was established in 1966.
*Comments*: The Wiener Tramwaymuseum is said to be the largest of its kind in the world, occupying four large sheds. It depicts the development of public transport in Vienna from the days of the horse-drawn streetcars, through the introduction of steam tramways right up to the modern trams of today. It was created on a private initiative to ensure that a selection of trams were saved from the scrap heap and subsequently renovated by enthusiastic volunteers to their original condition. All profits from the 'oldtimer' tramway specials tours are devoted to the renovation, repair and service of this museum's important collection. Not to be missed.

## 134  Vienna Tramways (operated by Wiener Linien)

*Location*: Vienna.
*Michelin map reference*: V4.
*Operated by*: Wiener Linien GmbH.
*Routes*: Vienna's tramway system is thought now to be largest in the world with a network totalling a  distance of 230 km. It was only previously exceeded by the network in St Petersburg but more recently many of that city's routes have had to be closed due to lack of maintenance.
*Journey times*: Vary according to route taken - consult local timetables.
*Gauge*: Standard by adhesion only.
*Electrified*: Yes, 600 V DC.
*Livery*: Red and white.

One of the many Vienna Trans; depicted here on 6th July, 2007, is a class E1 (2-section car) No. 4508 built by Lohner/Rotax as part of the 4400 series. *Author*

***Rolling stock***: Given the size of the network and the frequency of services, the fleet of trams is extensive. It includes class 'A' 5-section ultra-low floor cars built between 1995 and 2003; class 'B' 7-section ultra-low floor cars built between 1995 and 2005; class 'E2' 2-section cars built between 1977 and 1990; class 'E' 2-section cars built between 1959 and 1966; class 'E1' 2-section cars built between 1967 and 1976; class 'C3' trailer cars built between 1959 and 1962; class 'C4' trailer cars built between 1974 and 1977 and class 'C5' trailers built between 1977 and 1980 and also between 1985 and 1990 (*source: Platform 5*).
***Places to see***: Vienna, what more can one say? Given so many beautiful buildings it is difficult to know where to start but do not miss the cathedral, the Stephansdom in the Stephansplatz which is the focal point of the inner city, accessible by the U1 and U3 underground lines.
***Contact details***: Wiener Linien GmbH, Erdbergstrasse 202, A-1031 Wien. Telephone: 01 7909-100. E-mail: via 'kontakt' on the website.
***Website***: www.wienerlinien.co.at (de)
***Operating dates***: All year round.
***Comments***: Vienna's extensive tram network has more than 30 routes. The Vienna tram, known to locals as the 'bim', is an efficient way of getting around the city with trams on most routes departing every five to 10 minutes. Trams run underground in some parts of the city centre. The tramways are integrated within a network of Vienna's bus, S-Bahn and U-Bahn services (*see next entries*). The author strongly advises visitors to Vienna by car to park on the outskirts and take public transport into the centre. Traffic is impossible.

## 135 Vienna S-Bahn (Wien Schnellbahn)

***Location***: Vienna.
***Michelin map reference***: V4.
***Operated by***: ÖBB.
***Routes***: The Vienna S-Bahn serves the Greater Vienna area with 10 routes: S1 operating Wiener Neustadt-Floridsdorf and Mödling-Gänserdorf; S15 Hollabrunn-Hütteldorf; S2 Meidling-Mistelbach; S3 Stockerau Meidling, Meidling-Hollabrunn and Hütteldorf - Stockerau; S40 - Franz-Josefs Bahnhof-Tulln Stadt; S45 Hütteldorf-

Handelskal; S50 Westbahnhof-Tullnerbach-Pressbaum; S60 Südbahnhof Ostseite-Bruck a.d.Leitha; S7 Floridsdorf-Flughafen Wien and services to Erzherzog-Karl Strasse and Wolfsthal; and, S80 Südbahnhof Ostseite-Hausfeldstrasse.
*Journey times*: S-Bahn timings vary according to the journey taken.
*Gauge*: Standard by adhesion only.
*Electrified*: Yes, 15 kV AV 16.7 Hz on the S-Bahn.
*Rolling stock*: S-Bahn rolling stock is mainly class '4020s' built between 1978 and 1987 by SGP/BBC/Elin/Siemens.
*Contact details*: Wiener Linien, Erdbergstrasse 202, A-1030 Vienna. Telephone: 01 7909-100. E-mail: via the website or kundendienst@wienerlinien.co.at
*Website*: www.wienerlinien.co.at (de)
*Operating dates*: Daily all the year round.
*Comments*: The S-Bahn is well integrated in Vienna's transport system including the U-Bahn, bus and tram networks. 'Schnellbahn' translates from German to mean 'fast railway'.

### 136  Vienna U-Bahn

*Location*: Vienna.
*Michelin map reference*: V4.
*Operated by*: Wiener Linien-Wiener Stadtwerke-Verkehrsbetriebe (WL).
*Routes*: On the U-Bahn there are five routes numbered U1 to U6. U1 travels from Reumanplatz to Leopoldau; U2 operates from Schottenring to Karlspaltz; U3 is routed between Simmering and Ottakring. U4 conveys passengers from Hütteldorfer Strasse to Heiligenstadt; U6 connects Siebenhirten with Floridsdorf which is the longest journey on the network at 17.4 km with a journey time of 36 minutes. There is no line U5 in the network. From the 1960s to the 1980s all long-term plans included a line U5, but the traffic predictions for the route were never promising enough to justify building the line. Had the line been built it would have travelled the following route: Hernals-Alser Strasse-Landesgericht-Scottentor-Schottenring-Taborstrasse-Praterstern-Ausstellungsstrasse-Stadion to Stadlauer Brücke. Today the total distance of the network is 61.6 km of which 32.5 km is underground. Karlsplatz is an important junction with the U1, U2 and U4 converging. There a total of 76 stations.
*Journey times*: On average U-Bahn trains run every five minutes and four minutes at peak times. These times extend to 7-8 minutes in the evenings.
*Gauge*: Standard by adhesion only.
*Electrified*: Yes, 750 V DC is collected from a third rail on the U-Bahn.
*Rolling stock*: There are four main types of rolling stock in service. On Lines U1, 2, 3 and 4 standard 'U', 'U2' and 'U11' stock is deployed and operated automatically using the LZB system. Line U6 (Stadtbahn) uses light rail stock of the 'E6', 'C6' and 'T' types with overhead current collection and optical signalling.
*Contact details*: Wiener Linien, Erdbergstrasse 202, A-1030 Vienna. Telephone: 01 7909-100. E-mail: kundendienst@wienerlinien.co.at
*Website*: www.wienerlinien.co.at (de)
*Operating dates*: Daily all the year round.
*History*: Plans to build an underground railway in Vienna go back to 1843, when Heinrich Sichrowsky submitted plans to the city council, but it was another 50 years until the construction of an urban railway system in Vienna began. The origins of the present-day U-Bahn go back to 1898 when Otto Wagner's *Stadtbahn* (Metropolitan Railway), a full-sized railway, operated with steam engines and was managed by the

Class U1/U11 set No. 2261/3261 on the U2 line at Karlsplatz U-bahn station on 6th July, 2007. *Author*

Federal Railways. Today's city transport is based on the *Stadtbahn* which is now mainly lines U4 and U6. The network was electrified in 1925. A converted underground tram tunnel was built in the 1960s to become line U2. New lines have been added since 1969 (i.e. lines U1, U3, and U6 extensions). Further modernisation followed in 1976 and improvements have continued since.

*Comments*: The U-Bahn is well integrated into Vienna's transport system including the S-Bahn, bus and tram networks.

### 137 Wiener Lokalbahnen (WLB)

*Location*: Vienna.
*Michelin map reference*: V4.
*Operated by*: Wiener Lokalbahnen AG (WLB).
*Route*: The WLB runs the only private, completely electrified twin track railway in Austria. Its Vienna (Wien Oper) to Baden route is in part operated as a tramway on the public transit infrastructure and in part as a railway for the conveyance of freight. The total track length is 30.4 km with an additional 5.6 km of servicing and connecting tracks. About 40 per cent of daily commuters to the south of Vienna use the WLB.
*Journey time*: The journey between Baden and Wien Oper takes 1 hour 2 minutes.
*Gauge*: Standard by adhesion only.
*Electrified*: Yes. The power supply is provided through 10 electric rectifier systems with feed supplies every 2.5 km. The electric rectifier systems transforms the current from 10 or 20kV to about 620 V DC. After the rectification through a bridge, an open circuit voltage of about 1000 V is attained.
*Rolling stock*: Type '100' and the more modern type '400' powered passenger carriages.
*Contact details*: Wiener Lokalbahnen AG, Eichenstrasse 1, Wien A-1120. Telephone: 043 1 90344. E-mail: verkehrskontrolle@wlb.at
*Website*: www.wlb.at
*Operating dates*: Daily all the year round.
*Tariff*: Single adult tickets are priced on a zone basis varying from €1.70 for the Centre/Inner zone to €5.40 for Centre/Inner zone and two outer zones. Children and dogs travel for just over half of the adult price (2007).

*History*: The Wiener Lokalbahnen AG began operations in 1888 with concession for the local rail route from Vienna to Wiener Neudorf (and related routes) being transferred to the *Aktiengesellschaft der Wiener Lokalbahnen* from the original New Viennese Tramway Society (NWT). In those days the wagons in Baden were still hauled by horses, whilst on the route between Vienna and Wiener Neudorf steam-driven trains were operated. In 1894, the horse tramway in Baden was one of the first to be electrified followed, in 1907, with the construction of the twin track railroad system between Vienna and Baden.

*Comments*: Tram-style passenger trains as well as considerable freight traffic (a subsidiary company since September 2007) operated on their own line as well as on to other open access rail networks. Wiener Lokalbahnen also offers *Nostalgie* train services and private charter excursions using two types of vehicle. First, is an 1899-built k.k. *Hofsalonwagen* the first quadruple axis motor coach of the *Aktiengesellschaft der Wiener Lokalbahnen* which began life serving local traffic around Baden. Between 1908 and 1911 it was transformed by Int. Schlafwagengesellschaft in Vienna and made into what it can be seen as today. From 1911, it was used exclusively by members of the Royal Family for their journeys between Vienna and Baden. In the 1920s it was then used for Royal leisure trips throughout Austria. In 1955, it was sold to the VEF (Verband der Eisenbahnfreunde). Then, in 1973, on the initiative of the local railway museum in Niederösterreich and with the support of the Wiener Lokalbahnen, an extensive restoration was undertaken. Since 1977, the *Hofsalonwagen* has been available for charter on all routes of the Wiener Lokalbahnen. The *Oldtimer-triebwagen* Nos. TW 223, 230 and 231 were built in the Grazer wagon factory between 1927 and 1928 and were considered at that time as very modern and elegant motor coaches with leather seats, mirrored glass, and highly polished wood. In 1954, they needed to be modernized and upgraded to conform to prevailing standards. They continued operating until 1989 when they were replaced with modern rolling stock. In 1990, they were restored to their original design and condition including the use of the original paint scheme and the former LWB coat of arms. Since 2004, WLB has also operated bus services through its subsidiary company, the Wiener Lokalbahnen Busbetrieb GmbH.

Wiener Lokalbahn's tram No. 119 *Margot* with a more recent 2001/2005 City Tram No. 404 photographed on 6th July, 2007 in the Karlsplatz in the heart of Vienna.   *Author*

## Vorarlberg

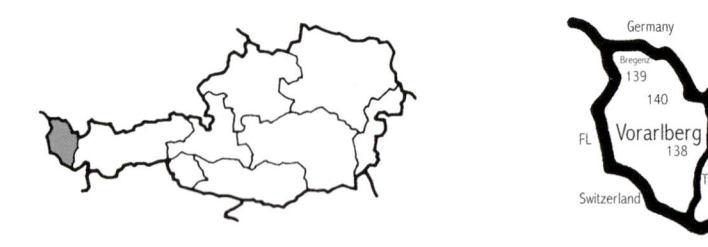

Vorarlberg is the most westerly state in Austria. With a geographical area of 2,601 sq km it is the eighth smallest in the country with only Vienna being smaller. It also has a small population with 372,791 inhabitants (eighth in size out of the nine states). It has borders with only one other Austrian state, Tyrol, but has international frontiers with Germany, Switzerland and Liechtenstein. The state capital is Bregenz on the eastern shores of Lake Constance (Bodensee).

### 138 Montafonerbahn [MBS]

*Location*: Bludenz, 21 km south-east of Feldkirch and 53 km south of Bregenz.
*Michelin map reference*: B7.
*Nearest main line railway station*: Bludenz on the Westbahn (line numbers 501 and 601 and timetable numbers 400 and 401).
*Operated by*: Montafonerbahn Aktiengesellschaft.

Montafonerbahn's Swiss-built two-railcar set No. ET 10.108/ES 10.208 approaching Lorüns on 11th July, 2007.
*Author*

*Official line number*: None allocated.
*Timetable number*: 420.
*Route*: From Bludenz to Schruns, a total distance of 12.7 km.
*Journey time*: 20 minutes.
*Gauge*: Standard by adhesion only.
*Electrified*: Yes, 15 kV AC 16.7 Hz.
*Rolling stock*: Electric locomotives: 1927/8-built class '1045' Nos. 01 & 03. Electric railcars: class 'ET 10' Nos. 103 & 104 (formerly diesel-powered and converted in 1961), 1990/4-built class 'ET 10' Nos. 107 & 108, 2000 Stadler/Adtranz-built class 'ET 10' Nos. 109 *Ernest Hemingway* & 110 *Anita Wacter*. Diesel locomotive: 1956 KHD-built class 'V10'. Finally, a former ÖBB class '5081' No. 12 which has been converted into an overhead line maintenance unit and carries the number X 10. 903.
*Contact details*: Montafonerbahn Aktiengesellschaft, Bahnhofstraße 15, A-6780 Schruns. Telephone: 05556 9000 Fax: 05556 72789. E-mail: office@montafonerbahn.at
*Website*: www.montafonerbahn.at
*Operating dates*: Throughout the year daily services operate hourly from 0500 hours to 2300 hours with extra half-hourly services at peak times.
*Tariff*: Local fare structure applies.
*History*: The line was opened in 1905.
*Comments*: The railway has its depot at Schruns where a large collection of electric railcars of various vintages can be found. The company also operates steam-hauled summer specials. ÖBB rolling stock also travels this route.

## 139 Rheinschauen

*Location*: Lustenau, 17 km south of Bregenz which is on the Bodensee (Lake Constance).
*Michelin map reference*: A-B6.
*Nearest main line railway station*: Lustenau Markt on official line number 504 and timetable 401 or St Margrethen on the Swiss border with help from SBB's timetable number 880.
*Operated by*: Rheinschauen Museum.
*Route*: From the museum at Lustenau to Rheinmündung, a total distance of 10 km.
*Journey time*: 30 minutes.
*Gauge*: Narrow (750 mm the only gauge of this size in Austria) by adhesion or rack only.
*Traction*: Steam- and electric-powered (750 V DC).
*Rolling stock*: Five diesel locomotives of which four are named as *Juno, Miki, Susi 2* and *Maikäfe*. Three diesel-electric locomotives named *Heidi, Urs and Elfi*. Two steam locomotives - a 1910-built *Widnau* ex-St Gallen and a 1921-built *Liesl* ex-Maffei. There are also 12 passenger coaches including two ex-Mariazellerbahn and 1 ex-Bregenzerbahn. There are a number of goods wagons.
*Contact details*: Rheinschauen, Hochster Strasse 4, Lustenau, A-6893 Telephone: 05577 20539 Fax: 05577 20539 18. E-Mail: verein@rheinschauen.at
*Website*: www.rheinschauen.at (de) and www.ingr.co.uk/dienstbahn.html (de).
*Operating dates*: Beginning of May to mid-October mainly on Fridays, Saturdays and Sundays but also some Public Holidays and Santa Specials in early December. Opening hours are 1300 to 1700 hours. When the trains are running they leave at 1500 hours.

Some coaches of the Rheinschauen. *Author*

Formerly ÖBB's 1940-built D3 No. 2091.08 crossing the River Bregenzerach near Schwarzenberg on 12th July, 2007. *Author*

*Tariff*: Museum admission for an adult is €3 and for a child (of school age) is €2. A combined museum and *E-lok*-hauled train journey is €8.50 for an adult and €4 for a child. A combined museum and steam-hauled train journey is €9.50 for an adult and €4.50 for a child (2007).
*History*: This was an electrified 750 mm gauge railway built for the transport of stones for flood protection dams from a quarry at Koblach to the Rhine mouth on Lake of Constance. Quarry trains were taken out of service on this line in 2005.
*Comments*: Some of the staff speak excellent English and are very helpful. A British group of enthusiasts chartered a train in 2007.

## 140 Wälderbähnle (Bregenzerwaldbahn)

*Location*: Bersbuch, 29 km driving distance south-east of Bregenz.
*Michelin map reference*: B6.
*Nearest main line railway station*: Dornbirn on the Westbahn (line number 601 and timetable number 401).
*Operated by*: Bregenzerwald Museumsbahn.
*Route*: Bezau to Schwarzenberg, a total distance of 6 km.
*Journey time*: 23 minutes.
*Gauge*: Narrow (760 mm) by adhesion only.
*Traction*: Steam- and diesel-powered.
*Rolling stock*: Steam locomotives: 1902-built U 25 *Bezau* and 1931-built Uh 102. Diesel locomotives: 1940-built D3 formerly ÖBB's No. 2091.08, 1943-built 0-6-0 dh No. D1 *Hilde*, 1961-built No. D2 *Margreth*, and a collection of passenger carriages and other wagons.
*Places to see*: The market town of Bezau, one of the principal communities of the Bregenzerwald, houses a folk law museum. Not far away at Mellau the Kanisfluh mountain should be seen with its five sides dropping 1,300 m to the valley floor - dramatic!
*Contact details*: Bregenzerwald Museumsbahn, Nr. 39, Langenegg, A-6941. Telephone: 06664 466 2330. E-mail: info@waelderbaehnle.at
*Website*: www.waelderbaehnle.at (de en).
*Operating dates*: From 26th May to 7th October, 2007 with some additional excursions in November and December. Likely to be similar dates in future years.
*Tariff*: On the steam-hauled train an adult return is €7.50 and single €5.50 and for a child (6-14 years) €3 and €2.50 respectively. On the diesel-hauled train an adult return is €6 and single €4.50 and for a child €6.50 and €2 respectively (2007).
*History*: The Bregenzerwaldbahn was opened on 15th September, 1902 and ran its operations on the route from Bregenz to Bezau (35.4 km). Unfortunately, in July 1980, there was an enormous rockslide which caused total disruption to continuous train services on the route. In 1983, a limited service was operated from Kennelbach to Bregenz but by the end of January 1985 the railway was finally closed. However, in the same year the Association Bregenzerwald Museumsbahn was founded with the objectives of safeguarding historic rolling stock and where finances permit to restore items to working order. This it has successfully achieved and now operates an excellent and popular tourist train service.
*Comments*: There is a covered museum where the trains and carriages are housed and where there is also a small shop which sells souvenirs. The Association also produce an interesting newsletter in German.

# Chapter Six

# Austria's Rail Freight Companies

### 141 Salzburger Eisenbahn Transport Logistik (SETG)

*Location*: Salzburg.
*Michelin map reference*: L5.
*Operated by*: Salzburger Eisenbahn Transport Logistik GmbH.
*Traction*: Electric- and diesel-powered.
*Gauge*: Standard.
*Rolling stock*: Class '1116' *Taurus* electric locomotives by Siemens, class '1115' electric locomotives by Bombardier, G 1700 diesel locomotives by Vossloh (Kiel) and class 'V100' (213) by MaK (Kiel).
*Contact details*: Salzburger Eisenbahn Transport Logistik GmbH, Fürbergstrasse 42a, Salzburg, A-5020. Telephone: 0662 45 75 67-0 Fax: 0662 45 75 67-19. E-mail: office@setg.at
*Website*: www.setg.at
*Comments*: SETG operates the following freight services: 1) Ecco-Shuttle-Züge (timber) from Germany with up to four shuttles per week from various loading points in Mecklenburg-Western Pomerania and Brandenburg via Passau into Austria. 2) Ecco-Cargo twice a week connections carrying wood from Schleusingen and Schweinfurt in Germany to customers in Austria. 3) Ecco-Cargo 'Unterweser' operating six times weekly, carrying wood products from Kirchweyhe in Lower Saxony to Austria. 4) Ecco Cargo-Netz from the port of Brake on the River Weser (accessing the North Sea near Bremerhaven) to Austria, and 5) Ecco-Cargo (Knoten Köln-Eifeltor) offering freight transit on routes Köln-Eifeltor-Dusseldorf-Reisholz - Neuss-Hessentor and Köln-Eifeltor-Bergisch Gladbach between three and five times each week.

### 142 LTE Logistik und Transport GmbH

*Location*: Graz, 243 km south-east of Salzburg.
*Michelin map reference*: S7.
*Operated by*: LTE Logistik und Transport GmbH.
*Official line number*: Graz.
*Routes*: Freight running: Marchegg to Liesing (cement), Kirchdorf-Liesing (cement), Burghausen (Germany)-Simbach-Marchegg-Ziar and Hronom (Slovakia) (coke) and Graz-Duisberg (containers).
*Gauge*: Standard.
*Rolling stock*: Three Bombardier Traxx F140 Cs - Nos. 9480 0185.528-7 *Hermine*, 9480 0185.529-5 *Michael* and 9480 0185.524-6 *Sonja*; two Vossloh G 1206 LTE 2150.9s - LTE 9381 2150 901-3 *Birgit* and LTE 9381 2150 902-1 *Brigitte*; a Vossloh G 1700 - No. LTE 2170 001-8 *Johanna*; and two Siemens 'Eurorunner' ER 20s - Nos. LTE 2016 903-1 and LTE 2016 904-6.
*Contact details*: LTE Logistik- und Transport-GmbH, Reininghausstrasse 3, A-8020 Graz. Telephone: 0316 5987-289 Fax: 0316 5987-238. E-mail: e-mail: office@lte.at
*Website*: www.lte.at
*History*: LTE is a joint venture between Porr Infrastruktur and Graz-Köflacher Bahn und Busbetrieb GmbH (GKB) (*see entry* 77).

## AUSTRIA'S RAIL FREIGHT COMPANIES

*Comments*: LTE is an open access operator. Interestingly, LTE does not have a depot as such but operates mobile maintenance teams. LTE, mentioned here for its freight operations, also has a relationship to Graz-Köflacher Bahn und Busbetrieb GmbH (GKB) which also preserves and uses historic material (*see entry 77*).
LTE has subsidiaries in Slovakia and the Czech Republic.

### 143 Rail Transport Service (RTS)

RTS's *Eurosprinter* No. 1216 901-9 passes Timelkam on 1st July, 2007.   *Author*

*Location*: Graz, 193 km south west of Vienna.
*Michelin map reference*: S7.
*Operated by*: RTS - Rail Transport Service GmbH.
*Gauge*: Standard.
*Traction*: Electric-powered at 15 kV AC 16.7 Hz and diesel-powered.
*Rolling stock*: Some 1965-77-built Series 2143 by Simmering Graz-Pauker AG (SGP), 2004-6-built Series ER 20 by Siemens and 2002-6-built by Siemens *Eurosprinters* Series ES 64 U2 & ES 64 U4.
*Contact details*: RTS Rail Transport Service GmbH, Puchstraße 184 a, A-8055 Graz. Telephone: 0 316 2161-3351 Fax: 0 316 2161-3398. E-mail: office@rts-austria.com
*Website*: www.rts-austria.at
*Comments*: RTS is a subsidiary of the manufacturing company Swietelsky, one of the biggest European companies in the field of railway track with RTS transporting its track-laying machines. Through the establishment of a subsidiary RTS Rail Transport Service GmbH has also been established in Munich since 2006. RTS currently has 45 employees.

### 144 Cargoserv

*Location*: Linz and other various Voest Steelworks locations throughout Austria..
*Operated by*: Cargoserv's parent company is Voest Alpine.
*Gauge*: Standard.
*Traction*: Electric-powered (15 kV AC 16.7 Hz) and diesel-powered.

*Rolling stock*: Cargoserv operate four 2003-built Siemens *Eurosprinters* ES 64s and three 1969-built class '1504' diesels.
*Website*: www.cargoserv.at which links to www.voestalpine.com
*Comments*: Cargoserv is part of Voest Alpine which operates its own steel-carrying trains over the ÖBB lines between Steyrling and Linz. Voest Alpine has five divisions: Voestalpine Stahl GmbH (steel), Boehler Uddeholm AG (stainless steel), Voestalpine Rail Systems GmbH (rail manufacture), Voestalpine Profil GmbH and Voestalpine Automotive GmbH. A number of the Voest factories have marshalling yards, Linz, for example, having a large internal factory network.

## 145 Rail Cargo Austria

*Locations*: Rail Cargo Austria offers 16 locations throughout Austria - Wolfurt, Bludenz, Brennersee, Hall im Tirol, Wörgl, Salzburg, Wels, Linz Stadhafen, Enn Hafen, Krems a.d. Donau, St Pölten, Vienna NW, Vienna FH, Graz Süd and Villach Süd.
*Operated by*: Rail Cargo Austria AG as an independent company of ÖBB.
*Gauge*: Standard.
*Traction utilised*: Electric- (15 kV AC 16.7 Hz) and diesel-powered.
*Rolling stock*: Given the relationship with ÖBB the full range of latter's fleet is available to Rail Cargo Austria AG. The *Taurus* range by Siemens-Krauss-Maffei (classes '1016', '1116' and the new '1216') can be regularly observed hauling freight not only in Austria but also into neighbouring countries. However, the use of other classes is far from exclusive for mixed-goods work but it is not within the scope of this book to pursue in detail freight workings.
*Contact details*: Rail Cargo Austria AG. Telephone: 05 7750 Fax: 05 7750-700. info@railcargo.at
*Website*: www.railcargo.at (de en).
*History*: Since January 2005, Rail Cargo Austria AG has been an independent company previously having been the former ÖBB Freight Transport Division.
*Comments*: Rail Cargo Austria AG, in co-operation with its subsidiary Speditions Holding AG, is an international provider of transport and logistics services.

The aptly named *Hercules* class '2016' is akin to the diesel version of the electric *Taurus* class '1116'. On 29th June, 2007 No. 2016 078.4 is seen with a freight train at Lambach on the Westbahn. *Author*

# Chapter Seven

# Funicular Operations in Austria

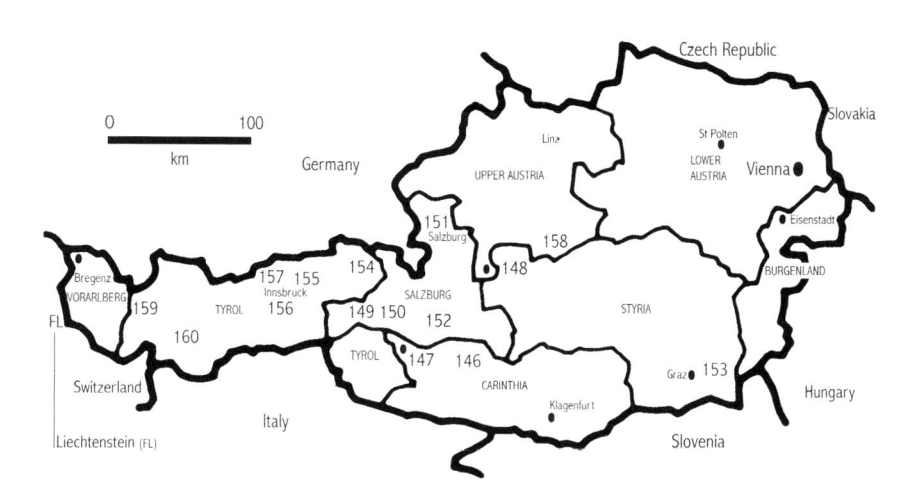

## 146 Kreuzeckbahn*

*Location*: Mölltal Valley at (Unter) Kolbnitz 56 km north-west of Villach.
*Michelin map reference*: L8.
*Nearest main line railway station*: Kolbnitz on the Tauernbahn (line number 806 and timetable number 220).
*Operated by*: Österreichische Drauwerke AG, A-9815 Kolbnitz (Carinthia).
*Route*: From Tratten (alt. 605 m) to Kreuzeck Bergstation (alt. 1,211 m), a height difference of 606 m over a total distance of 1.28 km.
*Maximum gradient*: 74 per cent.
*Journey time*: 11 minutes.
*Contact details*: Österreichische Drauwerke AG, A-9815 Kolbnitz and also Touristikbüro Reisseck, A-9815 Kolbnitz. Telephone: 04783 2060 Fax: 043 4783 2160.
*Website*: www.peak.at/reisseck/Tourismus/kreuzeckbahn.htm (de)
*Operating dates*: End of June to mid-September only.
*History*: The Kreuzeck Funicular first opened on 9th October, 1974.
*Comments*: Is marketed as the 'Panoramabahn Kreuzeck'. On the route there is a magnificent view of the Reißeckmassiv. At the terminus it is possible to hike to Bergwanderungen, Keuschenwaldalm, Bernitschalm, Mühldorfer Alm and the Salzkofel mountains, all over 2,000 m.

---

* Not to be confused with the one in Germany near Garmisch-Partenkirchen.

### 147 Pasterzen-Bahn

*Location*: Heiligenblut, 122 km north-west of Villach.
*Michelin map reference*: K7.
*Nearest main line railway station*: Lienz on the Drautalbahn (line number 707 and timetable number 223).
*Operated by*: Großglockner Cable Car GmbH.
*Route*: From Freiwandeck car park (alt. 2,212 m) to Pasterze glacier (alt. 2,356 m), a height difference of 144 m over a total route distance of 212 m.
*Maximum gradient*: 95.5 per cent.
*Journey time*: 2 minutes.
*Contact details*: Tourismusverband, A-9844 Heiligenblut. Telephone: 02824 2002.
*Website*: www.grossglockner.at
*Operating dates*: The access road (Hochalpenstraße) is only open in the summer months.
*History*: Was opened on 15th September, 1963.
*Comments*: The *Großglockner-Hochalpenstraße* (High Alpine road) is probably the most famous Austrian Panoramic road. There are many vantage points on the route giving magnificent views of the Hohen Tauern. One of the best is from the car park at Freiwandeck and from where the funicular travels directly to the Glacier Village. Perhaps, because of climate change, the route to the glacier gets further away each year. In recent years, there have been several proposals to install a new cable car to the present location of the glacier but these have been rejected for environmental reasons. The *Großglockner-Hochalpenstraße* is closed in winter from early November to May the following year. There is a charge of €28 (day ticket) for a car to travel the High Alpine road when it is open in the summer months. The tariff gets cheaper if a ticket for more than a one day is purchased (2007).

### 148 Hallstätter Salzbergbahn

*Location*: Hallstatt, 78 km south-east of Salzburg.
*Michelin map reference*: M6.
*Nearest main line railway station*: Obertraun Dachsteinhöhlen on the Salzkammergutbahn (line number 306 and timetable 170).
*Operated by*: Österreichische Salinen AG.
*Route*: From the roadway (alt. 513 m) alongside the Hallstätter See to the mine (alt. 808 m), a height difference of 295 m over a total route distance of 548 m.
*Maximum gradient*: 81.5 per cent.
*Journey time*: 3 minutes.
*Places to see:* The fantastic views of the UNESCO World Cultural and Natural Heritage Region - Dachstein-Hallstättersee.
*Contact details*: Österreichische Salinen AG, Salzwelten Reisedienst Birgit Ellmer, Wirerstraße 10, A-4820 Bad Ischl. Telephone: 06132 200 2490 Fax: 06132 200 4400. Email: info@salzwelten.at
*Website*: www.salzwelten.at/cont/salzwelten/en_salzwelten_hallstatt_salzbergbahn.aspx
*Operating dates*: End of April to the beginning of November from 0900 to 1800 hours daily.
*Tariff*: An adult return on the funicular is €8.50.
*History*: The funicular was opened on 1st May, 1980.

Funicular No. 2 descends to its base station on the Salzbergbahn on 30th June, 2007.
*Author*

**Comments**: The funicular takes visitors up to the 'Salzwelten' where are the oldest salt-mines in the world dating back 7,000 years. The guided tour through the 'Salzwelten' takes 70 minutes but three hours should be allowed for the whole visit. Children under 4 years of age accompanied by a parent can be taken free of charge on the funicular but at that age are not allowed to enter the mine.

### 149 Kaprun

*Location*: Kaprun, 91 km south-west of Salzburg.
*Michelin map reference*: K7.
*Nearest main line railway station*: Zell am See on the Giselabahn (line number 601 and timetable 201) and also accessible from the Pinzgauerbahn (*see entry 65*).
*Introduction*: Gletscherbahnenen Kaprun AG originally operated three accesses to the summit of the Kitzsteinhorn. These were: Section 1 (Kaprun I) opened in December 1965 and running from Kapruner Thörl ((alt. 928 m) to Salzburger Hütte (alt. 1,897 m). Section 2 (Kaprun II), also opened in December 1965, ran from Salzburger Hütte (alt. 1,897 m) to Krefelder Hütte (alt. 2,452 m) and Section 3 (Kaprun III) ran from Krefelder Hütte (alt. 2,452 m) to Kitzsteinhorn NW-Grat (alt. 3,029 m). Kaprun II suffered a catastrophic fire in November 2000 tragically claiming the lives of 155 people, it has not operated since. To replace Kaprun II 'Glacier Jet 1'

a double-cable railway was opened in December 2001 and in October 2002 'Glacier Jet 2' a single-cable railway was opened. Kaprun III started life out in November 1966 taking skiers to within 175 m (in altitude) of the summit of the Kitzsteinhorn (alt. 3,203 m). It was 2.2 km long and could carry 680 people every hour in a journey time of about eight minutes. It claimed to have at that time (and perhaps still now) at 113.5 m the highest cable car ropeway support in the world. It was replaced with the Gipfelbahn in 1990.
*Operated by*: Gletscherbahnenen Kaprun AG
*Route*: The Gipfelbahn rises 92 m over a journey distance of 257 m.
*Maximum gradient*: 37.8 per cent.
*Contact details*: Gletscherbahnenen Kaprun AG, Wilhelm Fazokas Straße 690, A-5710 Kaprun. Telephone: 06547 8700 Fax: 06547 7614. E-mail: office@kitzsteinhorn.at
*MandarfenWebsite*: www.kitzsteinhorn.at (de en).
*Operating dates*: All year round.
*History*: See the introduction above.
*Comments*: With the growing popularity of the Kitzsteinhorn in the 1970s, Gletscherbahnenen Kaprun AG decided to build a funicular railway with the majority of the track travelling underground. On 23rd March, 1974 the first alpine underground railway in the world was opened.

## 150 Lärchwand-Schrägaufzug

*Location*: Kaprun, 91 km south-west of Salzburg.
*Michelin map reference*: K7.
*Nearest main line railway station*: Zell am See on the Giselabahn (line number 601 and timetable number 201).
*Operated by*: Formerly Tauernkraft Werke AG now merged with the Verbund Austrian Hydro Power AG.
*Route*: From the *Talstation* (bottom station) (alt. 1,209 m) to the *Bergstation* (top station) (alt. 1,640 m) a height difference of 431 m over a total journey distance of 820 m.
*Maximum gradient*: 81 per cent.
*Gauge*: At 8200 mm, it is believed to be the widest in the world.
*Journey time*: 6 minutes.
*Places to see*: Kaprun is located in the Hohen Tauern National Park. The funicular/elevator takes visitors up from Kaprun to the Kitzsteinhorn glacier.
*Contact details*: Verbund Austrian Hydro Power AG, A-1010 Vienna. Telephone: 05 03 13-0.
*Operating dates*: All year round.
*History*: Was first opened in 1952.
*Comments*: Is reputed to be the largest elevator in Europe carrying 185 passengers and one 'driver'. Verbund Austrian Hydro Power AG also operate two other funiculars in this area: the Maiskogel-Schragaufzug with a 1600 m gauge over a distance of 1.44 km rising 755 m with a maximum gradient of 82 per cent; and, the Limbergstolen-Schragaufzug with a 800 mm gauge over a distance of 923 m rising 583 m on a maximum gradient of 87 per cent.

## 151 Salzburger FestungsBahn

SLB's Car No. 2 *Wolf Dietrich* descends from the castle in Salzburg on 1st July, 2007.
*Author*

*Location*: Salzburg, 189 km north east of Innsbruck.
*Michelin map reference*: L5.
*Nearest main line railway station*: Salzburg on the Westbahn (line number 401 and timetable number 101).
*Operated by*: Salzburger Stadtwerke AG. Salzburger Lokalbahn (SLB) (*see entry 66*).
*Route*: From the *Talstation* Festungsgasse (alt. 437 m) to the *Bergstation* Hohensalzburg (alt. 535 m) a height difference of 98 m over a total distance of 190 m.
*Maximum gradient*: 60.1 per cent.
*Journey time*: 58 seconds.
*Gauge*: 1040 mm.
*Places to see*: Salzburg with its Mozart associations annually holds a music festival (July-August). The *Dom* (cathedral), the *Schloss* (castle) and the Old Town are all worth exploring on foot.
*Contact details*: Salzburger FestungsBahn, Festungasse 4, A-5020 Salzburg. Telephone: 0662 44 801 500. E-mail: festungsbahn@salzburg-ag.at
*Website*: www.slb.at
*Operating dates*: All year round opening from 0900 hours and closing at 1700 hours from 1st October to 30th April but remaining open until 2200 hours from 1st May to 31st August and to 2100 hours in September each year.
*Tariff*: Entry to the *Festungs* (fortress) including the funicular trip is €10 for an adult and €5.70 for a child (6-15 years) (2007).
*History*: The funicular was opened in July 1892 and underwent a major refit in 1992.

'One up one down'. On 8th July, 2007, empty car No. 1 on its way down (*right*) passes fully-loaded car No 2 on its way u on the Grazer Schloßberg-Bahn. *Author*

## 152 Schlossalm-Bahn

*Location*: Bad Hofgastein, 88 km south of Salzburg.
*Michelin map reference*: L7.
*Nearest main line railway station*: Bad Hofgastein on the Tauernbahn (line number 806 and timetable number 220).
*Operated by*: Gasteiner Bergbahnen AG, section 1 of the ascent is the Schlossalm Standseilbahn.
*Route*: from the *Talstation* at Schloßalm (alt. 843m) to the *Bergstation* Kitzstein (alt. 1,302) a height difference of 459 m over a total distance of 1.251 km.
*Maximum gradient*: 48.5 per cent.
*Gauge*: 1200 mm.
*Journey time*: 2 minutes 30 seconds.
*Places to see*: In the summer the mountain station is the perfect starting point for hiking and mountain tours which offer breathtaking views of the mountains of the Hohen Tauern. In winter, four ski centres (Dorfgastein-Großarl, Schlossalm-Angertal-Stubnerkogel, Graukogel, and Sportgastein) offer variety for skiers and snowboarders of all ages and abilities.
*Contact details*: Gasteiner Bergbahnen AG, A-5630 Bad Hofgastein. Telephone: 06432 6455-0 Fax: 06432 6455-66. E-mail: info@skigastein.com
*Website*: www.gasteinertal.com/bergbahnen/
*Operating dates*: All year round for summer and winter pursuits.
*History*: The funicular opened on 15th September, 1964.

## 153 Grazer Schloßberg-Bahn

*Location*: Graz, 228 km south-west of Linz.
*Michelin map reference*: S7.
*Nearest main line railway station*: Graz on the Südbahn (line number 805 and timetable number 501)
*Operated by*: Grazer Verkehrsbetriebe.
*Route*: From the *Talstation* (alt. 353 m) to the *Bergstation* (alt. 461 m) a height difference of 108 m over a total journey distance of 210 m.
*Gauge*: Metre.
*Journey time*: 4 minutes.
*Places to see*: Tour on foot the Old Town and see the 16th century *Landhaushof* behind the 19th century *Rathaus*, both were seeing. There is reputed to be here the world's largest collection of ancient weaponry housed in the 17th century *Landeszeughaus*.
*Contact details*: Grazer Verkehrsbetriebe, Andreas-Hofer-Platz 15, A-8011 Graz. Herr Werner Hierzer is the Operations Manager for the Grazer Schloßbergbahn. His contact address is Steyrergasse 114 A-8010 Graz. Telephone: 0316 887 404 Fax: 0316 887 1818. E-mail: w.hierzer@gstw.at
*Website*: www.gvb.at/home/unsere_dienstleistungen/schlossbergbahn.php
*Operating dates*: All year round with services on Mondays to Wednesdays from 1000-2400 hours; Thursdays to Saturdays 1000-0200 hours (next morning); and, on Sundays 1000-2200 hours (2008).
*Tariff*: An adult return is €3.70 and €1.90 for a child. A single ticket is €1.70 and €0.90 respectively.
*History*: The funicular was originally opened on 25th November, 1894 and at that time it was steam driven. It was electrified in April 1900. A complete overhaul was made in 1961 and again in August 2004.

### 154 Hartkaiserbahn sometimes spelled Hartkaser-Bahn

*Location*: Ellmau, 86 km east-north-east of Innsbruck
*Michelin map reference*: I6.
*Nearest main line railway station*: Kirchberg in Tirol on the Giselabahn (line number 601 and timetable number 201).
*Operated by*: Recreation Centre Ellmau.
*Route*: From the *Talstation* in the village of Ellmau (alt. 818 m) to the *Bergstation* (alt. 1,525 m) a height difference of 707 m over a total journey distance of 2.317 km.
*Gauge*: Standard (1435 mm).
*Maximum gradient*: 46 per cent.
*Journey time*: 3 minutes 30 seconds.
*Places to see*: Ellmau is in the foothills of the Wilder Kaiser Mountains.
*Contact details*: Recreation Centre Ellmau, Weißbachgraben 5, A-6352 Ellmau. Telephone: 05358 2320-0. E-mail: bergbahnen.ellmau@skiwelt.at
*Website*: www.wilderkaiser.info/de/hartkaiserbahn/-1.html (de en nl fr it) www.bergbahnen-ellmau-going.at (de en).
*Operating dates*: All year round.


### 155 Hungerburg-Bahn

*Location*: Innsbruck.
*Michelin map reference*: G7.
*Nearest main line railway station*: Innsbruck on the Westbahn (line number 601 and timetable numbers 201 & 300).
*Operated by*: Innsbrucker Verkehrsbetriebe (Hungerburgbahn).
*Route*: From the *Talstation* (alt. 572 m) to the *Bergstation* (alt. 858 m), a height difference of 286 m over a total journey distance of 840 m.
*Maximum gradient*: 48.7 per cent.
*Gauge*: Metre.
*Journey time*: Just under six minutes.
*Places to see*: The Alpenzoo - Europe's highest zoo - at Weiherburggasse 37 and accessed via the Hungerburgbahn.
*Contact details*: Innsbrucker Verkehrsbetriebe (Hungerburgbahn), Rennweg 41, A-6020 Innsbruck. Telephone: 0512 58 6158.
*Website*: See www.wcities.com/en/record/,184112/120/record.html - no official site found.
*Operating dates*: All year round.
*Tariff*: Return tickets to Seegrube cost adults €18, €15 for seniors and students and €9 for children (2007).
*History*: The funicular was first opened on 10th September, 1906.
*Comments*: The funicular connects to the Nordkettenbahn cable car to Seegrube (alt. 1,905 metres) and on to the Hafelekarspitze (alt. 2,334 m). The views over the Inn valley are superb especially from the Seegrube Restaurant. (NB: Visitors travelling up to the Alpenzoo get a free ride (zoo tickets can be purchased at the station).)

### 156 Olympia-Bahn

*Location*: Axamer Lizum, 18 km south-west of Innsbruck near to Fulpmes.
*Michelin map reference*: F7.
*Nearest main line railway station*: Innsbruck on the Westbahn (line number 601 and timetable numbers 201 and 300). The Stubaitalbahn is not far away (*see entry 103*).
*Operated by*: Axamer Lizum Aufschließungs AG.
*Route*: From Lizumalm (alt. 1,572 m) to Hoadl-Gipfel (alt. 2,334 m) a height difference of 762 m, a total journey distance of 2.105 km. The funicular runs on a bridge construction over its entire length.
*Maximum gradient*: 54 per cent.
*Gauge*: Standard (1435 mm).
*Journey time*: Not known.
*Places to see*: The mountain station at Hoadl-Haus in winter offers excellent opportunities for skiing. In summer it is a great departure point for mountain hiking. The whole area of Kalkkogels present challenges. The highest peaks in the area are the Kalkkogel itself (alt. 2,558 m) and the Schlicker Seespitze (alt. 2,804 m).
*Contact details*: Axamer Lizum Aufschließungs AG, Fassergasse 3 A-6860 Hall im Tirol.
*Website*: No official site found but see www.axamer-lizum.at (de).
*Operating dates*: All year round. The winter months are defined as 'high season'.
*Tariff*: A day pass for an adult in high season (December to the end of March) is €29 and children €15. There are family tickets at reduced prices.
*History*: The funicular was opened on 20th December, 1975.

### 157 Roßhütte-Bahn

*Location*: Seefeld in Tirol, 23 km west-north-west of Innsbruck.
*Michelin map reference*: F6.
*Nearest main line railway station*: Seefeld in Tirol on the Karwendelbahn (line number 551 and timetable number 410 (ÖBB) and 960 (DB)).
*Operated by*: Bergbahnen Roßhütte.
*Route*: From the *Talstation* near Seefeld (alt. 1,235 m) to the *Bergstation* at Roßhutte (alt. 1,753 m) a difference of 518 m over a total journey distance of 2.41 km.
*Maximum gradient*: 37.2 per cent.
*Gauge*: 1244 mm.
*Journey time*: 5 minutes.
*Places to see*: At nearby Stams in the Inn valley is a Cistercian Abbey said to be one of the finest monasteries in Austria.
*Contact details*: Bergbahnen Roßhütte, Seefeld in Tirol A-6100. Telephone: 05212 24160 Fax: 05212 241629. E- mail info@rosshuette.at
*Website*: www.rosshuette.at
*Operating dates*: Winter months from November to Easter Monday.
*Comments*: From the Roßhutte *Bergstation* a cable car climbs Härmelekopf (alt. 2,041 m). A second cable car climbs to the Seefelderjoch (alt. 2,064 m). From both locations the Seefelder Spitze (alt. 2,221 m) can be accessed. The *Talstation* just off the main road at Seefeld underwent major re-construction in 2007.

Roßhuttebahn's car No. 1 makes its ascent from the *Talstation* on 28th June, 2007.    *Author*

## 158  Wurzeralmbahn

*Location*: Spital am Pyhrn, 23 km north of Selzthal in Styria.
*Michelin map reference*: P6.
*Nearest main line railway station*: Spital am Pyhrn on the Pyhrnbahn (line number 304 and timetable number 140).
*Operated by*: Hinterstoder-Wurzeralm Bergbahnen AG.
*Route*: From the *Talstation* at Pyhrnpassbundesstraße (alt. 804 m) to the *Bergstation* at Wurzeralm (alt. 1,426 m) a difference of 622 m over a total journey distance of 2.937 km.
*Maximum gradient*: 30 per cent.
*Gauge*: Standard (1435 mm).
*Journey time*: 4 minutes 20 seconds.
*Contact details*: Hinterstoder-Wurzeralm Bergbahnen AG, A-4573 Hinterstoder. Telephone: 07564 5275 Fax: 07564 5275 130. E-mail: info@hiwu.at
*Website*: www.hiwu.at
*Operating dates*: All year round.
*History*: The funicular was opened on 15th July, 1978 and underwent overhaul in 1995.
*Comments*: The holiday Pyhrn-Priel region totals nine municipalities - Windischgarsten, Edlbach, den Ski-Weltcup-Ort Hinterstoder, Klaus, Steyrling, Rosenau, Roßleithen, Vorderstoder and Spital am Pyhrn. Here a wide range of sports and other recreational activities can be enjoyed throughout the year (see www.pyhrn-priel.net).

## 159  Arlberger Kandaharbahn now referred to as the Galzigbahn

*Location*: St (Sankt) Anton am Arlberg, 107 km west of Innsbruck in the Tyrol region.
*Michelin map reference*: C7.
*Nearest main line railway station*: Sankt Anton am Arlberg on the Arlbergerbahn (Westbahn - line number 601 and timetable number 400).
*Operated by*: Arlberger Bergbahnen previously Arlberger Kandaharbahnen AG.
*Route*: From the Sankt Anton am Arlberg railway station to Gampen, an increase in altitude of 532 m over a total journey distance of 1.45 km.

*Contact details*: Arlberger Bergbahnen AG A-6580 Sankt Anton am Arlberg. Telephone: 054462352-0 Fax: 05446 2352-102. E-mail: office@abbag.com
*Website*: www.abbag.com
*Operating dates*: All year round.
*Tariff*: An adult return is €12 and a child travels at half-price (2007).
*History*: The original funicular was opened on 2nd February, 1973, its cost of construction rising over the two years of the project from 24 million schillings to 42 million. The funicular, for its entire length, ran on a steel viaduct up to the mountain station at Gampen. In the run-up to the Alpine World Ski Championships in 2001 in Sankt Anton, the entire facility was demolished and replaced by a cableway using gondolas. This facility, now called the Galzigbahn, is a spectacular cableway based on a ferris wheel which allows travellers to enter one of the 28 gondolas at ground level. This innovation has allowed the carrying capacity to be increased threefold, thus eradicating long waiting times to make the ascent or descent.
*Comments*: As with the cableway technology itself, the glass building designed by Tyrolean architect Georg Driendl is fascinating. It is possible to see into the transparent Galzig Valley station with its impressive ferris wheel and advanced technology; it is as good to see from the outside as it is from within!

## 160 Pitz-Expreß

*Location*: St (Sankt) Leonhard in Tirol, 93 km by road south-west of Innsbruck.
*Michelin map reference*: E7.
*Nearest main railway station*: Imst-Pitzal on the Westbahn (line number 501 and timetable number 400) then almost 40 km by road.
*Operated by*: Pitztaler Gletscherbahnen GesmbH & CO KG.
*Route*: From Sankt Leonhard (alt. 1,730 m) to Mittelberg (alt. 2,841 m), a height difference of 1,111 m, over a total distance of 3.786 km.
*Maximum gradient*: 37.6 per cent.
*Journey time*: 5 min 30 seconds.
*Contact details*: Pitztaler Gletscherbahn GesmbH & CO KG, Mittelberg, A-6481 St Leonhard. Telephone: 05413 86288 Fax: 05413 86288-150. E-mail: office@pitztaler-gletscher.at
*Website*: http://en.pitztaler-gletscher.at/aboutus/ and www.tirolgletscher.com
*Operating dates*: All year round.
*History*: It was opened on 23rd December, 1983. The tunnel lighting was improved in 2001 and between 2001 and 2003 some additional equipment was installed primarily to increase safety. The carriages which operate in pairs, have fire detectors and automatic carbon dioxide fire extinguishers, video surveillance and four emergency telephones to allow communication between passengers and the person controlling the motor for the carriages.
*Comments*: Underground funicular. From Mittelberg there is a 'panorama train' (*Pitz Panoramabahn*) opened in 1989 taking passengers up a further 601 m to Hinteren Brunnenkogel (3,440 m) and the ski area's Pitztal glacier. Incidentally, the terminus here is also the highest cable car station in Austria.

A *die (Deutsche) Bahn* Inter-City Express (ICE-T) electric multiple-unit train takes on its passengers at Linz bound for Munich on 1st July, 2007.   *Author*

Arriving at Scharnitz station on the Austro-German border is a morning service to Innsbruck on 28th June, 2007. *Die (Deutsche) Bahn's* locomotive No. 111 072-5 heads the train.   *Author*

# Chapter Eight

## Austria's International Railway Relationships

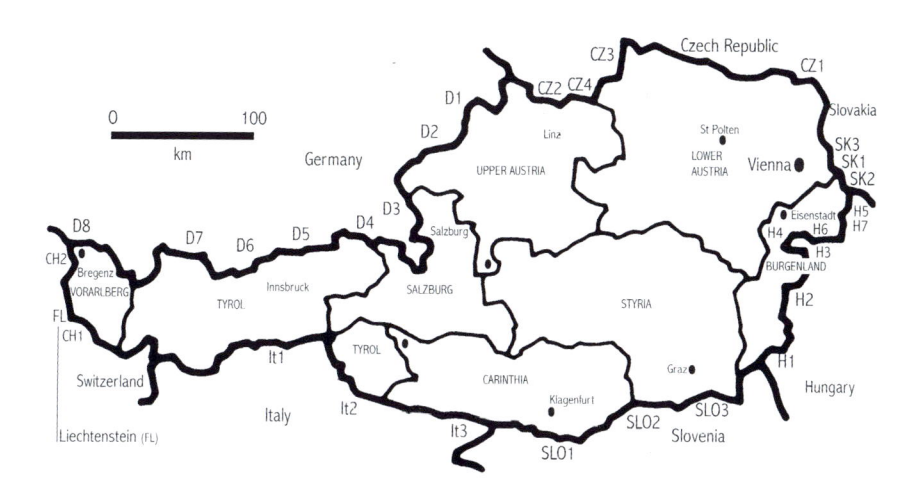

### 161 Germany

The German (D) border runs from the Lake Constance (Bodensee) near Bregenz south-west of München (Munich) and ends near Passau, south-east of München. The routes passing into or out of Germany and Austria (A) are:

*Border crossing D1*: Passau (D)-Pyret for the route from Wels to Regensburg (D).
*Border crossing D2*: Simbach (D)-Braunau am Inn for the route Steindorf bei Straßwalchen to Mühldorf (D).
*Border crossing D3*: Freilassing (D)-Salzburg for the route Salzburg to München (D).
*Border crossing D4*: Kiefersfelden (D)-Kufstein - for the route Wörgl to Rosenheim (D).
*Border crossing D5*: Mittenwald (D)-Scharnitz for the route Innsbruck to München (D).
*Border crossing D6*: Griesen (D)-Ehrwald for the route Reutte to Garmisch-Partenkirchen (D).
*Border crossing D7*: Pfronten-Steinach (D)-Schönbichl for the route Reutte to Kempten (D).
*Border crossing D8*: Lindau Reutin-Bregenz for the route Feldkirch to Lindau (D) and Sankt Margarethen (CH).

192 THE ESSENTIAL GUIDE TO AUSTRIAN RAILWAYS AND TRAMWAYS

To travel to and from the German towns of Garmisch-Partenkirchen and Kempton, *die (Deutsche) Bahn* trains have to travel through Austria. On 21st October, 2007 a Siemens-built diesel railcar set No. 426 028-7 has just departed Griesen (in Germany and on the border) headed for Reutte in Austria. *Author*

A *die Bahn* diesel two-car set seen here near Pflach (Austria) on 23rd October, 2007 *en route* to Garmisch-Partenkirchen (Germany). *Caroline Jones*

## 162 Zugspitzbahn

Zugspitzbahn's car No. 12 aided by the Riggenbach design rack rail leaves Eibsee for the steepest section to the summit station on 21st October, 2007. *Author*

*Location*: The Zugspitze mountain (alt. 2,962 m) near Garmisch-Partenkirchen in Bavaria which is 62 km by road north-west of Innsbruck.
*Michelin map reference*: E6.
*Nearest main line railway station*: Garmisch-Partenkirchen on the *die Bahn (DB)* route from Innsbruck via the Karwendelbahn on ÖBB official line number 551 and timetable number 410 (*see entry 100*). The DB timetable number is 960.
*Operated by*: Tourismus-Service Zugspitzland.
*Route*: From Garmisch-Partenkirchen to the summit station (Zugspitzplatt) is a total distance of 19 km.
*Journey time*: The total journey time is 58 minutes with the non-rack assisted section between Garmisch-Partenkirchen and Grainau taking 13 minutes, the rack assisted section between Grainau and Eibsee taking 10 minutes and the final and steepest section, also rack assisted, between Eibsee and the Zugspitzplatt taking 35 minutes.
*Gauge*: Narrow (metre) with rack/cogwheel assistance using the Riggenbach system.
*Gradients*: The train rises from 710 m to 2,600 m a height difference of 1,890 m. The gradient varies on the route. The Garmisch-Partenkirchen and Grainau section is 3.51 per cent, Grainau and Eibsee has a maximum of 14 per cent and the Eibsee to the Zugsplitzplatt reaches 25 per cent.
*Traction*: Electric-powered railcars and locomotives. The power supply is 1650 V DC.

*Rolling stock*: For the section between Garmisch-Partenkirchen and Grainau double-carriage railcars (Beh 4/8s) operate without rack assistance. Thereafter, and to the summit station, single unit rack-assisted railcars (Stadler-updated 1956-built Beh 4/4s) are used. For full technical details see www.zugspitze.de/pdf/TechnikZRB_neu.pdf (de).
*Places to see*: As with all Alpine peaks the views from the summit of the Zugspitze are breath-taking.
*Contact details*: Tourismus-Service Zugspitzland, Schmiedeweg 10, D-82496 Oberau. Telephone: +49 (Germany) (0) 88 249 3973 Fax: +49 (0) 88 248 890. E-mail: info@zugspitzland.de
*Website*: www.zugspitzland.de (de).
*Operating dates*: Daily all the year round.
*Tariff*: A day ticket (return journey) for an adult costs €37.50, for a youth (16-18 years) €27 and for a child (6-15 years) €22.50 (2007).
*History*: The building of the railway began in 1928, the section between Grainau and Eibsee being opened on 19th February, 1929 and the section between Eibsee and Schneefernerhaus on 8th July, 1930.
*Comments*: The service is very popular throughout the year carrying up to 600 persons per hour.

## 163 Switzerland

Austria and Switzerland (CH) share a border on the Bodensee (Lake Constance) near Bregenz. The border crossings are:

*Border crossing CH1*: Buchs (CH) and Schaanwald (FL)-Tisis for the route Feldkirch (via Liechtenstein - FL) to Zurich (CH).
*Border crossing CH2*: St Margrethen (CH)-Lustenau for the route Bregenz to Zurich (CH).

## 164 Czech Republic

The border runs along the northern international frontier of Austria. The routes passing into and out of the Czech Republic (CZ) and Austria are:

*Border crossing CZ1*: Breclav (CZ)-Hohenau for the route Vienna (via Gänserdorf) to Brno (CZ).
*Border crossing CZ2*: Satov (CZ)-Retz for the route Stockerau to Znojmo (CZ).
*Border crossing CZ3*: České Velenice (CZ)-Gmünd Nö for the route Sigmundsherberg to České Budéjovice and Prague (CZ).
*Border crossing CZ4:* Horni Dvoriste (CZ)-Summerau for the route Linz to České Budéjovice CZ).

Gmünd station witnesses a visit from Czech Railways diesel multiple unit No. 842 016-8 on 4th July, 2007. In the foreground is an ÖBB class '5047'. *Author*

## 165 Slovakia

Austria borders Slovakia (SK) to the east. The routes passing into and out of the Slovakia and Austria are:

*Border crossing SK1*:  Bratislava Petrzalka (SK) - Kittsee for the route Vienna (via Parndorf) to Breclav (CZ) and Prague CZ).
*Border crossing SK2*:  Bratislava Petrzalka (SK) - Wolfsthal for the route Vienna (via Vienna Airport) to Bratislava (SK).
*Border crossing SK3*:  Devinska Nová Ves (SK) - Marchegg for the route Vienna (via Raasdorf) - Bratislava and (CZ).

## 166 Hungary

Austria borders Hungary (H) to the east. The routes passing into and out of the Hungary and Austria are:

*Border crossing H1*:  Szentotthárd (H)-Mogersdorf for the route Graz to Körmend (H).
*Border crossing H2*:  Szombathely (H)-Rechnitz for the route Pinggau Markt via Großpetersdorf to Szombathely (H) (*crossing now closed*).
*Border crossing H3*:  Staatsgrenze-Sopron (H)-Deutschkreutz for the route Lackenbach-Sopron (H).
*Border crossing H4*:  Sopron Déli Pu (H)-Loipersbach-Schattendorf for the route Wiener Neustadt to Sopron (H).

Ebenfurth in Lower Austria is a frequent meeting point for Austrian and Hungarian trains. On 5th July, 2007 an ÖBB class '1116' encounters GYSEV's electric locomotive No. V43 320. *Author*

In Burgenland and Lower Austria it is a common sight to see Hungarian traction working both freight and passenger traffic as evidenced here on 5th July, 2007 with GYSEV-ROeEE's locomotive No. 1116 065-2 travelling the Pottendorfer Linie. *Author*

*Border crossing H5*: Sopron (H)-Baumgarten for the route Vienna to Györ and Budapest (H).
*Border crossing H6*: Fertoujlak Fertöszentmiklos (H)-Pamhagen for the route Frauenkirchen to Györ (H).
*Border crossing H7*: Hegyeshaslom (H)-Nickelsdorf for the route Vienna (via Parndorf) to Györ (H).

### 167 Gyor-Sopron-Ebenfurti Vasut (GySEV)

*Locations*: Ebenfurth, 13 km north east of Wiener Neustadt and Gyor in Hungary.
*Michelin map references*: V5 and east of X6 (off map).
*Operated jointly by*: ÖBB and GySEV and also operating on the Neusierdler Seebahn AG (Lake Neusiedl Railway Company) for the route Neusiedl am See to Fertoszentmiklós (*see entry 19 and border crossing H6 in the previous entry*).
*Routes*: a) Gyor (Hungary) to Ebenfurth (Austria). NB: Since 2001, the company has also operated b) the Sopron to Szombathely route (both towns are in Hungary).
*Journey times*: a) vary but on average 2 hours 40 minutes; and, b) 56 minutes.
*Gauge*: Standard.
*Traction*: Electric dual-powered 15 kV AC 16.7 Hz for Austria and 25 kV AC 50 Hz in Hungary.
*Contact details*: Gyor-Sopron-Ebenfurti Vasút Zrt. (GYSEV Corp.) Bahnhofplatz 5, A-7041 Wulkaprodersdorf. Telephone: +43 2687-6222 4; and also in Hungary: Gyor-Sopron-Ebenfurti Vasút Zrt. (GYSEV Corp.)Mátyás kir. u.19, H-9400 Sopron.
*Website*: www.gysev.hu
*Operating dates*: Daily services throughout the year.
*Tariff*: Consult GYSEV's website or that of ÖBB at www.oebb.at/vip8/oebb/en
*History*: In 1872, Baron Viktor Erlanger applied for and was granted a licence to establish the Gyor-Sopron-Ebenfurt Railway. His desire was to connect Gyor, which was one of the primary loading ports for Hungarian cereals, with markets to the west taking the shortest possible route but avoiding Vienna, which had by then become a serious obstacle for goods traffic. The railway began its life in the Austro-Hungarian Empire and was completed in 1879 but almost 40 years later suffered seriously as a consequence of the settlement treaty after the end of World War I hostilities. A new border was created between Austria and Hungary which effectively cut the line into two. However, provisions in two specific peace treaties of that time together with a commitment by Austria in 1923 ensured the continuing running of the railway until today. This is in spite of the impact of World War II and the post-war settlement which saw the occupation of Austria by Soviets until 1955 and Hungary after the uprising in 1956.
*Comments*: One of the prime functions of the company is to provide the passenger rail services between the western part of Hungary (Györ) and Austria (Ebenfurth). Since the break-up of the Eastern bloc countries post-1990 and later Hungary's accession to the EU in 2004, the amount of traffic between the two countries has increased significantly. The town of Sopron, formerly Ödenburg until 1918, and very close to Austria's Burgenland state, is pivotal in the region's railway network, with over 30 pairs of trains operating in and out of there each day. Wiener Neustadt, Vienna and Budapest are key termini in this company's operations. As it was from its very beginnings, the company plays a vital part in the movement of freight in that region of Europe.

A closer view of GySEV-ROeEE's locomotive No. V43 320 which had travelled the Raaberbahn to here at Ebenfurth on 5th July, 2007.  *Author*

Not related to the museum but perhaps of interest is GySEV's 2-6-2T steam locomotive No. 121 which is 'plinthed' at Neufeld an der Leitha station on the Raaberbahn south-east of Ebenfurth.  *Author*

## 168 Raaberbahn

*Location*: Sopron (formerly named Ödenburg) in Hungary.
*Michelin map reference*: V5.
*Operated by*: ROeEE-GySEV.
*Official line number*: The Raaberbahn being operated wholly by ROeEE-GySEV is not allocated an ÖBB line number. Border crossing H5 is described in *entry 166*.
*Timetable number*: 512.
*Route*: From Sopron to Ebenfurth via Wulkaprodersdorf.
*Journey time*: Mattersburgerbahn - 42 minutes and the Raaberbahn can vary between 37 minutes and 1 hour 11 minutes according to which train is taken.
*Gauge*: Standard by adhesion only. The maximum gradient is 1 per cent near Wulkaprodersdorf. Main line - single track.
*Electrified*: Yes, 25 kV AC 50 Hz.
*Website*: www.gysev.hu and www.erlebnis-bahn-schiff.at

## 169 Széchenyi Museum-Railway (GySEV Heritage Railway)

GySEV also operates Széchenyi Museum-Railway just over the border in Hungary near to Nagycenk and close to the Castle of Széchenyi. The museum railway is unusual in that much of the service is operated by children. Although the line is less than 4 km long, it is very popular with railway enthusiasts of all ages.
*Location*: Fertöboz just over the border in Hungary.
*Access*: There is no road access to the station at Fertöboz! The tourist line, however, can be accessed by a standard-gauge service from Ebenfurth albeit there are not that many trains operating. For example, the situation in 2007 was that trains departed Ebenfurth at 0741, 0759, 1139, 1339 and 1739 hours and returned from Fertöboz at 0746, 1211, 1500, 1607 and 2003 hours.
*Route*: Fertöboz via Bartátság to Kastéy, a terminus alongside the Castle of Széchenyi, a distance of 3.6 km.
*Gauge*: Narrow (760 mm).
*Traction*: Steam and diesel.
*Rolling stock*: Three Budapest-built steam locomotives: a 1924-built 0-8-0ST, a 1924-built 0-6-0ST and a 1949-built 0-6-0ST. There is also a 1950-built diesel locomotive. There are eight passenger coaches and two luggage vans used for the transport of cycles.
*Contact details*: GySEV Corporation Commercial Department, Mátyás kir. u. 19, H-9400 Sopron. Telephone: +36 99 517-244 Fax: +36 99 517-384. E-mail: ehackl@gysev.hu
*Operating dates*: Each year the museum-railway is run from early April until early October at weekends and all public holidays. In 2007, steam-hauled services operate on 8th, 9th, 16th, 17th and 30th April; 1st, 13th, 14th, 27th and 28th May; 3rd, 4th, 5th, 10th and 11th June; 8th and 9th July; 12th, 13th, 19th and 20th August; 9th, 10th, 16th and 17th September; and, finally, 7th and 8th October, 2006. On all other days the services were diesel-hauled. The pattern of operating is likely to be similar in future years. Special trains can be chartered on weekdays for a charge of 30,000 forints (Ft) for a diesel-hauled service and 90,000 Ft for steam-hauled. (NB: 1,000 Hungarian forints were worth £2.98 in January 2008.)
*Tariff*: An adult single ticket for the steam service is 440 Ft and for the diesel service cost 28 Ft. Return tickets cost twice the single fare. Children travel at half the adult

At Jesenice in Slovenia on 9th July, 2007 a variety of traction could be found. In the foreground is Slovenia Railways (SZ) electric locomotive No. 362 039 with No. 363-026 behind. To the left is a class '1116' carrying the SZ No. 541-007. Out of shot are SZ's No. 363-006, ÖBB's No. 1116 110-6 and No. 1144 222, the latter two waiting to double-head a freight train back into Austria through the Karawanken tunnel. *Author*

A rather quiet Dravograd station which currently seems to be the normal state of things there. On 16th October, 2007 all that could be found was a 'plinthed' 4-6-2 T steam locomotive No. 18-005 ex-Yugoslavian Railways (J2), ex-BBÖ No. 629.80 built by Krauss-Linz in 1927. *Author*

fares. A bicycle is transferred one way for 90 Ft. Depending on operational conditions, a passenger may have the opportunity to drive the little steam locomotive under the direction of the driver at a cost of 1,600 Ft. The railway company awards the successful 'driver' with a diploma.
*History*: The 760 mm narrow-gauge museum railway was built and opened in 1972 by the Gyor-Sopron-Ebenfurti Railway Company. The line had originally been standard gauge but was re-gauged by the company and extended from its original length of 1.2 km to 3.6 km. The steam locomotives and the railway carriages which are used were constructed in the early mid-20th century; a diesel-powered locomotive which is also used was built in 1950.
*Comments*: The railway operates a small museum which includes a number of interesting non-operational exhibits, i.e. seven narrow gauge locomotives, three of which were built in Budapest by a) Sigl Lokomotiv Fabrik, b) MÁVAG Lokomotiv & Maschinenwerke and c) Maschinenfabrik der MÁV. A fourth is of Orenstein & Koppel manufacture and the other three were built by Krauss, two at Linz and one in Munich.

## 170 Slovenia

Austria borders Slovenia (SLO) in the south-east. The routes passing in and out of Slovenia and Austria are:

*Border crossing SLO1*: Jesenice (SLO) via the Karawanken tunnel-Rosenbach for the route Villach to Ljubljana (SLO) and Zagreb (Croatia-HR).
*Border crossing SLO2*: Holmec (SLO)-Bleiburg for the route Klagenfurt to Dravograd (SLO) and Maribor (SLO).
*Border crossing SLO3*: Dravograd (SLO)-Lavamünd for the route St Paul to Maribor (SLO) (*now closed*).
*Border crossing SLO4:* Sentilj (SLO) - Spielfeld Straß for the route Graz to Maribor (SLO), Ljubljana (SLO) and Zagreb (HR).

## 171 Liechtenstein

Liechtenstein (FL) lies between Switzerland and Austria, but shares a rail border crossing with both countries. There are only 18.5 km of railways in the country which are owned and operated by the ÖBB. The border crossing is at Schaanwald (FL) - Tisis on the route from Feldkirch (A) to Buchs (CH) which is described earlier (*see entry 163*) as border crossing *CH1*.

On a bright sunny day in June 2007 ÖBB's 1144 208-4 double-heads with a new class '1216' No. 148-7 a vehicle-carrying train laden with heavy goods vehicles into the Brenner Pass station from Innsbruck. *Author*

## 172  Italy

Austria borders Italy (I) to the south and south-west. The routes passing into and out of the Italy and Austria are:

*Border crossing I1:*  Brenner/Brennero (I)-Brennersee for the route Innsbruck to Fortezza (I).
*Border crossing I2:*  Prato alla Drava (I)-Weitlanbrunn for the Villach to San Candido (I) and Brunico (I)
*Border crossing I3:*  Tarvisio Centrale to Arnoldstein for the route Villach to Udine (I) and Venice (I).

Tarvisio-Boscoverde station on 15th October, 2007. Italian Railways locomotive No. E 652-130 is coupled to an unidentified diesel *locotracteur* as it departs with a freight train for Udine on the Pontebbana route. *Author*

# Appendix

# UK's Austrian Railway Group

The Austrian Railway Group, based in the UK, was formed to promote interest in the railways of Austria from their inception through to the present day. Railways under all ownerships are catered for, as are standard and narrow gauge railways and tramways. Modelling Austrian railways is also actively pursued within the Group and a number of layouts are moved to various locations in the UK for other members as well as the general public to enjoy. The Austrian Railway Group also publish a journal quarterly which is free to current members and deals with a variety of topics and news about the Austrian railway scene. A comprehensive website has been written - www.austrian-railways.org/arghome.htm - which provides a mine of useful and interesting information well illustrated with high quality photographs. Linked to the website is a members' E-group (hosted by Yahoo!) which permits those members with internet access and the necessary skills to share messages, files and pictures and to seek as well provide a whole host of information on Austrian railway matters. Participation is restricted to ARG members and a few special, helpful friends who make special contributions to the group. Currently about one-third of the ARG members have joined the E-group. They include several people based in Austria, some of whom are vendors of Austrian models and railway literature and videos/dvds on the country's railways. Commercial advertising is not allowed, but members may advertise their own items for sale. Information on events and on new models, etc. is actively pursued. A number of individual booklets have been published by the Group about the railways in and around Linz, Vienna, Salzburg and Innsbruck and other rail centres. There are also booklets on Stern & Hafferl, the Erzbergbahnen and Austrian Signalling. Others are in the course of preparation (*see Bibliography*).

The author is a member of the Group and he actively encourages those who have an interest in Austrian Railways and/or have enjoyed reading this book to join without delay. The Secretary/Treasurer is Howard Lawrence and he can be contacted at 14 Wheatfield Way, Skegby, Sutton in Ashfield NG17 3EU. UK telephone number is 01623 455373. E-mail: howard.lawrence@ntlworld.com   Annual subscription for those resident in the UK is £13 and £15 for those living elsewhere in the world.

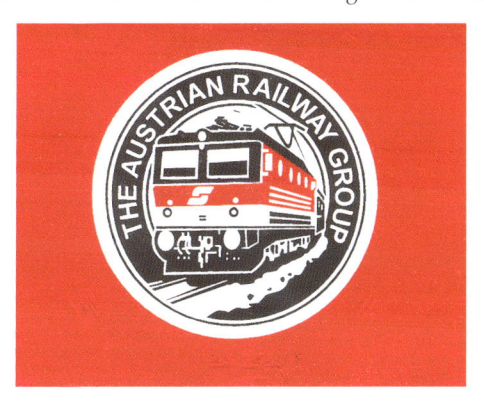

# Glossary

Glossary of some German language railway terms.

| German | English |
|---|---|
| Abteil | compartment |
| Ausbesserungswerke | works |
| Autowagen | vehicle carrier |
| Bahn | railway |
| Bahnbetriebswerke | depot |
| Bahnunternehmen | railway company |
| Bahnhof (Bhf) | station |
| Bahnsteig | platform |
| Baureihe | class (as in class '1116') |
| Betriebslänge | route length |
| Dampflok | steam locomotive |
| Diesellok | diesel locomotive |
| Doppelstockwagen | double-deck coach |
| Ellok (E-lok) | electric locomotive |
| Eigentumslänge | length of line owned |
| Erlebnis | experience |
| Eurospaische Bahnen | European railways |
| Fahrkarte | ticket |
| Fahrleitung | catenary |
| Fahrplan | timetable |
| Fahrplanmässig | scheduled |
| Fahrzeuge | rolling stock |
| Gleichstrom | direct current (DC) |
| Gleis | track/platform |
| Gepäckwagen | baggage car |
| Güterwagen | goods wagon |
| Güterzug | freight train |
| Hauptbahnhof (Hbf) | main station |
| Hauptgüterbahnhof (Hgbf) | main freight depot |
| Klasse | class (as in 1st class) |
| Liegewagen | couchette car |
| Lokführer | driver |
| Lokomotive (lok) | locomotive |
| Neigezug | tilting train |
| Normalspur | standard gauge |
| Niveauubergang | level crossing |
| Personenwagen | passenger carriage |
| Personenverkehr | passenger traffic |
| Rangierfahrzeuge | shunters |
| Reisezug | passenger train |
| Reisezugwagen | passenger carriage |
| Rollmaterial | rolling stock |
| Schienenbus | railbus |
| Schiff | ship or cruise boat |
| Schmalspur | narrow gauge |
| Schlafwagen | sleeping car |
| Speisewagen | restaurant car |
| Station | station |
| Steuerwagen | (steering) railcar |
| Strom | (electric) current |
| Trasse | train path |
| Triebwagen | (powered) railcar |
| Verspätung | lateness |
| Unfälle | accidents |
| Unterhalt | maintenance |
| Verschiebebahnhof (Vbf) | marshalling yard |
| Weiche | points |
| Zahn | tooth (cog railway) |
| Zug | train |
| Zugführer | guard |

# Bibliography

*Books and Journals*

*Austrian Railways - Locomotives, Multiple Units and Trams - European Handbook No. 3* by Brian Garvin and Peter Fox. Platform 5 Publishing, Sheffield 2005. ISBN 1 902336 49 6.

*Great Railway Journeys of Europe* edited by Tom Le Bas of Insight Guides, London 2005. ISBN 981-234-720-8.

*LGB Journal 2005*, published by Ernst Paul Lehmann, Nurnberg 2006.

*The Complete Encyclopaedia of Locomotives* by Mirco de Cet and Alan Kent. Rebo International, The Netherlands 2006. ISBN 13-978-90-366-1505-1 & 10-90-366-1504-4.

*The Encyclopaedia of Trains and Locomotives*, edited by Davis Ross, Amber Books, London 2003. ISBN 1-85605-792-5.

*The History of Trains* by Colin Garratt, Octopus Publishing, London 1998. ISBN 0-7537-0630-X.

*Austria*. Insight Guides, London 2006. ISBN -13 078 981 258 342 0.

*Die Mariazellerbahn* by Horst Felsinger and Walter Schober, 3rd edition, Verlag Pospischil, Vienna (de).

*Rail Centres of Austria - Linz* by Ron Ferguson et al. The Austrian Railway Group, Carlisle 2007.

*Railways of Salzburg* by Geoff Bird et al. The Austrian Railway Group, Carlisle 2002.

*The Railways of Stern und Hafferl* by Stephen R. Ford et al. The Austrian Railway Group, Carlisle 2006.

*Die Erzbergbahnen* by Mike Morton et al. The Austrian Railway Group, Carlisle 2005.

*The Mur Valley - Unzmarkt-Tamsweg-Mautendorf und die Murtalbahn* by Stephen R Ford. The Austrian Railway Group, Carlisle 2005.

*Eisenbahnatlas Österreich* (Rail Atlas Austria). Schweers + Wall, Köln 2005. ISBN 3-89494-128-6.

*Annual Report of ÖBB Holding AG*, Vienna 2006.

*Österreich mit dem Zug erleben* by Markus Inderst, Ronald Gohl & Hans-Bernhard Schönborn. Geramond München, 2000. ISBN 3-932785-72-X.

*Journal of The Austrian Railway Group (UK)* edited by Stephen Ford, Nos. 60, 61 & 62 (2006-2007).

*Die Eisenbahn in Österreich - Geschichte, Strecken, Lokomotiven* by Klaus J Vetter, Geramond 2007. ISBN 978-3-7654-7092-9.

*Das Heizhaus - Eisenbahnmuseum Strasshof - Band 1 Lokomotiven* by Rupert Gansterer. Museumführer Eisenbahnmuseum Strasshof, 1999.

*Die Alpen mit dem Zug entdecken* by Marcus Inderst. Geramond München, 2006. ISBN 3-7654-7187-9.

*Die Schonsten Alpenbahnen - Strecken - Zuge - Landschaften* by Dietmar Beckman and Bernd Eisenschink. GeraNova Bruckmann München, 2004.

*History of the Austrian Railway* by Alfred Horn and published by ÖBB on the internet (see website entries below).

*Durch Wälder und über Wiesem - Ein Jahrhundert Innsbrucker Mittelgebirgsbahn* Tiroler MuseumsBahnen, Innsbruck 2000.

*100 Jahre Strassenbahnen in Innsbruck 1891-1991 + 50 Jahre Innsbrucker Verkehrsbetriebe AG 1941 - 1991* Tiroler Museumsbahnen, Innsbruck 1991.

*Ihre Urlaubsspeitzialisten ... Erlebnis Bahn & Schiff ...fur Resiselust* ÖBB, Vienna 2007.

*75 Jahre Feistritztalbahn* Steiermärkische Landesbahnen, Graz 1986.

*Schaufenster volkskultur Forum Museum 2006* Volkskultur Niederösterreich, Atzenbrugg 2006. ISSN 1680-3434.

*75 Jahre Mittenwaldbahn* ÖBB undated.

## Maps

*Austria - Michelin National Map* No. 730 (2006). ISBN 13 978 2 06 711267 4.
*Carinthia* published by Freytag & Berndt. ISBN 978-3-7079-0304-1.
*Lower Austria* published by Freytag & Berndt. ISBN 978-3-85084-341-6.
*Steiermark* published by Freytag & Berndt. ISBN 978-3-85084-344-7.
*Tyrol* published by Freytag & Berndt. ISBN 978-3-7079-0306-5.
*Upper Austria - Salzkammergut* published by Freytag & Berndt. ISBN 978-3-85084-342-3.
*Vorarlberg* published by Freytag & Berndt. ISBN 978-3-7079-0445-8.

## Electronic Media

*Encarta, 2005 Standard Edition*. Microsoft Corporation.
*Encyclopaedia Britannica, 1999 edition*. Earthlink Network.
*The History of Austria* published by Wikipedia, the free encyclopedia (*see website entries below*) licensed to the public under the GNU Free Documentation License (GFDL).
*Oxford Interactive Encyclopedia*. TLC Properties Inc. 1997.

# Interesting Websites

www.oebb.at/en the official ÖBB website providing a wealth of information as well as timetable and fares information.

www.oakwoodpress.co.uk – publisher's website listing their UK and European titles (en).

www.rail-guides.eu – website written by the author to support this book and others (en).

www.railfaneurope.net

www.nostalgiebahn.at/

www.stern-verkehr.at/sverkehr/

http://cms.graztourismus.at/cms/beitrag/10001767/47303/DE

www.erlebnisbahn.at

reiseauskunft.bahn.de/bin/query.exe/en the on-line timetable for most European services.

www.fahrgast.at/~english.htm body representing passengers using Austrian public transport.

www.austria.info/english/ the official site for Austrian Tourist Information.

www.oebb.at/en/OeBB_Group/History_of_the_Austrian_Railway/index.jsp history of Austrian railways

http://en.wikipedia.org/wiki/History_of_Austria

# Index

The numbers refer to individual entries except those in *italics* which refer to pages.

| | | | |
|---|---|---|---|
| Achenseebahn | 95 | Höllentalbahn | 38 |
| Almtalbahn | 108 | Horse railway | 117 |
| Arlbergbahn | 96 | Hungary | 166 |
| Arlberger Kandaharbahn | 159 | Hungerburgbahn | 155 |
| Aspangbahn | 32 | Innsbruck Tramways | 99 |
| Attergaubahn (Stern & Hafferl) | 109 | International railway connections | *191* |
| Außerfernbahn | 97 | Italy | 172 |
| Austria - facts and figures | *7* | Kamptalbahn | 39 |
| Berkstecke Ybbstalbahn - *Ötscherland Express* | 33 | Kaprun | 149 |
| Bregenzerwaldbahn (Wälderbähnle) | 140 | Karawankenbahn | 25 |
| Brennerbahn | 98 | Karwendelbahn (Mittenwaldbahn) | 100 |
| Cargoserv - Voest Alpine | 144 | Knittelfeld Museum | 79 |
| Club 760 - Frojach Museum | 71 | Kohlebahn | 112 |
| Club Florianerbahn | 110 | Koralmbahn | 80 |
| Club U44 | 73 | Kreuzeckbahn | 146 |
| Czech Republic | 164 | Krumpen (die) | 40 |
| Danube (Donau) Express (Nostalgia - E6) | 11 | Lambach-Haag (Stern & Hafferl) | 113 |
| Donauländebahn | 128 | Larchwand-Schragaufzug | 150 |
| Donauuferbahn | 34 | Lauer Ostbahn | 41 |
| Drautalbahn | 21 | Lavamündebahn | 26 |
| Eastern Austria trips | 16 | Lavanttalbahn | 27 |
| Ennstal (Nostalgia - E7) | 12 | Lendcanaltramway | 28 |
| Ennstalbahn | 61 | Liechtenstein | 171 |
| Erlaufbahn | 35 | Lienz - Eisenbahn Freunde | 101 |
| Erzbergbahn | 74 | Liliputbahn | 129 |
| Erzbergbahn Museum | 75 | Linz Tramways | 114 |
| Facts and figures about Austria | *7* | Linzer Lokalbahn (Stern & Hafferl) | 115 |
| Feldbach - Bad Gleichenberg (StLB) | 88 | LTE | 142 |
| Feld Industriebahn | 36 | Märchenbahn aka Südbergenlandische | 20 |
| Franz-Josefs Bahn | 37 | Mariazellerbahn | 42 |
| Feistritztalbahn (Club U44) | 73 | Mariazell Museum | 43 |
| Freight railway operations | 176 | Martinsberg Lokalbahnverein | 44 |
| Frojach Museum (Club 760) | 72 | Mattersburgerbahn | 45 |
| Funiculars | *xx* | Middle Austria trips | 15 |
| Gaitalbahn | 22 | Mittelgebirgsbahn (IVF) | 102 |
| Gasteiner Hollenstein | 62 | Mittenwaldbahn (Karwendelbahn) | 100 |
| Germany | 161 | Mixnitz-St Erhard (StLB) | 90 |
| Gesäuse | 76 | Montafonerbahn | 138 |
| Giselabahn | 63 | Mühlkriesbahn | 116 |
| GKB (Graz-Köflacher Bahn) | 77 | Murtalbahn (StLB) | 81 |
| Gleisdorf-Weis (StLB) | 89 | Museums | |
| Gmunden Tramways (Stern & Hafferl) | 111 | Erzbergbahn Museum | 75 |
| Graz-Köflacher Bahn (GKB) | 77 | Frojach Museum (Club 760) | 72 |
| Graz Tram Museum | 94 | Graz Trams | 94 |
| Graz Tramways | 78 | Knittelfeld | 79 |
| Grazer Schlossbergbahn | 153 | Mariazell Trams | 43 |
| Gurktalbahn (KMB) | 23 | ÖGEG | 118 |
| GySEV | 167 | Pferdeeisenbahn Kerschbaum | 117 |
| Haager-Lies aka Lambach-Haag (Stern & Hafferl) | 113 | Schwechat Museum (VEF) | 130 |
| Hallein Salt Mines | 64 | SKLGB (Lokalbahn Museum) | 123 |
| Hallstätter Salzbergbahn | 148 | Steyrtalbahn Museum | 125 |
| Hartkaiserbahn | 154 | Strasshof Museum | 51 |
| History | | Südbahn Kulturbahnhof | 92 |
| Austria | *7* | Szechenyi Museum Railway | 169 |
| Railways of Austria | *13* | Tauernbahn | 69 |
| Höhenbahn | 24 | Tiroler Trams | 105 |
| | | Vienna Trams | 133 |

207

| | | | |
|---|---|---|---|
| Neumarkt Sattel | 82 | Steirische Ostbahn | 87 |
| Neusiedlersee (Nostalgia - E8) | 13 | Steiermärkische Landesbahn | 86 |
| Neusierdler Seebahn (NSB) | 19 | Stern & Hafferl | 124 |
| Nordbahn | 2 | Steyrtalbahn Museum | 125 |
| Nordwestbahn | 46 | Strasshof Museum | 51 |
| Nostalgiebahn in Kärnten | 29 | Strudengau (ÖBB Nostalgia - E5) | 10 |
| ÖBB | 1 | Stubaitalbahn (IVF) | 103 |
| ÖBB Nostalgia (Erlebniszug) | | Südbahn | 4 |
| Donau (E6) | 11 | Südbahn Kulturbahnhof | 92 |
| Ennstal (E7) | 12 | Südbergenländische aka Märchenbahn | 20 |
| Neusiedlersee (E8) | 13 | Sudwestbahn | 52 |
| Reblaus Express (E9) | 14 | Switzerland | 163 |
| Schneebergland (E3) | 8 | Szechenyi Museum Railway | 169 |
| Strudengau (E5) | 10 | Tauernbahn | 67 |
| Wachau (E4) | 9 | Tauernbahn Museum | 69 |
| Wiener Alpen (E2) | 7 | Tauern Tunnel | 68 |
| Zauberberge (E1) | 6 | Taurachbahn | 70 |
| ÖGEG | 118 | Thörlerbahn (was StLB operated) | 93 |
| Olympia-Bahn | 156 | Tiroler Museum | 105 |
| Ostbahn | 3 | Traisentalbahn | 53 |
| Österreichische Bundesbahnen (ÖBB) | 1 | Tramways | |
| *Ötscherland Express* (NÖBL) | 33 | Gmunden | 110 |
| Pasterzenbahn | 147 | Graz | 78 |
| Peggau-Ubelbach (StLB) | 91 | Innsbruck Tramways | 99 |
| Pinzgauerbahn | 65 | Linz | 113 |
| Pitz-express | 160 | Postlingbergbahn | 118 |
| Pontebbana | 30 | Vienna | 134 |
| Postlingbergbahn | 119 | Traunseebahn (Stern & Hafferl) | 126 |
| Pottendorfer Linie | 47 | U-Bahn | |
| Pressburgerbahn | 48 | Serfauser Alpen | 104 |
| Pyhrnbahn | 120 | Vienna | 135 |
| Raaberbahn | 168 | Verbindungsbahn | 131 |
| Rack/cogwheel systems | 17 | Vienna | |
| Radkersburgerbahn | 83 | S-Bahn | 135 |
| Rail Cargo Austria AG | 145 | Tram Museum | 133 |
| Reblaus Express (ÖBB Nostalgia - E9) | 14 | Tramways | 134 |
| Rheinschaeun | 139 | U-Bahn 136 | |
| Rosenthalbahn | 31 | Voest Alpine - Cargoserv | 144 |
| Roßhuttebahn | 157 | Vorchdorferbahn (Stern & Hafferl) | 127 |
| RTS (Rail Transport Service) | 143 | Vorortlinie | 132 |
| Salzburger Festungsbahn | 151 | Wachau (ÖBB Nostalgie - E4) | 9 |
| Salzkammergutbahn | 121 | Wachtl-Express | 106 |
| S-Bahn - Vienna | 135 | Wäldbahnmuseum | 54 |
| Schafbergbahn | 122 | Waldbähnle (Bregenzerwaldbahn) | 140 |
| Schlossalmbahn | 152 | Waldviertlerbahn | |
| Schneebergbahn | 49 | (Alt Nagelberg to Heidenreichstein) | 56 |
| Schneebergland (ÖBB Nostalgia - E3) | 8 | Waldviertlerbahn (Gmünd-Groß Gerungs) | 57 |
| Schoberpass | 84 | Waldviertlerbahn (Gmünd-Litschau) | 55 |
| Schwechat Museum (VEF) | 130 | Waldviertler Eisenbahnmuseum | 58 |
| Semmeringbahn | 50 | Wechselbahn | 32 |
| Serfauser Alpen-U-Bahn | 104 | Westbahn | 5 |
| SETG | | Western Austria trips | 18 |
| (Salzburger Eisenbahn Transport Logistik) | 141 | Wiener Alpen (ÖBB Nostalgia - E2) | 7 |
| SKLGB (Salzkammergutbahn Lokalbahn | | Wiener Lokalbahn | 137 |
| Mus'm) | 123 | Wurzeralmbahn | 158 |
| SLB (Salzburger Lokalbahn) | 66 | Ybbstalbahn (Waidhofen - Lunz) | 59 |
| Slovakia | 165 | Ybbstalbahn (Waidhofen -Ybbitz) | 60 |
| Slovenia | 170 | Zauberberge (ÖBB Nostalgia - E1) | 6 |
| Southern Austria trips | 17 | Zillertalbahn | 107 |
| Stainzerbahn | 85 | Zugspitz | 162 |